Sh*t A Teacher Thinks

(and sometimes says)

by Paul Bentley

The names and identifying characteristics of the individuals depicted throughout this book have been changed to protect their privacy. Any resemblance to actual persons, living or dead, is purely coincidental.

Cover design by Paul Bentley using Cover Creator

ISBN 13:978-1456348007
ISBN 10:1456348000

To my lovely wife: The best teacher I know and the one who set the standard.

CONTENTS

Acknowledgements

I'd like thank all the students I taught, and who taught me, and all the teachers and administrators I worked with over the years. Without you and your sharing, your engaging personalities, conversations, and electric moments, this book would not have been possible. Thanks for the memories and for giving life a swift kick forward.

SEPTEMBER – Long and Hard

She's staring off into space. It's the second day of school, there's a summer reading assignment in front of her, but she's not writing. *Shit, here we go again,* I think. How many times have I seen that same clueless look? A thousand? Ten thousand? The girl's unprepared and bored. Not panic stricken that she's starting the year with a zero. Not concerned about early impressions. She's thinking about lunch, or the Welcome-Back-Dance, or getting to the lav. I look around the room. There are a bunch of them.

Mr B, a lank haired boy says without raising a hand. Are you retiring after this year? I heard you were. . . I notice the putz isn't very good at feigning interest, or sincerity. Just another pathetic delaying tactic. They have thousands of them.

This gets the girl's attention along with the rest of the zoning out teen zombies. They're happy for the diversion and to see how this teacher guy reacts. It's part of the drama of the typical public school classroom. No need for books. This is where the life's real lessons will be played out and learned for this bunch.

I glance at my seating chart, recognize his family name, and give him a short look trying to decide in a picosecond whether to cut him off, totally ignore him, tell him to raise a hand, remind him others are working, smile noncommittally, tell him to fuck off, etc. He looks like a wise guy, but not tough.

Well, I say, I honestly don't know for sure. . . I'm pausing and smiling and many in the class are looking up now. . . It's probably 90% that I will retire, but the one-oh could come through though I don't know why you think I'd be telling you before I announce it to the administration unless you think we're good buddies or something. . . His eyes go up, so do a lot of others around the room. This is what they like: off topic jibber-jabber shit. I say, Like maybe we've got some karmic connection going or something. Shared DNA, one gene pool. . . I'm laying it on thick, but I might as well establish the pecking order right off. I smile wider and finish with, Is that definite enough for you?

And just like that I show him I know the game and can wise guy with his gnat brain. I practice the belief that a little humorous sarcasm can be just the thing if not overdone or mean spirited. Intent is everything. Smiling definitely takes the edge off.

He nods not sure what I just said but happy at what he perceives to be a successful diversion.

Coin Toss, Teacher Ball – *Set the tone early or a long tough year will be even tougher. If you want to talk shit with them remember, it's all about infotainment. Dish it up with style.*

Not You, That Idiot In Your Seat – *First impressions and first grades do count, dingbats. Well established averages are hard to pull down, hard wired impressions are difficult to change. If you act like a duh from Animal House and metaphorically crush beer cans on your forehead, don't ask for a recommendation or to borrow lunch money.*

It's late summer, the school year's just begun, and I feel that adrenaline rush that goes with first day and reconnecting. It's my 32nd year and probably my last. I'll be 60 in the spring, that's enough. I'm tired. I never could imagine as a beginning teacher reaching the end, can any twenty-something? You contribute to your pension, get that first statement from the retirement board showing your projected retirement in a thousand years when the polar caps are gone and the water's lapping at your desk, and you think, *Will I even live that long?* And then the years inextricably pass along with the hair, skin tone, and forceful whiz. Colleagues come and go, some become friends, and you miss them and the memorable students. Of course, there are always the social networking websites where reconnect is easy, but then what? Remember me? Remember the old days? Remember the time you– And they say, Cheez Bentley, you still teaching? Thought you'd be pickled with gin by now. Or in a rest home. Still teaching huh? What are you, some sort of Viagra fueled, sado/masochistic deviant?

Crocodile Tears – *Sentiment is best practiced at home fussing over a cat or dog. Fish are good too and will most approximate many classes.*

Listen Up Numbnuts – *If you think your teacher is an inhuman drone who doesn't have a life, remember that he/she probably doesn't. But neither do you.*

I teach at rural high school that serves two small towns in a backwoods corner of the state. The school complex is set on a pretty rise alongside a secondary highway and is surrounded by woods and the homes of Generation X commuters with families. The parents want better for their kids, and the kids want better too. Better usually means more, and more expensive, which the students frequently get: late model cars, iphones, itoys, charge cards, seashore vacations, i.e. worth through consumption, the stuff of upward mobility. Most wear designer labels and name brands like a second skin. It's a life of, You have chosen wisely, even if the labels are knockoffs or seconds.

I have the usual 5 classes this year, including four level 2 classes, the lowest level. No problem. The level 2's are made up of teens who will mostly wind up going into the family business/trade, matriculating at some tech/community/small name college, enlisting in the armed forces, getting arrested or pregnant or married or some combo. Why some of these hand-teaches-the-brain types are not in trade/tech school now is a question I have every year though I know some can't get in. Public schools like ours have to take everyone, the tech/trade schools don't. Others lack the ambition of even a thick shelled crustacean. It's easier just to flunk here.

Most of these level 2's are the generic good kid with real world aspirations and I sincerely like most of them. Four of the five tradesmen who work on my house are former students. Many of the ones now finishing the assignment are sons, daughters, nieces, and nephews of these kinds of alumni. No big deal. Any teacher who hangs around long enough gets the descendants and relatives.

Mr. B, a homeboy says the third day of World Literature. You had my mother. She says you're the only teacher in this school who taught her anything. . . I smile. The compliment seems sincere. What's your mother's maiden name? I ask. The boy tells me, and I rack my memory. The name definitely rings a bell, but I can't put a face to it. Later at home I pull out an old grade book and find her name and a class photo I stapled in. Lean. Animate. I check the grades. Average, with flashes of A's. Not a scholar, not a dimwitted mice brain either. A middle roader, good kid. I show the picture the next day to the son, but not the grades. He gets a kick out of it, and we now have a bond, though who knows if that'll have any academic effect. I ask the class who has a mother, father, aunt, uncle, brother, sister who had me for a teacher, and half the hands go up.

The Ties That Bond *– It's true that the apple doesn't fall far from the tree. Usually. To know the relative is to usually know the current student. But never say, You're a chip off the old uterus/penis. Don't even use the apple analogy. They know it's true.*

Heads Up Kiddo *– Sucking up is definitely a good thing and using a family connection is OK unless your family is illegal or pushing. And keep it sincere. If sincere isn't in your emotional grid get involved with the theatre people and learn to fake it.*

I'm on caf duty. It's duty not every teacher gets, but I had it last year, I have it again this year, and I wonder if they're trying to tell me something. Duty's for an hour at a stretch once a week, and about as much fun as watching varicose veins. I have the door shift, and I'm supposed to check the comings and goings of teens who can't wait to get to lunch, then can't wait to sneak off. Two boys with soccer shirts try to walk out past me without a word.

- Excuse me. Where are you going?

Boy 1 - We're not in here.

- What do you mean?

- We don't have lunch now.

- So why are you here?

Boy 2 - Our coach is going to be here.

- Now?

Boy 1 - No, later.

- So why are you here now?

Boy 2 - We had to talk to someone.

- Where are you coming from?

Boy 1 - Study.

- Do you have a pass to come here from study?

Boy 2 - We're going to the band room.

- Do you have a pass to go there?

Boy 1 - No. Because we have to see our coach.

- But not now. That's later.

- That's right.

- So do you have a pass?

Boy 2 - No, we're not in here now. . .

This could go on forever, I'm shoveling air. These two turtle farts probably don't know the Abbot and Costello Who's On First routine, but they have it down pat. I sigh, smile, and wave them on.

Keep It Lite – *There are times when school should be a happiness factory, especially at lunch when it helps the digestion. If you find nothing funny, try tickling yourself. Or giving yourself a private scratch.*

Charm Schoolers – *You don't have to be smart or in the right as long as you have charm and good manners. It works more often than not. Politicians, lawyers, celebrities, and restaurant hostesses know this. Detention is filled with dumbshitskis who don't.*

We're in a dry, hot spell. There's been little rain in August, and the extended forecast is for an uninterrupted streak of more. My room is hot, the new windows don't open all the way. A maintenance man tells me there are *stops* preventing the windows from going all the way up. He tells me it's no big deal to have them removed, he just needs a special tool. He's been telling me this for a year now and the stops are still in.

Support This *– It's very important to be in tight with the support staff. Janitors, secretaries, caf workers can do a lot more for you than you can do for them. But don't let them jerk you around too much. It's not like they're real support like a bra or jock strap.*

I thought I had this room all straightened out last year only to return a week ago and find that the emergency shower in the upstairs science room ran for 14 hours straight this summer and totally flooded my basement crib. The ceiling caved in, the sheetrock walls were ruined, I lost most of my good posters along with many, many sets of books, some out-of-print. The first day back I find drywall dust all over, electrical outlets without covers, too few desks, a water logged file cabinet, and 4 computer stations with no computers. Some salvaged but water stained and musky material is piled up in a corner.

It sucks big time, but I roll up my sleeves and get dirty.

I'm used to new rooms. At one point I was in 6 different ones in 7 years. This is my third one now in little over a year. It's never easy. Fat-assed janitors in the past have told me it wasn't their job to move furniture. I've scrapped paint after sloppy painting jobs, hunted down missing file cabinets and missing boxes of books and supplies, scrubbed Venetian blinds that were crusted with dirt, mopped up water leaks, remodeled closets, reglued laminate counters. I even vacuumed bare concrete floors during a renovation when a piss weasel custodian refused saying, What's the point? It'll only get dirty again.

Room Enough To Grow *– You can wait and play the union card, and it'll never get done. Or, like Nike, just do it. Pimp that room. No one will probably* *notice. But this is where you live a third of the day. It's also the best digs some of your students have.*

Cattle Call – *Your own teen room back home may be a dump and fit only to reflect your own inner turmoil or to hide from the world. But here it's the floor, not ground. Don't spit, litter, or park your goddamn used gum.*

New schedule changes this year: The administration's taken three of our weekly duty periods and replaced them with mandatory department meetings which they now call PLC's (Professional Learning Communities). This is a kick-in-the-ass. Teachers need the study hall time for prep and to correct papers. We're sour. The four veteran English teachers are grumbling. The four new ones aren't happy, but without tenure they're lucky they get to choose their own cafeteria food.

Sidebar: In the #1 best selling business book of all time *Who Moved My Cheese?* author Spencer Johnson depicts 2 mice and 2 little-people forced to find new cheese in their maze world. The message? Paradigms shift so go with the flow, embrace evolution, adapt or die. It's vocational Darwinism that mice have no problem accepting. Tiny people, and obstinate fucktards, do. Still, the change sucks.

A head pencil sharpener tells us we'll be discussing and revisiting course philosophies, essential questions, benchmarks, state frameworks, learning activities, rubrics, needs assessments, data analysis, tracking, common formative assessments, modeling, Connecticut competencies, etc. I have little idea what it all means. Creating edspeak is what Ed.D's do. Over-degreed bastards.

Kiss KISS Goodbye – *Be aware that there'll always be the latest educational fad du jour, the wheel will be reinvented many times in your career. Some can be ignored; most like kidney stones will pass on their own, though you may piss blood first.*

Poor Smurf Cookies – *Think your teacher's ignoring you? He/She might be preoccupied with meeting the class objective, which has to fit the course philosophy and essential questions, which need to fit state competencies, all while hoping you the student meets the day's benchmarks as determined by the course rubric matched to your skills, IEP, and, of course, all predetermined by a needs assessment and all subject to change. Teacher's not ignoring you. It's not that personal.*

I have 3 sophomore World Literature classes, 1 senior Drama, and 1 senior Film. The sophomores are mandated to take World Lit, and some are resentful, many unmotivated. It shows. Within a week discipline notices are mounting, and grades are redlining. I invent a new phrase: Zero Liners. I have a half dozen+ whose grades are a horizontal line of zeroes.

All boys. Serial fuckups.

I ask one of the dullards privately, Aren't you afraid of failing? You need this course. He says unemotionally, No. I keep it unemotional myself, and say, You realize you're digging yourself into such a hole that it might be difficult to pass for the year after this quarter? I show him the math. He shrugs. I try again. You don't care? No, he says. Think your mom would care if I called? I'm pulling out all stops – mom's usually a trump card, but he's still unfazed. Probably not, he says unflinchingly, she's used to it. Really? I ask rhetorically. So how did you get to be a sophomore? He shrugs again, and I'm getting the strong feeling this kid's hard wired for apathy. Still, it's the beginning of the year, so it's too early to let him veg out. I say, Let me guess. Your teacher last year didn't assign much homework or check it, you did most of the in-class work, and maybe got some online help – summaries, that sort of thing. Besides, you really believe you can make a comeback if you want to, despite the numbers, and in a worst case scenario you're hoping I'll cut a deal with you at the end of the year to get you by. . . He looks surprised, like I'm fucking Copperfield and just told him what card he's holding. I say, A deal ain't going to happen, no way. You don't get to take a prolonged vacation on your cyber blog then come waltzing back. I can't make you work. Can't tase you, bro. But your standardized test scores are good, you've got potential, and it won't take much work to pass, though you should be aiming a lot higher. I'm hoping you'll like most of the literature enough to make you *want* to read and write. I'm here if you need me.

It's positive reinforcement: the p.c. professional thing to do. But my hopes aren't high. This 16-year-old is one of those ballsy blockheads that makes you wonder if the parents got the sperm and egg from a consignment shop. A prime example of arrested development, a student whose growth stops nightly in front of a HD screen watching the latest YouTube, whose idea of a classic film is *Night Of the Living Dead.*

No Three Strike Rule *– Keep communication open, and document meetings/ emails/phone calls. It's a lot of work but if you don't CYA, it could be C-YA if you're nontenured and just plain hassled if you are.*

Wanted Dead Or Alive *– If your teacher's quietly letting you fail, it means you've been judged F On Arrival. Something's wrong. You both can't be on a* *mental sabbatical. Life's supposed to be a hassle, a tack up your ass. Teacher isn't doing you any favors.*

Boys Town: In this 1938 movie Father Flanagan says, There's one thing I know for sure: There's no such thing as a bad boy. . . Spencer Tracy is very convincing and I believe him. He doesn't say though there's no such thing as an unmotivated or lazy ass boy. There are. More than enough to make teaching a challenge and for a movie sequel.

Flashback: A Level 2 father accuses me of pushing his son too hard. Earl isn't going to college, he tells me. If I'm pushing too hard, I reply, I'd rather do that than push too little. I'm going to give Earl the background that if he changes his mind about college he can go. You're not paying me to sell your son short. . . The old man's a hard nosed, old school, blue collar worker who probably wouldn't mind if I even called Earl a lazy and shiftless deadbeat, which he is, but I don't. The skin-headed son starts doing the work.

Use my name! the student snarls when I tell him to get off the desk and sit in the chair. I repeat calmly, Get off the desk, and sit in the chair. He slips off the desk with all the speed of oozing breast milk, and repeats, Use my name! I look at my seating chart while he says a third time, Use my name! He's a second tier wise guy, but this appeal is not that. And I understand what he's saying: I'm a person, an individual, look at me, talk to me. . . Years ago I kicked a boy out of lunch who's throwing food. As I walked him to the office he says, I only threw one little thing, I wasn't the only one, why are you picking on me? He has a point, but I go rote, SOP. It's easy to do after a hundred conversations on roughly the same thing. I'm not picking on you, I say. You're the only one I saw. You know the school rules, I don't make 'em.

Nothing says you have to get a warning. If you don't like the rules, talk to the assistant principal about them. . . He looks at me strangely, there's a long pause, and he says simply, Talk to me. I don't know what he means and I repeat, Talk to the assistant principal. He gets angry and yells, Talk to me! TALK TO ME! Then it dawns on me what he means, but I'm too committed now to playing it by-the-book, following the path of least resistance to truly interact. I drop him off at the office, and that's that.

But it isn't because now, decades later, a boy the same age with shorter hair and different style clothes wants me to use his name. He's right, I'm wrong. I make a point of memorizing his name and not forgetting it.

Auld Lang Syne – *A name might not seem like much, and it is hard to remember 100+ students, and becomes harder still as you get older and those thousands of past names and faces intrude. But you have to try. Otherwise, you might as well put quarters over your eyes and drink your fill of embalming fluid.*

The Who From Whoville – *If you want to be a nameless and faceless aught in the classroom, no one can stop you. But then don't be surprised or insulted when the office calls and you hear the teacher say, Who?. . Don't make us resort to DNA testing to ID your dead ass.*

On the very first day I started teaching, I start off with a name game. The first student in the first row says his/her name. The next student repeats the first student's name, then says his/her own. This continues through the next 25-34 students. And I start the second day remembering almost everyone and quickly discard the seating chart.

As the years go by, the name game goes, the seating chart stays out longer, and I take to learning names through osmosis. One year two girls inadvertently switch seats on the second day, but because I associate a name with a seat, I continually call them by the wrong name. I call on one girl, and while I'm looking at her, the other girl answers. I think they just can't hold their answers, as if there's a weak mental prostate. And it takes quite a while before I realize the error. By then I've memorized the wrong names, and, sad to say, I'm in trouble for the rest of the year if I ever have to address them without my seating chart.

The Name Game *– Sherlock Holmes said the mind is like an attic and we shouldn't clutter it up with unneeded shit. In our own information rich age, what to toss out is the question. But the names have to stay. At least for the run of the course. Then go Alzheimer's if you want.*

What's in a name anyway? Seems to me some of my parents try for uniqueness simply by taking a common name and convoluting the spelling: Kayte, Aric, Mashel, Karie, Shawna, Kryste, Lora, Aimee, Kristyn, etc. I've had a lot of them, but Shakespeare never said a rose is a roze. Names can be tough. One year I have a Kristina, Kristen, Kristin, and Christine in the same class. They all insist on subtle differences in pronunciation, and I never do master it. At one point I suggest calling them Kris1, Kris2, Kris3, Chris4, but they nix it.

I bestow an occasional nickname. I call a Richard, Ricochet because everything I say bounces off him. Another boy becomes Secret Weapon because he constantly surprises me. A girl I dub Vanya because she's pretty and makes everything into a presentation. And the students don't spare my name. Over the years I hear: Get Bent, Mentally Bentley, and Dentley. They ask me my first name and I say, Mister. You're lucky it's not Moore.

Do Not Remove The Label – *Names are serious business on report cards, progress reports, attendance records, diplomas, paychecks, and tombstones. Otherwise, it's just a point of reference so you don't have to say, Please stop talking, Mr. Butt Hole.*

Mr. Bentley, are you coming in tonight for Back-To-School Night? a student asks. It's the middle of September and it's that time of year. Like I have a foking choice, I want to say, but I smile and say, Of course. And I hope all your parents will be here. I look forward to meeting them. Meanwhile the bubble above my head says, Like bloody hell.

Back-To-School Night is curriculum night. Parents follow their children's schedules, and teachers have 10 minutes a class to explain the programs. One year I have an ACL done. I'm homebound, so I tape an 8 minute segment. I'm sitting back in a overstuffed chair while my cats crawl across my lap and above my head. At the end I say, Thank you for coming and would someone please hit the stop and rewind buttons. . . Parents comment on it for years. They remember the cats.

Animals 1, You 0 – *You can knock yourself out, but an animal will steal the show every time, even the ones they're cutting up in bio.*

Pissing Into The Wind – *You students might not be happy with the curriculum, your parents might not be happy with the curriculum, but nothing is going to change because of a complaint or two on Back To School Night. Bureaucracies are resistant to change. Stupidity has a long half life.*

It's not supposed to be a conference night, and most parents are good about not trying for a personal update. But there's always a scattering of kidults who ignore policy. They hang back, big smiles on their faces, trying for *the word*. I'm patient this year, age has its advantages, and squeeze them all in. It's a big change from earlier years when I had the Sartre attitude that hell is indeed other people, especially hovering helicopter parent types. After the night's over I meet another teacher in one of our parking lots. We sit in a darkened car in the backskirts and have a beer which is cold and energizing after a friendly, but dull night. We keep a sharp lookout. It seems like an adolescent stunt, and I wonder how many students, teachers, and staff have done this same thing.

There Are Enough Saints – *Not every rule has to be followed, but be careful of the ones you choose to ignore. We live in moralizing times, and the moralizers/crusaders can make your life fucking miserable.*

Student Don't Tread On Me – *Your teacher is human, just like you. It's the one great common trait you share. Still, there is distance. There are other goddamn role models.*

I get an email there's a PPT (Planning and Placement Team) meeting for one of my SPED (special education) students. No big deal. Sometimes when we go, we get to say our piece and leave. Other times they want us to stay for the whole thing, an endless go-round litany of the same observations: he works well in class but doesn't like homework; she never volunteers but is otherwise very sociable. . . I barely know the student at this point, have virtually nothing to say, and anything they say to me is always put into writing. I wind up telling them I don't feel well at the last minute and go home.

Sometime Yes, Sometimes HELL No *– There are meetings to go to, and meetings to ignore. Be aware that administrative dipsticks feel every meeting should be attended but meetings are what they do, their raison d'être. For teachers, meetings are best at Hubble range.*

Viva Las Student *– If you hate meetings you might want to consider becoming a teacher. If you love them, and are flexible enough to kiss an ass or two, educational administration might be just your thing.*

Teachers get an email that our yearly objectives are due by the end of the month. We're given a prepackaged, district-wide one, and individually have to come up with a personal one. I don't know what this year's district objective means, not totally, i.e. it's written in edspeak. Our new teachers are like: Are they kidding, what does this mean? I shrug and tell the neophytes not to worry. Somehow the coordinator will see the district objective's met and to just say on their own paperwork that all meetings were attended and all procedures followed and to accumulate a stack of papers on whatever because no one is going to read them, and to make up a table of impressive stats on whatever because no one is going to check them. And to put their efforts and time into their personal goal.

My own personal goal is simple: To survive another year. Beyond that I have to create a new course entitled African Americans In Literature and Film. I tried for years to get this course approved. Now I have to write the curriculum and get new books approved and ordered by the middle of January when the course kicks off. And only 2 students are signed up for it.

Objective Burma *– Perhaps objectives don't improve teaching or do anything but keep the boss happy. But every job has them and at least yours don't involve playing Errol Fucking Flynn and hacking through jungles and killing overacting Asians.*

I get my objectives in but don't make an appointment to talk about them. The bosses and I both know there is little point to all this. I'm at the end of my career; it's either this year or next. And if I don't meet objectives, what's the penalty? You're fired? Do them again next year? We have at least one teacher who's had the same objective, or variations of it, for years. On going. The relentless quest for perfection. Olympic caliber sandbagging.

A month later when we finally do sit down we both smile and are amiable. I'm told that it's a tough year to hit near the end of my career but what can one do? There's sympathy, head-bobbing, but no break, no slack, no stroking, not even a friendly pat. . . Shit. Ha. OK. I know this is nothing new, i.e. it's SOP whether you're a beginning or ending teacher. Lockstep regimentation, treating all equally, distributing an age-old objective/ observation model without regard to seniority, sex, or smarts. I suppose some might think, *Damn heartless/unimaginative fucktoid*, but I don't. The game's on, and if I can now game them I will.

Break A Leg: A very few years ago we English teachers are given a jump in our numbers of students, and I get 2 short of max. A couple of big honchos come to talk to the department. When they're done, I go to the blackboard, draw a horizontal rectangle, and say, This represents the time and energy that any of us have. I get a yardstick, measure the rectangle, and say, It's about 1'x2'. Then I say, You've just added on this amount, and I extend the rectangle to the right by 6 inches. But, I say, our time and energy are finite, they have to stay constant at 1'x2', so I chop 6 inches off the left portion of the rectangle and say, This represents cutting back on numbers of compositions and overall assessments because there's only so much time and energy and we're already using nights, weekends, and vacations for school work. You add more (and I extend the rectangle to the right again), we have to hack off more (I chop more off on the left) because finite is finite, there's only so much we have to give, and we're giving it all now. Every last bit. I sit down and think, *KMA*.

There's an eerie silence. I realize at the time I'm flirting with insubordination, but there are times when a frontline soldier has to go over the top and lay it out there. Epilogue: I don't get into trouble, but nothing changes either, except for my cutting back. The others carry on as usual and get less sleep.

Knock Your Dead Ass Out – *Don't shortchange the students but also do what you have to do to survive. Only you know how tough this job is and if you're looking for sympathy or help or gratitude, talk to the mirror. Or rescue a dog.*

Bueller, Bueller? *—Stressed to the max? Feeling gutted and filleted? Pull a Ferris Bueller and take a day off. I know teachers aren't supposed to say that but my generation turned on and dropped out so to a boomer taking a day off is just some mild mental ovulating.*

Snippets: One of our young teachers in the department asks me to co-produce and edit the student newspaper with her. I tell her she's very pretty, but it's not enough. Too much work, sorry. At my age it’s honesty, not sexual harassment. And she takes it as such.

Two girls are walking down the hall ahead of me, and I overhear: He was so like, like. . . You know. . . Other girl: Yeah.

Girl-To-Boy in a study hall: What was your favorite part of *Hairspray*? Him: When it ended.

One of our nontenured teachers in the department comes into my room before school.

- Can you help me out? Some parents think my composition grades are too low. They're giving me a hard time.

- Sure, no problem. Damn parents. Give me a photocopy of the compositions you already graded and want me to check. Get the names and your grades off. Give the same set to any other tenured teacher in the department. We'll mark them and grade them and sign them, and you can give them all to the parents as proof that your grading is on the mark, provided it is of course.

First Year Phone Conversation:

- Hello. Mrs. Fullson?

- Yes?

- This is Mr. Bentley calling, Anthony's English teacher. He said you wanted me to call you.

- I did. We don't understand the grade on his last composition.

- You don't understand it?

- No.

- Aren't there comments written all over it?

- Pretty much.

- Do you understand the comments?

- I guess so.

- So, you understand the comments but you disagree with the grade?

- That's right. You gave him a C+. I read his composition myself and I think he deserves an A.

- How many other compositions did you read?

- What do you mean?

- Did you read any of the other compositions in the class?

- No, of course not. I just read his.

- Well, I read 100 others and I can assure you that in relation to the others his composition is a C+. I read a few of the others out loud. Did Anthony tell you that?

- No.

- Well, I wanted the class to hear what the best ones sounded like. Tell Anthony if he still thinks his composition is as good as the ones I read, to bring his composition back in either before or after school, or during lunch or study, and we'll go over it line-by-line. If I made a mistake I'll change the grade. I don't want him to feel cheated.

I no sooner hang up on that first questioning parent than I realize my ingrained standards need to be put into writing, and I invent my General Writing Checklist. It's a list of about 15 characteristics of good writing with space for the writer and 2 peer editors to checkoff and comment. Over time I create many other checklists for various kinds of compositions, but the General Writing Checklist never changes and still today accompanies each specific composition checklist.

This sounds very basic in the 21st century, but it wasn't when I started. Teachers back then just assigned compositions, and it was a student guessing game to decide just what the teacher wanted. Some regarded what I was doing as an infantile writing-by-the-numbers and poo-poo'ed it. As the years rolled by, I slowly shared my checklists, others modified them and over time started calling them matrixes and rubrics but I never stopped calling mine checklists. The checklists were my attempt to take a subjective area like composition and make it as objective as possible. I still feel it was one of the best things I did in education.

***Nothing Up This Sleeve** – Students can't rise to your standards if they don't know what they are. On the other hand if you've clearly communicated them, you've just belayed a lot of voice mails and iquestions. Everyone is happy. Or at least not iP.O.'ed.*

***You Can Handle The Truth** – Ask, ask, ask. Speak up if you have questions. The teacher can almost read your mind, but not fucking quite.*

Another veteran teacher and I grade three compositions from the non-tenured teacher, and it turns out the most we three differ is a half letter grade on one composition. I'm a little surprised but not shocked. So much for the notion that young teachers don't know what they're doing. This generation is the most highly trained I've ever seen. Much more highly trained than the critical parents. The parents don't let up. Damon Runyon would call it humming from mosquitos, and it eventually gets administration's attention. In the end it's a real cluster fuck and no one's happy.

It's nearing the end of September and my two senior classes are in good academic shape. Seventy-five percent have either an A or B. Out of my sophomores, however, 24% are failing, and I'm wracking my brain to understand why. And how? How did they get to be sophomores? They tell me they didn't do anything last year either. Two of last year's freshmen teachers are gone, so I can only imagine what kind of standards they had. Probably a lot of emphasis on in-class work, and homework checks that were sparse or superficial, if at all. I debate: Should I weigh homework less, in-class work more? It'll take that little of a change to make the percentages more palatable. . . If I were a beginning teacher, I probably would. But I've been doing this for too many years and I know what's fair and what the average student can and should handle. Besides I've told innumerable administrators, If you let me drop homework and grade just what students do in-class, I'll probably never have a failure again. Can't do that, I'm told, students need homework. Even, I ask, if it's setting up some of the recalcitrant monster fuckup types for summer school or a repeat of the course? Yes, administration says. Students have a right to fail. But it seems bassackward to what I should be doing, I say. Shouldn't I be taking them where they are (unmotivated) and acknowledging that at 16 or 17 a radical turnabout is unlikely and giving them some coasting room? Just assign the homework, I'm told. How about removing the hard core nonworkers, I persist, the ones who really could use some cognitive steroids and putting them in a self contained class with lower standards? Just assign the homework, I'm told.

Suck It Up *– Spike Lee said, Do the right thing, and traditionally the right thing is not dumbing down a course, putting expectations down on the deck because a few fail. As Ernest Hemingway should have said, The scum also rises. Sometimes.*

If Only *– Flunking? Don't like your teacher? Don't like your course/school? The futurist Buckminster Fuller said that you never change things by fighting the existing reality, you change it by creating a new model that makes the old obsolete. So, what new goddamn model will you create to replace school?*

Guidance Room Conference: A few other teachers and I meet after school with the parents of a failing student. After we give our updates and assessments, Dad in his ten-piece suit turns to Percivale and says angrily, You know what's going to happen if you don't get your grades up? You're *not* going to have much of a future. What you do now will determine the course of your life.

Bullshit, I think, and can't help interrupting with a polite but firm, Well no, that's not actually totally true. I've had a number of failed students over the years who have gone on to some very successful careers. Not all, but enough. I'm certainly not recommending or condoning failure now. I just hate to see Percivale leave here thinking his future's over if he fails World Lit. It's not.

Sidebar: There's a huge list of famous high school dropouts including George Gershwin, Wendy's founder Dave Thomas, billionaire Richard Branson, the Wright brothers, Tom Cruise, Cher, and many more. No sense in denying that today's failure *can* become tomorrow's success story. Students know how to Google.

I half expect Dad to explode, or implode, but nothing happens other than some head nodding. I've just given Percivale a free Get Out Of Jail card and later ask myself why. Why did I try to de-flower the myth that high school is the be-all end-all? Was it good guidance, was it even the truth or just a reaction to dad's pontificating and his Brooks Brothers' stature? It ultimately doesn't matter. Percivale's work picks up and his grades improve. Who knows why. A bell tinkles, an angel gets his wings.

September comes to an end. The month did not zip by for me, the school day seems longer than ever, 5 hours would be plenty. William Glasser: There are only two places in the world where time takes precedent over the job to be done: school and prison.

Retirement at the end is looking better and better but it's far from a lock, and there's always *perhaps*. Perhaps administration will ease up, perhaps my sophomores will see the light on their own road to Damascus, perhaps October will be better, and the Superus Perhaps – perhaps the Red Sox will win the pennant and World Series.

Perhaps.

OCTOBER – Everything But Wipe Their Asses

Progress reports come out, and my voice mail and email increase, but life is good because it's autumn in New England. Let them question grades, carp, bitch, cry to guidance, insist the other grade level teachers are easier. I'm impervious. Extra help is available everyday, I tell them. But I can't do the basic reading and writing for you. And I refuse to wipe any ass but my own. Even before the leaves start to turn there's a crispness in the air, a bit of a chill that's invigorating. I love this time of year.

Paul Bentley, your guidance counselor wants to see you, my Latin 1 teacher says.

- What?

- Go to guidance.

- Why?

- I don't know. Just go.

- Who's my guidance counselor?

- Mr. V wants to see you.

It's October, and Bentley the freshman is getting called to guidance, which means leaving the building, crossing street, and finding this Mr V in the other building. It only takes 2 minutes and I'm knocking on a door frame and staring at a tiny, gray haired Polish man whose last name is so long he's simply called Mr. V.

- You want to see me?

- Who are you?

- Bentley. Paul.

- Come in. . . He doesn't offer a chair so I stand there awkwardly while he fumbles through some papers. He looks up, says my address – I nod. Says my phone number – I nod. Says my date of birth – I nod again. I'm wondering if this is it, i.e. verifying personal information, when he hits me with the biggy: What do you want to be when you grow up?

- Huh?

- What do you want to be when you grow up? . . . No segue, no transition from small talk to the crux of life itself. What do I want to be? What does any 14-year-old want to be? I used to want to be a superhero and rescue exotic women but I can't tell him that. Then I wanted to be a cowboy and a soldier, but no more. With scarcely a thought I say, An English teacher.

- An English teacher, he repeats and writes it down. OK, you can go back to class.

And just like that my future has direction, though to this day I don't know why I said English teacher. English teaching back then is spelling and diagramming sentences, business and friendly letters. Up to 9th grade there are no novels, poetry, drama, film, or creative writing in our curriculum. English has all the appeal of skinned knees and wearing glasses. The English teachers themselves are wide ties and puckered vaginas.

But I do like to read and write, and we do have books in our house: *The Untouchables*, *The F.B.I. Story*, *The Power Of Positive Thinking*, a set of Collier's Encyclopedia.

I don't see Mr. V again for 3½ years when he calls me down again and asks, Do you still want to be an English teacher? – Yes. Where're you going to college? – UConn. And that's my high school guidance experience. Pathetic, or at least that's what I think for years until one illuminating day I realize that by asking me that most basic question: What do you want to be? in a formal surrounding Mr. V forced me to look ahead. Seriously. And that's a big deal. Teens live in the moment, the latest zit or hard-on can be an all occupying thought. A future glance, imbuing a sense of calling, is a very big deal. And while I'm sure it didn't work for all, or even most, it did for me.

Touching The Future *– It might be a cliché to say life's best lived with a sense of calling, but it's true. And if a person doesn't feel that way, he/she should try something else. Life's too short for self-flagellation and beating the piss out of yourself.*

Hand On Student Shoulder *– Latch onto what you know and love in life. Just don't get charged with stalking.*

I give my Film class the screenplay *Brian's Song* on a Thursday. One of my D students isn't here when I pass the book out and doesn't show up until the following Monday when I give her the book and bring her up to speed adding, The test is this Thursday.

- Don't I get an extension? She's pretty in a world-weary Veronica Lake sort of way and is probably used to catching some breaks.

- Are you going to read it? If not, you might as well take the test Thursday. . . I'm blunt but logical given the fact she hasn't read anything yet.

- I'll read it.

- OK, then take an extra week. But don't tell me you're going to read it, then not read it. Don't jerk me around. *Opps*, I think, but the jerk-me-around gets no reaction.

- I'll read it.

- OK.

Burn Unit *– Better to err on the side of compassion than to be accused of being unfair. Unfair generates ill-will, and phone calls. Unfair gets your house egged and your car keyed. Plus it's just. . . not. . . nice.*

Playing With Matches *– Teacher cut you some slack? Pay it forward. Cut him/her some slack. Pay your debts, even the psychological ones. Don't be a cheap fuck.*

Turns out the girl doesn't read *Brian's Song*, doesn't take the test. I collect her book two weeks later and give her a zero. She takes it with a shrug. What was that extension all about, saving face in front of the class? But they know she's nearly flunking. These douchetards know everything about everyone. When I want to know anything about school business, I just ask them. They're human wiretaps, i.e. connected and willing to tell.

The student looks at me sleepily, her dark eyelids are half drawn shades. She has a literature quiz in front of her, but she's not writing. I know the possibilities only too well: drugs, alcohol, partying the night before, too many extracurriculars, a job. She flips the quiz over without writing and puts her head down between her arms. I remember only too well my first somnolent student. It was a 14-year-old boy who had a morning paper route. He used to fall asleep every afternoon, and come spring I'd let him alone for 5 minutes before waking him. He wasn't much of a student anyway, the job was important to him, but most importantly he was a helluva a baseball player, I'm his coach, and the 300 second catnap is the difference between him being sharp on the field and not. For me it's a balancing act between academics and let's-be-proactive-go-team-go. If an administrator ever asked, I'd toss in safety too.

This female student I don't know much about. I take a shot and say, Job? She partially picks up her head and nods in agreement. Later I find out she's a counter worker, fast food, 15 hours during the week, 5 hours last night, and I'm annoyed. This girl's mother has already contacted me concerned over her poor grades and mom's letting her work all these hours during the week? Amazing. String theory of education. Work, sleep, class – all different dimensions that interweave here. Life appears to be separate particles but it's all a homogeneous whole where public education's concerned. Right now sleep appears to be the dominating dimension. I let it go, and the girl settles down for a nice autumn nap. No problem-o. Perhaps her unconscious will absorb some of today's lesson. W.H. Auden: A teacher is someone who talks in someone else's sleep.

Sidebar: When the famous writer and artist Henry Miller (*Tropic Of Cancer*, *Tropic Of Capricorn*) was in high school, his art teacher considered him so inept that he told Miller not to bother coming to class. Miller went on to paint thousands of watercolors that were praised by international critics. Biblical Thought: He who is last, will wind up first. Twenty-first Century Educational Appendage: Not usually. Life’s not a goddamn fairy tale.

Mr. Bentley, can I go to the lav? The boy looks bored, and no doubt wants a break and maybe some penis stimulation.

- I don't know. *Can* you?. . . I'm staying in character and busting his ass just a bit. The boy looks even more bored now but picks up his cue.

- *May* I go?

- Sure. Just fill out your passbook.

He does, I sign it, and 10 minutes later he saunters back in, smiles for everyone, and slides back down prepared to clock gaze till the bell.

- Excuse me. Even as I say it I think, *Here we go*. You were gone for 10 minutes.

- So?

- The lav's next door. I'm figuring 10 seconds to get there, another 10 to get back, 2-3 minutes total.

- I really had to go. And you're supposed to wash your hands for 2 minutes.

- Really? Who told you that?. . . Sidebar: It's a new one and I'm always interested in the latest.

- We learned it in health.

- Sounds appropriate for surgeons. But that still doesn't account for 10 minutes unless you have a bladder problem in which case you need to bring in a note from your doctor.

- I got a drink too.

- There's no water fountain around here.

- I went over to the gym.

- That's quite a walk. But your pass was only for the lav.

- I can't get a drink too?

- Not a 10 minute one.

- The drink wasn't that long.

- You can't wander the halls.

- I ran into a teacher who had to tell me some stuff . . . This is standard Q&A stuff, and he knows enough to say *teacher* rather than *friend.*

- Who?

- My guidance counselor. Call him if you don't believe me.

He's gambling, figuring I won't want to be bothered, won't even want to ask him who his counselor is. All too much trouble: get the name, look up the phone extension, get the counselor's voice mail, play phone tag, etc. It's a good strategy putting the work on me, but I learned long ago to reverse it.

- Tell you what. I'll hold off writing you up until the end of the day. . . I pause and take a yellow form out of my top drawer. . . You bring me a note from your guidance counselor saying when, where, and for how long you two talked, and I'll forget the discipline notice. Let you slide on wandering off for a drink. Fair enough?

- Why don't you just call him now?

Ralph Waldo Emerson: Conversation is the laboratory and workshop of the student.

This student could blow smoke forever. But I can't, and neither can the class.

- (stern look, the exaggerated calm of customer service) I. . . don't. . . have. . . the. . . time. . . *You* were the late one. *You* take care of it.

Fini. End of discussion, turdwad.

The student's look tells the class, It's not fair, but he doesn't say anything more. The day passes, the bright yellow form can't be ignored, and when the students leave I write the boy up and put it into the discipline officer's mailbox early the next morning. No big deal. The boy could get just a warning, provided it's a lone offense. If not, he could get anything from an hour's detention to Saturday morning in-school. Sky's the limit for a repeat turdwad.

Heart Of Lettuce *– Students are not zen masters or camels. They need movement, physical releases, and water. But they need to do it all in waaaay under 10 minutes, just like NASCAR.*

***On Your Marks, Get Set** – Your teacher understands that poopie, wee-wee, and wah-wah are natural things. But let's not make any of them into a project. There's only a grade for being a whiz, not taking one.*

When female students take prolonged breaks, a natural excuse is that it's their time of the month, and I've had several females over the years who were not shy about saying it. Or they just lower their eyes and say something along the lines of, Mr. B, I was gone a long time because it's that, you know, umm, time, ahh, you know what I mean. Since there's no debating this, especially for a male teacher, the only thing to do is to insert common sense and err on the side of compassion. Plato: Be kind. Everyone you meet is fighting a hard battle. If a female, or anyone, is habitually asking to go to the lav, you need to track it and get the office/nurse/parents involved. You might be doing the student a favor, though probably not.

I proctor the PSAT's one Saturday morning. I've done it many times. The students arrive with their #2 pencils, calculators, large mugs of coffee, muffins, and we get down to the business of charting their future. At least that's what most of the prep speakers tell them. I don't. I say, Want one of the top hundred competitive colleges? Want cutthroat competition and an academic future of study, study, study? Then better ace it all. But if not, if you're aiming at Community College, Unheralded College, School Of Mixology, Cooking Academy, Big Rig Driving School, Institute of Hairdressing and Barbering, the Armed Forces, bagging at Wal-Mart, etc. don't sweat it because they don't care much about this test. And besides, there's little you can do at this late date except panic yourself and black out. . . I'm trying to be comforting. And honest. They take the test, I read and watch the clock, and a little after 11 they're gone and I'm on my way to a football game. Undoubtedly it'll be a more exciting afternoon for all of us and in many cases, no less important.

Stanley comes in to see me after school. It's been years since I've seen him, but I recognize him immediately: same bowl-cut hair, same conservatively styled out-of-fashion clothes, still heavy with the same soft pinkish skin that I associate with puberty, and still shy and soft spoken. Stanley's one of those fringers every teacher worries about. Some students complain he smells and I have to get the nurse to talk to him about hygiene. A pretty brunette who at first is willing to talk to him and appears to be one of his few friends later complains he's bothering her, though I think he's just talking to her as anyone might who's lonely but doesn't really know how to converse. He isn't allowed to read Arthur Miller because of a few swear words and I have to find an alternate book. Socially he plays the buffoon at times to include sticking his finger up his nose which gets the wrong kinds of laughs.

I'm doing all right now Mr. B, Stanley tells me, but I've decided I want to go to college. I couldn't go before, I didn't have the money. But a relative's going to pay, so I want to go before it's too late. . . He's wondering if I'll write him a recommendation. You were my favorite teacher, he tells me and I'm touched. Of course I'll write you a recommendation, I tell him and he's all smiles. Just give me a couple of days, then stop by and I'll hand it to you. Happy to help. He thanks me, we shake hands, and I see him to the door.

A couple of days later I print out multiple copies of his recommendation on school stationery, put them in a folder, and leave it out on the desk all ready for him when he comes. But he never does. Not that week, not for the rest of the year. No visit, no note, no phone call, no email. Stanley vanishes as quickly as he appeared, and at first I'm annoyed before I realize his world probably collapsed, again. Probably lost his financing, if he ever had it to begin with. Maybe it was all just an excuse to come in to see an old familiar face and a space where he'd been treated civilly and where he'd enjoyed some success.

Don't Get The Fair Or The Fare – *Life isn't equal, students aren't equal. Try to give the impression of treating all equally, but don't. There simply are ones who need more, and you have to be ready, willing, and even eager to give them that more. More is a great gift. And sometimes it doesn't end.*

You Start With A Stack Of Chips – *Not everyone in your life will adapt to you or make allowances for you. Family members, friends, pets, and teachers might. Just don't get all kissy-ass over it. It's just the way it is. For now.*

My seniors are having a discussion and for some reason one of them is describing a grizzly bear. He says, It was fucking huge! and keeps talking. The others pause, none of us are quite sure what we just heard, everyone is looking around, then the laughter starts. The boy stops talking and looks around puzzled. I ask him, What did you just say? What? he asks. What was it you just said? I repeat. I didn't say anything, he says and he's totally unaware of saying anything out of the ordinary. You said the bear was fucking huge, I tell him. No I didn't, he says after a moment's reflection. Yes, you did, I insist, but I'm smiling and laughing along with the rest of the class. He looks around, sees he's wrong, and finally smiles himself.

Swear By It – *Just as laughter's an important part of life, laughter's an important part of the classroom. And there's no sense in denying a filthy word at an unexpected moment isn't funny. It is, or Redd Foxx and George Carlin would have died paupers.*

All The World Loves A Clown *– A classroom is a classroom, and Comedy Central's Comedy Central. There may be a very occasional overlap, but for the most part keep your public shtik clean. There are fucking teachers present.*

The bell hasn't rung to start class yet, and this class is having their usual freewheeling time with nearly everyone standing and exchanging lots of trash talk.

- You fucking bitch! a boy yells at a girl across the room.

- What did you say? I jump right in. Bell or no bell, a double expletive with emphasis on the F word needs attention. This isn't a faux pas, not the grizzly bear slip.

- Freaking, he says defiantly and doesn't miss a beat.

- Out! and I jerk my thumb towards the door. You know where to go. And let me remind you, it's a zero for the day. He grabs his gear, doesn't protest, doesn't say a word, cares little about this class, less about the zero. He walks out and leaves the door open. I walk over and close it softly feeling not good, not bad, just frustrated. I normally believe what happens in the classroom, stays in the classroom, i.e. I like to handle my own discipline, but this particular student has pushed it once too often, and his Planet Me attitude needs a new orbit. At least for today.

It's an ominous start, but the bell rings and things settle down.

Thirty minutes later another boy is frantically waving his hand.

- Mr. Bentley!

- What?

- This thing is leaking.

- What thing? He points under his desk, and I have to move around mine for a better look. Sure enough, water is seeping around the edges of a round metal plate in the floor directly under him. I know what the plate is. It's the cover for the sewer line that runs directly under my room from the girls' lav next door. I tell him to change his seat and tell the class, Keep an eye on it. Let me know if it gets worse. I go to the phone and barely pick up the receiver when I hear, It's getting worse!. . . I see the puddle spreading fast and tell them, Go back to lunch – they just ate – and stay there until further notice. As they're gleefully leaving, water starts shooting fountain-like 2 feet into the air out of the four screw holes that don't have screws. Did someone just flush a toilet? It's actually quite pretty once you get beyond the fact this is waste water.

A janitor and boss arrive. There's plenty of disgust all around. A wet vac is started and the girls' lav locked. The plate's pried off. It turns out that the screw-in plug on the line has not been screwed in, and floating in the water now is a brown turd. Gross. More than I need to see of my students. Another maintenance man enters and starts a mechanical snake. I'm told that despite being warned-and-rewarned our females persist in flushing their tampons and sanitary napkins down the toilets. The line gets clogged, and this time the backup is taking refuge here in my basement crib. I'm told this is going to take awhile and that I should be looking for another room for my afternoon classes.

I make sure nothing of importance is in the bottom drawer of my main file cabinet which sits on the floor directly in the path of this pestilential pond, then go in search of a room for next period. I could involve the main office, but this is faster and I have a room inside of two minutes. All's well that ends well.

Boy Scout Redux *– Be prepared, expect the unexpected. There's no planning for the unexpected – how could there be? But expect it, and don't go to pieces even when your classroom turns spontaneously to crap. Literally.*

Tiny Bubbles In The Line *– We live in a disposable world but please dispose of things properly. Some things don't dissolve, others don't sink. Hope floats, it's true, but no one breaks out a 50 foot snake for that.*

Kids Say the Damnedest Things: The film class has watched *Wings*, *It Happened One Night*, *Gone With the Wind*, *Pinocchio*, the 2-hour documentary *Victory At Sea*, *Peyton Place*, and *Some Like It Hot* so far. I show them the award winners and we move chronologically forward. Out of them all *Gone With the Wind* draws the most humorously written comments. One student says, The Yankees raised the price of Terror (instead of Tara, the plantation). Another, possibly with a Latin background, calls Tara, Terra (which it is), while a female says, Rhett gives in to the temptation of Scarlett's charm. This is understandable since he is a man.

It's Monday, and I'm collecting the latest composition. One of my zero liners tells me, I'm on holiday. I ask another for his and he shrugs. I ask, Did you work your part-time job Sunday? No, he says. Saturday? No. Last Friday? No. . . I tell him, Guess you're not supporting a family either, but even that wouldn't be excuse enough. I tell them both, You don't want to do anything, don't want to be part of the class, that's your choice. (Reflection: Why do the worst behaved have the best attendance, or does it just seem that way?). I understand you're bored, why wouldn't you be? You're both unprepared daily, and most days don't even want to work when you're here. You have the right not to work and to be bored.

I move them to opposite corners in the back of the class and tell them, This is a semi-permanent change. I'll consider moving you back if-and-when you show a proven pattern of work. Don't want to work? Read a magazine or do other schoolwork. No ipods, iphones, e-games, or making any noise whatsoever. Make noise and you're outtahere. Put your heads down and sleep if you want, but don't snore.

Flashback: Same situation years ago. There's no way this student can remotely pass. I tell him, From now till the end of the year I'll write you a pass to the library, computer room, guidance, or anywhere else within the school you want to go. No sense in wasting time here. Maybe you can run some laps, weight lift, build something in wood shop, do something constructive. He's puzzled, then elated. You mean I don't have to come here anymore? he asks incredulously. Just to get a pass and sign out, I tell him. I have to know where you are if the office calls.

He immediately signs out and does so for a couple of weeks. Then I notice he's hanging around more-and-more, not signing out. He's not doing any work, but he's not being disruptive either. I ask, Don't you want to go anywhere? No projects to work on? He shakes his head. Another teacher tells me he's lonely and hurt that I don't seem to care about him anymore. I set him free, but freedom isn't what he needed, or wanted.

Like A Circle In A Spiral – *Not every baby bird flies when shoved out of the nest, not every student soars when released. The only constant is gravity, whose preferred direction is down, and it takes work and balls to overcome it.*

For Want Of Want *– Want independence? Immortality? Peace in our time? Unconditional love? A tax free life?. . . None of them happen in undergrad life. And none of them happen in postgrad life either. Actually, none of them ever happen, ever. And that's the truth, Ruth.*

Our parent conferences this year are 5 minutes each with 2 minutes in-between. There are 22 slots on each of two nights, 44 slots total. A student presents the individual teacher with a signup form if the parent wants a conference, and the teacher fills in a time. All the English teachers this year fill in the 44 slots fast, with an additional 20-30 parents who want phone calls because they can't get scheduled.

During the conferences a bell rings every 5 minutes, and like a sheepdog you keep 'em moving. No problem. Not usually. Occasionally you run over and the next parent feels shortchanged. Or a parent is late and you're tempted to take the on-deck person who's usually a mom. And maybe you do, then the scheduled parent shows up and you could just flip-flop the two, but the late parent already has a full schedule, so you grab a phone number, or stay late, or get dirty looks and angry words and a cloud of dust, and think cheeeezz what the hell was that all about?

Words, Words, Words *– During conferences, stay on schedule even if it means gibbering away on fast forward. Just slow down for the key phrases: Great young person, positive influence, winning personality, will go far, talks good shit, etc.*

Student Nudge *– If you want to toss out the conference signup form or the letter from the main office saying it's conference time, go ahead. It's OK with your teacher and will put you on the FOT (Friend Of Teacher) list if you let* *him/her know, provided your parents aren't some of those rare out-to-lunchers the teacher actually should meet and talk to.*

Out of my 44 slots this year, only 23 of mine are filled. I'm the envy of the English Department and claim a department record. Twenty-three is so few, in fact, I believe it'd be a school record if not for P.E. and Culinary. Even when we've conflicted with the World Series, the mothers pour into English like we're having a clearance sale on A's. I chalk up my low numbers this year to a preponderance of Level 2 students and the fact report cards haven't come out yet, though some of my students bury or change them anyway. I have one student flat out tell me his parents have never seen a real report card or progress report.

Out of the 23 signed up, 21 show up. No problems, some of the usual requests, i.e. contact me if the grade goes down, if she misses an assignment, if he sneezes, if she farts. I always reverse it and suggest it would be more effective and quicker if *you ma'm* would initiate the contact and email's best, or have the guidance counselor send around a daily/weekly progress sheet – whichever you prefer ma'm. Overall Scene: I talk, they talk; I frown, they frown; I smile, they smile. I sneak looks at my watch and always try to end with a positive remark or two.

Out of all the conference nights over the years only two stand out. One involves a student with a really unique voice: low and gruff, that doesn't fit his A average. The parents come in, we're sitting facing each other and I'm pointing out his grades in my grade book, showing them the corresponding papers in his portfolio, and all of a sudden without realizing it I'm imitating the boy, talking low and gruff, and going, So haaay Mr. Bentley, I'm not gettin' dah question. Yah want both dah literal an' metaphorical, is dat it?. . . And as I'm talking the parents' eyes are getting wider and wider, and all of a sudden I realize what I'm doing, stop instantly and flip the record over, i.e. I raise my voice an octave and say without missing a beat in my best King's English, He's been a fine student, a fine boy, and I see no reason to think he won't go far. . . The parents are aghast, I'm totally embarrassed, but I don't know what to do. I really like their son a lot, know I'm way out of line, know I should apologize, but just want my stupid ass shit to vanish instantly like a belch and not be brought up again.

I don't apologize then or later. I get small.

Tears And Fears And Feeling Proud – *Be willing to use the "s" word and to really be sorry when you do. It's all about intent and perception. A truly contrite person is an object of sympathy, a serial offender is not.*

Student Aside – *Your teacher wants to praise you to your parents, so try to give him/her some material to work with. Fact: You can't write the parent/ teacher conference script yourself. It's not like changing a report card.*

The other memorable conference involves a paraprofessional in our school who's also one of my parents, unbeknownst to me. We've been experiencing a large turnover of peripheral staff and I'm way behind learning names. The lady shows up for a conference, I greet her at the door recognizing her as a fellow staffer but wonder why she's here. It's apparent she wants to sit down, so we do, and I'm staring at her hoping something will click when she says, So how's my son doing? I realize I don't know her name, didn't look to see who my next conference is, and I'm staring blankly back at her. Our eyes are locked, the conference sheet is right in front of me on the desk but for some reason I can't look down. There's a long pause, a looong pause, and she finally says, Sean, my son is Sean. Sure, I chime back glancing down at the column of names and their classes, Sean, of course. Well, to begin with he's still doing. . .

And again, I don't apologize, though we both know I shouldn't be dancing a victory dance in the end zone either. I'm happy there's no black box recorder. Closure: I never again make the mistake of imitating a student – at least not in front of the parents. And post-Sean I always know who my next conference is, i.e. I don't need a post conference one-on-one with the aspirin bottle or my own conscience.

My senior Drama class has read *Oedipus Rex* (which one teacher mistakingly calls Maximus Rex), *Everyman*, *As You Like It*, *The Miser*, *Beggar's Opera*, and *The Pirates Of Penzance.* They learn the language of theatre and reviewing, and they write their own reviews. It's the best student writing I get all year, insightful and biting. And it's a pleasure to read.

A Barrel Of Monkeys – *If it's fun for them, it can be fun for you. Assignments that offer only tedious regurgitation will disenchant them and slowly kill you. Flannery O'Connor: There's many a bestseller that could have been prevented by a good teacher. . . If you get that, you get it.*

Double Dog Dare You – *The world needs creativity and constant rebirth. And so do you. Never let a teacher stifle your need to create even if it's done outside of school. S.E. Hinton wrote the The Outsiders while still a high school student. What bozo busting way-nutz originality's in you?*

See me, the email says from one of the administrators. I hate that. No subject line, no indication of why or when, but I go and Boss is busy. For the next day Boss is always busy with someone, or out, or on the phone. But, See me, so I continue to try. Finally I get in.

- Did you throw Wilbur out of your class?

- Two days ago? Yes.

- You didn't write him up?

- I gave it to another boss.

- So what happened?

- He came in late for the 7th time. I told to get his work out, he didn't, and then we jawed and I threw him out.

- Did you call him an idiot and say duhh?

- I don't remember. Probably. I probably said he was acting like an idiot.

- This is an argument we can't win with the parents.

- I know. My only excuse is the class is driving me crazy. It makes me stick my foot in my mouth every once in awhile so thank God it's only a nine.

We both smile. Boss wants the names of all the troublemakers in that class. They get called down next period en masse and read the riot act. Nothing changes, but it's good to know something at least has been tried and that there's support from the office. It's going to be a real odyssey with this group.

Sidebar: I was hired 32 years ago when a veteran teacher was driven out by rowdy students. The instructions to me then were simple: Get control of the class back. I got it back and haven't relinquished it since. Undefeated, teacher-in-chief, though at times playing bad cop is no fun and playing it too often is a soul killer. I try for balance. I'd rather teach than micro-ramrod, but every few years a genetically mutated group comes along from hell. A teacher can either step up or step aside. There's not a lot of choice.

Testosterone Shot *– When behavior becomes an issue, when it comes down to it's either them or you, always remember: it's you. And anyone else who wants to learn.*

Turkey Shoot *– Your teacher has little interest in talk. Think of your teacher as Yoda and remember, Do, or do not, there is no try. Forget the jawing. Forget the con. Just, do. Do-be, do-be, do.*

Sidebar 1: The author S.E. Hinton trained as a teacher, but never became one because she said she lacked the nerve and physical stamina. Teachers know exactly what she means. You give up days, nights, weekends, all to teach, grade, and prepare. The phrase work-free-holiday does not exist. You wear name brands like Armani, Gucci, Valentino, Givenchy, Rolex, etc. only in your dreams though you'll be expected to dress sharply. You'll be hard pressed to meet an average mortgage, will paper bag your lunches and eat them in your room to save time, dip into your own pocket for supplies, get p.o.'ed parents calling for trivial matters. Everyone will think they know your job better than you. Some parents will preface remarks with, Back when I was a teacher, omitting they only lasted a year or two because they couldn't take it. Board of Ed members who were poor students and hellions themselves will pile local mandates on top of state ones. Other professionals won't give you a level gaze. You'll eat takeout pizza and rent dvd's and call it a night out. You'll be gutted by 8 p.m. and wake up with correcting ink on your fingers and a pile of fallen papers on the floor. And maybe at the end of your career you'll be burned out and cynical, and think it's all been a big waste of time. But if it was, it was a terrific waste of time that only you and a few other pigheaded balls-to-the-wall idealists could, and would, do.

Sidebar 2: Certainly, there are other professions that ooze nobility, are full of stress, involve long hours, serve a real public need, all for little thanks and less pay. But Jeff Bridges in the movie *Starman* wanted his son raised as a teacher, so it's got to be a good/great thing. Or at least an alien thing.

A half dozen of us teachers are having a meeting in guidance with a parent. My turn, and parent expresses disbelief that his son isn't doing the homework and is getting zeroes because of it on the daily quizzes. He gives me an understated, Really? and says, I want to see my son's latest quiz. . . I go back to the room, get it, and hand it over. Across the quiz the boy's written, I didn't read. Why he wrote that – there are several that do – I have no idea. Most of the thumbers-up-the-ass just doodle or leave the paper blank. But bless his little sprained brain now. Dad's jaw tightens. It's like he's just scraped the black paint off the Maltese Falcon and realizes he's been conned. Attitude drops a millimeter, but no apology. No, You were right after all. Not even a, Well I'll be damned. Just, I'll talk to him.

Send In The Clowns – *It's incredible how willing some parents are to believe a 16-year-old and to disbelieve a 59-year-old. Apparently blood is thicker than common sense, and umbilical cords have a fucking high tensile strength.*

Fall Guy 101 – *Go ahead and blame detentions, poor grades, cafeteria food, and even bad hair days on the teacher. Some of us are even old enough to take the blame for the Kennedy assassination and the Beatles' breakup. The ozone layer, global warming, and the Titanic would be pushing it, though with some fart sniffing parents who knows?*

Eavesdropping Timeout: Overweight boy to boy in front of him: I used to be handsome when I was small. Now look at me.

Girl-to-friend in hallway: My guidance counselor talked to me for 45 minutes, and it was about nothing.

My wife's been an elementary teacher for 37 years. She's on bus duty and hears one first grader say to another, My parents are getting divorced. Dad hates mom, Mom says Dad's a liar, and mom's got a big zit on her forehead. Wife's kindergartner chimes in with, Ohhh, that hurts.

I happily report to a mister & the missis that their son has the second highest average in my 3 sophomore classes and is close to having the highest. They're as thrilled, as I am. It's always a pleasure to have a male excelling in what's traditionally a female dominated field. It's been a decade since my best student was male, and I'm as puzzled as anyone by this gender gap as there's no shortage of crack male reporters, best selling male authors, brainiac male lit professors, etc. Why males don't succeed more at this secondary level is a puzzle. The out-and-out smartest two students I ever had were male, i.e. they had the 2 highest IQ's that I'm aware of though neither had the highest class average.

Flashback: Janos is in my honors 7th grade class back in the days when it's a junior high, and we have 4-tier grouping. Janos reads all the time, pretty much a book a day, and can divide his attention so I let him read. He devours everything from fantasy to science and even reads during lunch. . . It's the beginning of the year and I'm going over ten new vocabulary words. I say each word to see if anyone knows what the word means before we work with it. One of the first words is *drone*. Janos is reading, but his hand is the lone one up, so I call on him. Drone is a low humming sound, like the drone of the engine, he says scarcely looking up from his book. Very good, I reply and start to move onto the next word but his hand is still up. Janos? Drone can also mean a male bee, as in the drone serviced the queen. Right again, I say and pause because his unwaving hand is still up and it surprises me. He's got everyone's unwavering attention. Janos? Drone can also mean a plane that's remotely controlled as in the air force shot down the drone. Now he puts his hand down. The class is thunderstruck, and I realize that I've just witnessed a display of intelligence that is unprecedented in my experience. And I'll never see the like of it again.

A Stephen Hawking's Universe – *You're going to have a lot of smart students in your career, but if you're lucky you'll get one so brilliant that you'll need to relinquish the title Teacher and replace it with Guide. Be gentle with your guidance. This is Starman's child.*

3,2,1 Blastoff! – *There is always someone brainier and less brainy than yourself. Comparisons tend to give a false sense of superiority or inferiority, so avoid them. Be gentle with yourself. You too are a Star Child (maybe Starbucks too).*

A girl presents her chapter analysis – they each have a section of the book they're responsible for – and after a round of polite applause a student says to me, Mr. Bentley, I might not be smart, but I'm strong. Why he says this out of the clear blue I have no idea, but it makes sense to the class. Heads nod around the room and he gets some verbal endorsements. He's encouraged and wants to arm wrestle me. I decline. The class wants the contest, but we all know it's an everything-to-lose, nothing-to-gain proposition for me. I don't think I'll lose, but in any case this isn't gym or interage competition. I tell the would-be gladiator, This class is about brains, not brawn. Academic, not physical.

Another student takes the off-topic cue and says, I'm smart. I just don't try. Not often, anyway. I turn to her and say, I agree you usually don't try. But are you smart? Yep, she shoots back. OK, I say and I tell the class, turn to Chapter 12, pages 126-128. I pause, then ask the girl, Want to take an intelligence test from last night's reading? I don't wait for an answer but say, One of the characters says a witch cannot walk past two blessed needles stuck into a wooden door frame in the shape of a cross. . . I go over to the door. Imagine this is wood, I say, and I run my hand over the inside of the metal door frame. Imagine these are blessed needles, and I hold up two pencils. Question, and I look directly at the girl: How do you stick these into the frame to form a cross? Take your time. She doesn't and immediately says, Put them in at an angle. Like this? I ask and hold them diagonally against the frame. She nods. But, I say, that forms an X not a cross. They need to look like a traditional cross, like the letter t. I form one in the air with the pencils. She's puzzled and now takes some time. I wait, and wait, and finally call on a hand waver who says, Put them into the upper corner of the frame; one straight down, one straight across. That's it, I say and demonstrate.

I walk back to my desk and a male voice breaks into my thoughts.

- What are we doing next, Mr. B?

- What does your weekly assignment sheet say?

- I don't have one.

- Why not? I gave them out last Wednesday.

- I must've lost it.

- Didn't take long.

- No wait, I was suspended last Wednesday. I never got it.

- I sent one to the suspension room.

- I never got it.

- So why didn't you ask for one when you returned to class Thursday?

He thinks and speculates, We didn't meet.

- Really? What about the day after that? We had to have met on one of the days.

- (he shrugs) I don't know.

- Fine.

Everyone is now focused on the assignment sheet melodrama. Gone is brains not brawn, blessed needles, cross, etc. We've had an educational disconnect, an influx of universal randomness beyond even John Nash's equations. . . Thought: What if an ADT type alarm blew at these ADD times? Could students be auditorily blasted into focusing?. . I now have to shutdown and reboot. I hand him a new assignment sheet, forget about any closure, and we start an editing lesson.

Ice Cream Castles In The Air *– There's nothing like a practical demonstration to bring a lesson home, to make the abstract concrete. Students may even lock it in till the bell, or lunch, provided either comes soon and there's nothing else in-between.*

Educational Disconnect, Life Imitates Art: A state official shamelessly tells me what a wonderful social studies teacher she was back-when. Tells me how she'd have students march all around the classroom, over the chairs and desks to simulate the winter march from Fort Ticonderoga. Then I remember I saw it on *My Three Sons* years ago, just as this older former teacher obviously did. Life imitates art, though I now have my doubts she ever actually did the historical reenactment. Think it more likely she just psychologically adopted the tv episode (we call this plagiarism if a student does it in English) for whatever delusional, b.s., queen shit reason. I pause, then think what-the-hay, and tell her, Yeah, great lesson. I saw it on *My Three Sons*. You should sue the bastards for stealing your material.

Halloween. It's the end of the month, and time for *all* to be delusional and pretend to be someone/something else. Years ago I never overlook the holiday and from the first dedicate a lesson or two to it. In the earliest years. I shut the blinds, turn out the lights, and play the Orson Welles' radio broadcast of *War Of the Worlds* on LP. And just like that we're transported to an overrun New Jersey countryside with aliens blasting the shit out of pre-turnpike farmhouses. I let the students get into it, then stop the recording short and have them write an original ending.

Over the years I add *Dracula*, *The Devil and Daniel Webster*, *The X-Files*, and *The Twilight Zone*. I use six different Rod Serling scripts and the matching VHS tapes, and we really get into episodes like Eye Of the Beholder and The Monsters Are Due On Maple Street. Eventually it becomes a unit I name The Strange and Unusual and I incorporate a field trip to Salem. The students love it.

The Monster Mash – *Students love the paranormal and occult, but don't call it that. Don't even mention spiritual. Get an innocuous title, and stay away from real blood, Ouija boards, seances, and cemeteries. Consider letting the Goths run a class.*

Dress Up, Sugar Down – *Your teacher already thinks some of you are possessed. No need to do much more at Halloween.*

Over the years I let The Strange and Unusual go. No more *Phantom Of the Opera*, no more *Dr. Jekyll and Mr. Hyde*, which they think is a Saturday morning cartoon until I hand them the unabridged Robert Louis Stevenson. The unit goes, but the school celebrates the holiday now by letting the seniors dress up.

A student makes a shark costume and pushes himself through the halls lying on a skateboard. Another student dresses up like one of our math teachers and dons a long salt-and-pepper wig with matching full beard and flowing moustache. They stand side-by-side and we all have a good laugh. Girls hot for a way around our dress code show up as Playboy bunnies and rock singers. No one dresses as a stripper, though several of our postgrads have taken it up, or so I'm told. I arrive at school early and see a wrinkled old man limping down an empty hallway with a cane. Turns out it's one of our thespians, even in character when no one's around.

The air is getting colder, leaves are covering the ground. There's a senior class and staff barbeque during lunch with main office personnel doing the grilling – unexpected but nice. The Red Sox win the pennant and World Series – ass numbing unexpected, but very nice And I get thinking that just maybe there *is* hope for the year and my classes, and maybe things *will* work out. It’s unexpected, improbable, surreal, a Powerball long shot. But it would be very very nice.

NOVEMBER – For God, For Country, For School: Rah, Rah

Autumn sports are winding down, winter sports are poised to begin. I make it a point to check the results everyday. For some it's the most important thing they do and it's important to be aware of that. It's also a way to bond – Hey, great game yesterday! And a thing to hold over their heads – Want me to talk to your coach?

I used to coach cross country, and it's a sport that is special to me. I always felt kick-ass alive coaching on the back roads, trails, and dirt roads, running through a blaze of color and leaf scented air. Runner, writer, and philosopher Dr. George Sheehan: There's a time when running is enough. When it is enough to race the same races, run the same roads. Enough to live out the cycle upon cycle of the running year.

Cross country has no cuts and I like that. Runners cut themselves, i.e. it’s basically an everyman sport. Bring only legs and balls. A physically handicapped runner years ago just won't quit. He struggles his way over the course race-after-race, comes in a distant last, and gets the biggest round of applause. An indomitable “loser.”

Most of the ones who persevere are not possessed with the running gene but struggle onward anyway. A red-faced runner experiencing what author James Tabor calls *a carnival of pain* stops at the halfway mark, tells me he doesn't feel well, throws up, then takes off running again. A rookie who's never played a sport in his life starts crying during an early season workout, crosses his arms across his chest, and asks, Why does it have to hurt? The great Czech runner Emil Zatopek after numerous Olympic victories says, It's at the borders of pain and suffering that the men are separated from the boys. I say something less poetic like, So you know you're improving. Later I think of Knute Rockne's, You are going to sweat all the way out to your fingernails. . . It's really that simple. Accept it, overcome it, grow a pair.

Blood, Sweat, And Cheers – *Sports are important to many of your students. Rejoice with them, and be aware that games and practices take a substantial physical and mental toll. Still, unless someone's signed a professional contract, academics still are #1. No exceptions. Rah, rah, brain; cerebral pain.*

Diddle Dump Diddle – *Play your sport, eat supper, get the emails and phoning out of the way, take a nap. Wake up around 9-9:30 and don't go to bed again until all the homework is done. Note: E and cyber gamers are not interscholastic athletes and are not the concern of the school. So kiss off.*

Report cards come out. Email and voice mail increase, but not that much, and no one challenges the grades. My first year teaching I have a big poobah's son. After the quarterly report cards come out he calls me in. I'm talking to you as a parent, he tells me, not as your boss. My son's puzzled by the D you gave him. He's convinced his average is higher; is it possible you made a mistake? NOTE: This is an era before school computers and pocket calculators so everything has to be tabulated by long hand. Let me see, I tell big poobah getting out my grade book and pencil. I do the average once, twice, and my heart starts to race. *Oh SHIT! BIG mistake.* Sorry, I say not sure how to admit a two letter grade error. Your son's right. He has a B average, and I sit there blushing, wondering if I can collect unemployment after only 2 months on the job. It's OK, he tells me smiling. I don't know how you teachers figure out so many averages anyway. And just like that I'm back on the road to tenure. After this, I always eyeball the numbers first and approximate the average before actually doing the math. Guesstimation + crunching the numbers = Peace o' fucking mind.

Good news. A minor chief tells me all my zero liners have been warned that if they continue to disrupt the classes they'll be arrested on breach of peace charges. It's never come down to this before, but I'm impressed and I hope there's a fine that goes along with it. Money is what zero liners understand best since most have little of their own and when mom and/or dad has to pay there's all sorts of shit hitting the fan.

I mention the new rule to my next class and get a singular, So what? Same student, a real Godzilla fuckup, soon refuses to read orally, though the student reads fine orally. I give a second chance, a third reconsider, then I toss the nonparticipant out. I say, No homework, no willingness to work even when you're here, gets you *gone*. If you aren't willing to work, what's the point of you being here? There is no point. I'm not a life support system for comatose students. . . Quantum Physics: When I think about this incident later it's comforting to realize there's a parallel universe where I'm not only tossing the student but also calling him something amusing like a mute booger. But not here, and not today.

Years Ago Sidebar: I have a student refuse to read when I'm getting observed. It snowballs, and soon everyone's refusing to read and to participate, and I can see my evaluator's writing faster. Crux time, Ultimate Teacher time. I make it up as I go along, this is no situation I've had before, terra incognita. I say, I can see you don't want to do much today. That's fine. But starting today, right now, I'm recording class participation as a grade that'll be averaged in. It'll be classified as In-Class Average. No participation, or refusal to participate, earns a zero. Everyone will get plenty of opportunity both today and in the future. A reasonable answer will get you max credit, even if it's wrong. Your thoughtful effort is appreciated, and you will not be penalized for logical, honest mistakes. Remember, participate and you earn an easy 100%. Don't, and well, you'll miss a cinch opportunity to raise your average. Now, who wants to take the next question?

If You're Breathing Talk – *An unwillingness to work is a type of misbehavior and it's contagious. You have to act fast, even if it means recording more numbers to average. You'll never regret working too hard or caring too much. Hoo-rah.*

Powder That Kisser – *You can't throw a firewall up between you and the work. We're working, you're working. All for one, one for all. Rah, rah.*

Field Trip Time: I'm taking my senior Drama class, my A/B students from Film, and some jr/sr FOBs, i.e. students I like and trust, on a day trip to NYC. It's an annual event, and I bill it as the best field trip in the school.

At 6:15 a.m. the bus arrives at school for a 6:30 departure. I call out the names, make eye contact, count heads just to be sure, and by 6:35 we're off, all 35 of us. Flashback: In my early years as a coach I leave an athlete at MacDonald's after I ask, Is everyone here? and get back a rousing YEAH!

Hide And Seek – *You may want to lose some of your students but no, sorry, can't. The South Africans have a unity of life principle called ubuntu. We call our unity principle: roll call and head count. Ubuntu is spiritual, ours is physical. Trust the physical/empirical, even if you aren't a math or science teacher.*

I always sit in the front of the bus and talk to the other chaperone and the driver. It's pleasant and hopefully creates some synergy, i.e. maybe 3 adult brains working together can safely guide 32 randomly firing ones.

We get to Manhattan, but instead of running an avenue south down the island like every other field trip driver's done, this driver cuts west, crosses over the Hudson on the GW, then heads south in Jersey, and cuts back into Manhattan through the Lincoln Tunnel. We miss the express lane closing by 1 minute, and the driver's happy, but this seems like a crazy fucking way to go. He's following a GPS system called Jill and he seems happy with his e-female navigator but I'm getting doubtful fast.

Turns out to be an omen that will kick in close to midnight. But for now. . .

We get into the lower island and try to worm our way northeast. Jill seems to be taking us roundabout and I convince the driver to trust my map and me. This trip is a lot about trust, even when it involves just an old-fashioned pain-in-the-ass backseat driver. At Washington Square Park more trust comes into play when I give the students two-and-a-half hours of you're-on-your-own (armed with maps, emergency info, and buddies/ groups), go enjoy/learn about this macro pigeon-infested corner of Gotham. . . When they're back – breathless and 64 eyes wide open – I'm relieved. Only 2 students have ever gotten lost down here, but it's enough. Trust is fine in theory but can be a bitch to practice.

I give them more time around Lincoln Center, then we rendezvous and walk to the Museum Of Modern Art via Central Park. A student asks if this is where Holden Caulfield hung out, another if John Lennon was shot near here, someone remembers a Survival episode, another recalls seeing the horse and carriage rides in a movie. I point out the Plaza and mention the play/movie *Plaza Suite*. They're more interested in the hot dog and pretzel vendors.

At MOMA students charge into the newly renovated galleries while the other chaperone and I sit in the sculpture garden. The quiet is nice, I'd take a nap if I could. When we eventually get to an upper floor, one of my seniors gives me some faux shock and a, Mr. B there are lots of nudes on this floor! as if he's just walked the green mile and gotten a jolt. I know he just wants a reaction, so I say, Swell. At last I'm going to find out what one looks like. . . Bah bing!

Keep Your Pants On – *1. You can tell them the human body is beautiful. Just don't show them yours or ask to see theirs. 2. Even your most conservative parents will accept nudity in a museum. Just keep it off the bus.*

BMOC – *You can't shock your teacher. He's seen the world via Travel Channel and Google. . . And behave yourselves in public. Your teacher isn't into herding cats, leading snipe hunts, or filling out missing person reports.*

At 7:30, after they've had more free time, we're standing on 41st in front of *Rent*. I've been bringing groups here since it opened in the 90's. I feel it's important for the young to see creations that mirror their own generation, even if the creations are cutting edge. *Especially* if they're cutting edge.

The other chaperone calls out names. They walk past me, I make eye contact and hand each student his/her ticket. Thirty-four people, thirty-four tickets, perfect. It wasn't so simple the first year. One student missing. I send everyone in and wait. A few minutes before eight he comes running up, sweating, out-of-breath. He's honest. Hooked up with his girlfriend, a college freshman, and, Well, you know how it is Mr. Bentley. Yeah, I know. And I can't help smiling both from relief we don't have to dredge the East River for his sperm soaked corpse, and from memories of what it is to be young and in love. He's a Romeo who found his balcony, and now we have to find ours.

Turns out we're about the only ones up here on this Thursday night. Play is closing soon. What a far cry from the standing room only crowds of the 90's. Still, the students are excited to see it, and so am I. No student's ever hated it, most love it. I can still hear one turning to me at intermission and saying in a flush, I don't have a clue what's going on in this play Mr. B, but I love it! Love it!

Rent is a big hit again tonight, with many of my students knowing the libretto and story. We get out at 10:45. Past groups have hung around for autographs, but there are no groupies this year – not like when the original cast or Joey Fatone of N*Sync played.

The bus is nowhere is sight, and I send scouts west to reconnoitre. I get on my cell and call the driver. He's shocked. Why, I'm right near the theatre he tells me. I look around. There isn't a bus in sight. I walk east to the corner. I'm standing at 41st and 7th, I say to him. Where are you? Right there, he shoots back. The question flashes through my mind, Is there another 41st and 7th ? I ask, Can you see the theatre? I'm at 7th and 41st, he repeats. This goes on for 45 minutes. At one point I'm standing in the middle of the street yelling, You get that fucking bus here now! Right NOW! The students who hear me are agape, and I apologize, and silently kick the driver's ass, a bus driver who probably fell asleep, woke up late, hit the midtown traffic snarl, then isn't big enough to admit it. I'm not blaming Jill.

At 11:30 our bus rounds the corner onto 41st. We quietly climb aboard, and after two head counts, we're off. The driver apologizes, plays dense dipstick dumb, and I let him. I'm tired, the other chaperone's tired, the students are exhausted. Many fall asleep. About 10 miles from the school I have the driver turn on the inside lights and I walk the aisle playing smiling drill sergeant. The many students who are driving have to be wide awake when they get behind the wheel.

We pull up to the school at 1:45 a.m. I remind the students not to leave anything, check to see that eyes are wide open as they file past, check the bus for litter and personal items, and thank the driver as I climb off. He wants to know if I'm going to report him to the company. I tell him I'm going to tell the company exactly what happened. I don't tell him his $50 tip is as gone as he was.

Aftermath: The bus company manager refunds me $200 for inconvenience, apologizes profusely, and wants to be assured she hasn't lost our business. . . The students are still excited about the field trip days later. They talk about the pot smoking in Washington Square Park, playing hackysack with a street man, getting propositioned by a hooker, and the quality of the escalators in MOMA, etc. i.e. the lessons of the street, i.e. the users, pimps, prostitutes, panhandlers, and pervs provided the best education/theatre they got.

La Vie Boheme *– Trust in people under 20. the magic of the big city, and take some advice from Rent: No day like today.*

The Tango Maureen *– Be a good kid, the kind a teacher wants to be seen with in public and maybe you'll find yourself going on more field trips. And trust people over 20, especially teachers, and yes even drivers. Most of them have your best interests at heart.*

A nontenured teacher complains that a parent called him at home 9 o'clock on Sunday night. Parent wanted the rubric for a composition due the next day. Teacher can't believe he's getting rousted at home on a weekend. I suggest to him he tell his classes that he's in school from 6:30-4 most days, and those are the business hours. I tell him if he doesn't nip it fast, it'll only get worse. I know fictional teachers are available round-the-clock on tv and in the movies, and I know some in real life are. But a teacher has to decide early on what kind of teacher to be: slave, or merely dedicated, and while both are sweatbacks, one gets no break and the other gets to at least pee, shower, and scratch in peace.

In my own nontenured years a parent calls early one evening and my wife hands me the phone.

- Mr. Bentley, this is Mrs. Wingnut.

She's slurring her words badly and I know she's had a jar or two.

- What can I do for you?

- Is Stephen failing?

- Yes he is. He doesn't do the homework and is putting in little effort.

There's a pause though I doubt the F average is any great shock. She now talks with a really agitated bug-up-her-ass passion.

- I want you to start hitting him.

- Excuse me?

- I want you to start hitting him. That's his problem. He needs to get belted around.

She's overwrought but serious; I'm stunned and puzzled. *Hit him?* What to say? There's nothing in teacher training that prepares you for moments like this. After not much thought I say, I can't do that. In the first place it's not allowed. Secondly, I don't think it would help Stephen. It isn't what he would respond to.

- You're not going to hit him?

- No.

- Well, someone's going to hit him, either the principal or me, but someone's gonna hit him.

- I think it'll have to be you. Goodnight, Mrs. Wingnut.

The Walls Of Jericho *– Robert Frost said, Good fences make good neighbors. If you give out your home address, home phone, or home email, you have no fence and have to expect visits from parents. Some will be wingnuts. Others will be REALLY fucking nuts.*

Both Sides Now *– As difficult as it is to imagine, your teacher has a life outside school, just like you. The two should intersect only if you can mow a lawn, shovel snow, rake leaves, shingle a roof, or install a swimming pool. And for not much money.*

I return a phone call from a mother's questioning her son's latest composition grade. Despite the same basic explanation on the composition itself, I patiently explain it all again. She listens and says, It's just that it's very discouraging for him. He tried really hard, and I don't know if he'll try again after this. Oh, I'm sure he will, I say. The comments also show he can do B work, if not higher, when he wants. Parts of his composition were that good. So, it's too late to change the grade? she continues undeterred and relentless. She suspects I could change it, still wants me to change it, and I'm tempted to change it just to end this. But I'm not going to. Not even if hell freezes over. Not if she offers money, sex, or faster internet. I say, It's almost never too late to change a grade. But there's no reason to change this one. Remember, your son didn't make the minimum length. *Minimum!* There was a time when that in itself would have gotten him a F, so in a sense he's already gotten a break.

There's nothing left to say. She wants a full psyche massage and satisfaction, but they ain't happening. And a class is starting soon. I say, But there *is* good news. The marking period's just begun and there are another eight weeks for him to pull up his average. Plenty of time. Also, I recommend he see me with his rough draft next time and we can work on it together. And I might give extra credit near the end of the semester, so that's another way to minimize this grade.

These are all practiced standard lines. As an ace in the hole, I usually return phone calls 5 minutes before the bell. The vast majority of calls don't need more than that, and when the bell rings, which the parent can hear, you say, I've got a class now, but I think we've covered everything. If anything changes I have your number and will be sure to get back to you. Thanks, and have a nice day.

I Couldn't Have Done It Alone – *Like the Tim Robbins in the movie Bull Durham, you have to learn the clichés, the proper lines. The vast majority of questions/problems have standard, time proven responses. Just don't sound bored as shit when you're delivering them. You have to be an actor, not a form letter.*

And Behind Door #4 – *If something is explained to you in class verbally, is further reinforced in writing, and is reiterated constantly, what don't you understand? Grades are not changed because you don't like them and having mom/dad plead your case won't work unless your parents believe in quid pro* *quo and own a bank, a home on the Riviera, or a Ferrari dealership. Got it, dunce packer?*

The students are busily working when out of nowhere a student says, Mr. Bentley, your hair's getting really white. I smile and respond, Thank you for letting me know. I thought it was just falling out. Now, go back to work.

Students think nothing of making personal remarks like this. Scientists tell us a teen's prefrontal cortex, the part responsible for controlling impulses, is not fully developed for another decade. Add to that the fact their dopamine levels – the chemical that allows us to triage, to prioritize – are not at optimal levels yet, and you have these outbursts of what I used to call verbal diarrhea. The understanding side of me knows they're more observations than critical comments and are not intended to be hurtful but rather just displays of spontaneous insight as irrelevant and as personal as they might be. Still, I can't imagine ever talking like this to one of my former teachers back when teachers were teachers, students were students, and everyone was thankful for the difference. Over the years I've been told I have a gut and a combover, wear funny shoes, have a scar on my face, walk like a duck, dress in mismatched shirts and ties, see the world through old fashioned glasses, and have a weird voice. I usually thank the observer, and sometimes I volley. Sometimes I point out that I see myself shaving everyday, so I know my face. Sometimes I tell them I'm not inclined to take fashion advice from anyone who wears sneakers, jeans, and a t-shirt everyday, i.e. the student fashion trifecta. The underwear and socks, I don't know about, but I suspect some rarely change/wash those either.

Many classes ago I'm walking down the hall and I hear behind me, You're getting really bald, Mr. Bentley. There's a real big round spot on your head. I turn around and here are two students I don't know, have never even seen. I smile and say, Got a minute, follow me. They balk. We'll be late, one says. Don't worry, I assure them. I'll give you a late pass and this isn't going to take long.

A few doors down is the boys' lav. I lead them in and stop in front of the sinks and mirrors. Look, I say and I point to their reflections. What? they ask, and I continue to point and repeat, Look, look at yourselves. They slowly turn toward the bank of mirrors and I say, The next time you feel like making fun of me, remember what you're looking at in these mirrors,.

There's a delay, it sinks in, then one gets really angry. We can get you fired for saying that! he spits out, and I reply, I don't think so, but you can go ahead and try. And who are you anyway? I don't know you, never saw you, and you make personal remarks to me? I think I have a better shot at getting you a detention, or suspended, than you have of getting me fired. But why don't we all get to class now and think about it. . . Uncivil slugs.

The next day the aggressive one goes out of his way to be polite, and that's how it is until he graduates, while I do, in fact, get balder.

Reflection: This was not a shining educational moment for me, but I'm young and inexperienced with being insulted, am definitely human, and can only plead temporary insanity. Still, it's major league overkill, and the teacher/student relationship should not be adversarial. This isn't court. On the other hand, it'd be nice if *nice* were a two way street. Shit, yeah.

A Deal You Can't Refuse – *It's not all business; it is personal at times. If it weren't, you'd be a automaton, not a teacher. Still, it wouldn't hurt to develop thicker skin. Your hearing and prostate will go naturally.*

Student Insight Be Damned – *Anything personal you want to tell your teacher he/she probably already knows or doesn't need to know. Not every* *observation/revelation needs an audience. Keep a journal and keep it private. Some of your opinions certainly suck.*

I'm standing on the narrow counter in my room taking down the boxes above my cabinets. I step sideways, miss the counter, and launch into space. I come down on a desk corner, land on one foot, then careen headfirst into the wall so hard I crack the drywall, leave embedded hair, and blackout.

I come to seconds later on my back. I shake my head and the class is staring at me like I'm Rodney Dangerfield and just pulled off the ass-over-teacups Triple Lindy. There's dead silence, no one asks if I'm OK, so I wisecrack and thank my zero liners for not kicking me when I'm down. I get to my feet still shaking my head. I ask if anyone saw what happened and admit I'm not sure. They get excited and talk fast. One tells me I stepped on the top of a wheeled chair and when it rolled, I flew off. They're amazed I'm not dead or hurt, and so am I. I *am* foggy. If I had my wits about me, this'd be an excellent opportunity to segue into vocabulary. Proprioception = the body's understanding of its place in space. It allows us to perform a task without concentrating on the movement. It's what I lacked. . . I could also segue into Greek mythology and teach the story of Icarus who flew too close to the sun and had his wax wings melt. If I were still teaching middle school my team would get an IDU (interdisciplinary unit) going.

But this is high school. I fill out an accident report and never do find the playbooks.

On The Wings Of Eagles – *Keep a low profile. Don't stand on counters, desks, wheeled chairs, or students. You're not Superman or Peter Pan. Dumbo, at times, maybe.*

A Time Not To Jump Into It *– When your teacher tells you to fly, to soar, this should not be taken literally.*

I order a DVD on early black film but am told the film can't be purchased from the usual vendors, but if I get it on my own I'll be reimbursed. I get a new copy on Ebay, use Paypal to pay for it, and submit my Paypal voucher but am told I need to show my Visa bill. Blame the other office, I'm told. I go to the other office with the DVD itself and my Paypal statement. Two underlings refuse to honor it. I finally have to see a big boss. Big Boss tells me Paypal is too new and they really don't recognize it. I point out that Paypal's been around for years and is accepted worldwide. Big Boss finally gives in, and I go back to first office, reiterate previous conversations, and get reimbursed out of petty cash. All this over $10.

Chump Change *– You'll buy a lot of supplies over the years out-of-pocket, and that's just the way it is. But try to keep it to a minimum and never take no for a final answer until it comes from a big boss. Your time is valuable, but so is your money, even if it is American.*

Reality Check *– School is not the be-all, end-all. But if it ever comes down to your daily, double tall toffee nut latte with the extra expresso shot, or school supplies, you need to get academic and not be more fucking hyper.*

A fairly new student comes in near the very end of the period. She shows me a pass, but I'm not impressed and motion for her to follow me into my office, a.k.a. the hall for a confidential mano-a-girlo. I come right to the point.

- Your attendance record stinks. You've been out every fourth day, have several tardies, and make up nothing, which means you take zeroes for everything you miss. You're borderline failing.

She looks surprised, almost stunned. What did she think we were doing when she was out? Playing Yahtzee? World Championship Poker?

- Are there health reasons you're out and don't come back for makeup? I don't need specifics.

She shakes her head, no. *What else can it be?* I wonder. One student missed every Friday because her mother worked that day and the girl had to baby-sit her sister. Another girl was kept home regularly by mom because the divorcing mom was lonely and depressed and wanted company. One boy had anxiety attacks brought on by school but it was OK to work full-time at a customer service desk. Some students cut school to work, some have serious health problems. But I haven't heard anything about this girl who now seems lacquered with cluelessness.

- Look, I say with my best secular compassion, if you can't help being out, you can't help being out. But if you can, I suggest you get here. And on time. I don't know the rules in your last school, but absences and tardies here can mean loss of course credit, even if you pass, even if you make up your work. When you're out, bring in a note, and get a makeup sheet from the main office and get it filled out. I'm not going to remind you constantly to make up your work, but if you have the sheet, maybe you'll remember on your own. I want you to succeed, but you have to want it too.

So Simple Yet So Basic *– Woody Allen said that 80% of life is showing up. In school the other 20% is showing up on time. Don't assume that every student knows this or is tracking her/his own attendance record/academic average. Students usually just track each other. And you.*

Take THAT! *– It's a good idea to know the attendance policy and to know which teachers enforce it. The ones who don't aren't doing you any favors. Every hurtful act isn't a physical knee to the groin.*

I've worked with teachers who traditionally miss 20-30 days a year. This is not good. I once worked with a teacher who was going through a home crisis and was 5+ minutes late to every class, everyday, because of hanging out in the faculty room between periods and talking about it with anyone who would listen.

Bottom Line: Humane teacher behavior is always expected; human behavior less so. Teachers can't major in frailty. Suck it up, man-up, lady-up, put on that happy face or crack some skin trying.

The attendance officer and I have a major disagreement over one boy's tardies. I have the student down for 10 in my record book, but the attendance czar says I entered only 5 into the computer. It's the difference between an after school detention and a Saturday detention with parent conference. I don't know how I could have missed entering so many. . . After weeks, it dawns on me. Like most teachers I take attendance both electronically and by hand to start the class. I don't submit the electronic till the end of the period because a student's status frequently changes, e.g. an absence becomes a tardy, and once the electronic's submitted you get logged off and it's a royal pain to keep logging back on. Lightbulb Moment: This new attendance program is logging me off anyway (though the screen doesn't change) after so much inactive time so that when I finally do submit attendance at the end, it doesn't go through, though it appears to. And that turns out to be the explanation.

Stupid ass machine.

2001: A Space Odyssey *– The computer on your desk is not conspiring against you, though it may seem that way at times. Your mantra should be: It's making my life easier, it's making my life easier, and maybe one day it will. Maybe you'll also be voted Homecoming King/Queen.*

Classroom Snippet Timeout: At the end of *The Crucible* one of our American Lit. classes is asked to comment on the main character John Proctor who's had an affair and gotten his wife pregnant. One student writes, You can't condom John Proctor. Teacher: That was half his problem.

A student shows me a drawing he did of fennel for a class herbal research project. I tell him, I don't see any yellow. He says, Use your imagination.

My Film class is watching *American Grafitti*, and there's a scene at a high school dance when a teenage girl is coming on to a young male teacher and he takes her away for a *talk*. A girl in class asks, Was that a teacher? Me: Yes. Her: Where were they going? Boy in class: He was giving her an oral exam.

The class novel is over, and I'm collecting books. I say, Get your books out, and when I call your name give me your book number and bring the book up.

- We're turning in our books today? one mystified boy asks and looks around at books magically appearing.

- That's right.

- I asked you last week and you said you didn't know when.

- The plans weren't made out then, but they were the next day and it's on this week's assignment sheet. You were given one.

He shrugs. I walk over and show him the sheet. He shrugs again and cracks, Who reads that?

- I do, and you're supposed to. . . I sigh, he looks exasperated, I react. Think you'd read it if I had you copy it over by hand every time you don't know what's going on That's how I make them out. By hand. And I remember them.

Learning Theory: Hand teaches the brain, though I'm not sure anything, even the Black Hand could beat remembrance into this ossified wazoo.

I don't mention his unpreparedness is on the increase, or that I can't really make him write things out as punishment, as was expected in the old days when I began. What I can do is offer him choices, i.e. do you want an unprepared for the day, or would you prefer to write out this week's assignment sheet in long hand? I don't give him a choice and mark him unprepared. This zero will come off his in-class average.

He's visibly annoyed now and sulks like a pansy-waisted thumb-sucking wuss. Five minutes later he stages a power play: one of his legs is draped over his desk, calf exposed, and he's leaning back arms crossed. He's assuming the pose of the alpha male, posturing, a testosterone high fatgut. Body language = embodiment of faux power = fake it till you make it. I'm tempted to say, If I had a blimp sized gam like that I sure-as-hell wouldn't put it on display. But I don't. Instead, it's my turn to shrug. I give him a looong look, the leg stays, and I finally say, Take your leg off the desk. Simple and direct. No misunderstanding. He takes his time, slowly swings it over and down, then goes into what I simply call, The Look. Voodoo type. Curse me forever type. I ignore him, and 10 minutes later he's back bouncing around again like the one dimensional, South Park caricature he is.

Absolute Zero – *What some call petty distractions are not always petty. The most valuable lessons some of your students will learn involve being* *prepared for class and manners. And some could use a course in just those two things.*

Miss Manners Says – *You probably wish your teacher would just ignore you and let you drift off into La La Land. No way. Reality might be an illusion, as Einstein and Richard Bach theorized, but it's a persistent one, and your teacher and you are in it together. Till June. Rah. Rah. Fucking rah.*

It's getting colder out. We come back after the 3 day Thanksgiving break and a ripple of excitement runs through the class one frosty morning. Light snow flurries are falling in the alley between our wing and guidance. The scattered flakes look huge, magic little carpets carrying hopes for a snow day, but they melt as they hit the window ledge and ground. Students stare memorized as if they've never seen snow before, like maybe it's anthrax or a dusting of cocaine. Then it starts.

- Mr. B, do you think we'll have a half day?

- What about an early dismissal, Mr. B?

- I walk to the window and stare at the white sprinkling coming down. I'd like a half day too, but this snow isn't stacking up. Time for an old leg pull.

- No, there won't be any early dismissal today, we'll be here till 2. Anyone remember the old Indian saying: Snow like cornmeal, snow great deal. Snow big flake, snow big fake?

I laugh, they frown, and November rolls over confetti-ed in white.

DECEMBER – Getting On, Getting Off

The time between Thanksgiving and Christmas is unique in a school. There's an intense feeling of countdown and calendar watching. Red and green start to appear. A tree's decorated in the foyer. Teachers rush to finish books, papers, and projects before the big 11 day holiday break figuring forgetfulness generally sets in after only a weekend away, 11 days away produces amnesia.

Students pray for snow days and dream of no homework and free time.

Holiday drives kick off. Clubs collect food, paper items, and scarves for the needy. Groups sell cookie dough, poinsettias, and custom gift-wrapping to raise money. Winter sports gain momentum. There'll be a pep rally before the break. Field trips get squeezed in before we get snowbound.

December gets hectic. It's a month that sometimes needs a break from itself.

Mr. Bentley, the girl says energetically chewing her gum, so like ahhh, what do you want for Christmas?

I look up and smile; the girl smiles back. I usually do get two or three gifts a year at various times so her question isn't outrageous. Still, the students who give me gifts are mainly the ones I write recommendations for, or the ones who think I'm an OK pretty cool dude, or at least not Kingfish Asshole. This particular girl doesn't fit any category. Doesn't take years of experience to see her question is just the usual bull cant said to kill time.

I look at the clock, there are only a few minutes left in the period, and I figure what the hell, it's December, let's go where the season takes us. Over the river and through the bare-ass woods. . .

- Do you really want to know?

I ask this with a serious look, as if she might actually be giving me something. She perks up as if she can't believe I'm going to go along and looks around to be sure everyone appreciates that she's getting teacher off track. Then she says, Sure.

- I'd like a hair transplant, liposuction, and a facelift.

- Really? she asks.

- Sure, why not? I'd like to do my part to glamorize the school for the holidays. A few students laugh. They like self deprecating humor on a teacher's part. The girl isn't laughing. She's studying me like I'm in 3-D Imax and I can see she's thinking: Yeah, like good idea.

- No, I say, just kidding, I've changed my mind. . . I lean over the metal podium and say, I don't want that at all, I don’t want anything. I’m going to give you a present. Does anyone know what, Beauty is in the eye of the beholder means?

There's a pause, then a bunch of students talk all at once. They know.

- But that's only part of it, I say. There's another truth which is even more important: Beauty is in the eye of yourself. If you truly think yourself beautiful, attractive, or at least cute or interesting, that's how you'll be perceived. People will believe whatever self image you yourself believe as long as that's what you project.

I take a breather and let it sink in. I can see puzzlement and skepticism. True story time.

- When I was in high school, there's a girl, a neighbor, who is Ms. Everything. She's bubbly, energetic, involved, extremely popular, and *cute*. Everyone says she's cute. Adorable. One day we're standing at the bus stop in a group and I take a really hard look at her. I study her eyes, nose, face, hair, and figure. It dawns on me that she's very average physically, nothing exceptional at all, but that she herself doesn't believe that, doesn't project that, believes in fact she's cute, plays the cute role, and in doing so becomes cute/adorable/huggable, and convinces everyone else of it, including me. She sprinkles pixie dust and creates magic. And cute is my lasting impression of her to this day.

At this point I should say to the girl, I like your hairdo. New, isn't it? Or I should compliment her on her shoes. Girls like that. But I don't and the class is left with just the story.

They Came Bearing Gifts – *Students take looks very seriously. Compliment them whenever you can, especially when they change hair style, makeup, and fashion. Help them believe in themselves. It's the best holiday present you can give, even if it is cheap as shit.*

Mirror, Mirror On The Wall – *Like David Copperfield, strive to be the hero of your own life. Some of your classmates opt for cosmetic surgery to this end, but that means mega-dollars and never passing a mirror. An attitude adjustment is free, much longer lasting, and makes a much better gift. Honest daydream believer.*

Woody Allen Snippet: Beauty is in the eye of the beholder. Should the beholder have poor eyesight, he can ask the nearest person which girls look good.

My sophomores finished the American/Mexican novel *Bless Me, Ultima*, the Haitian novel *Taste Of Salt*, and are currently reading *Goodbye, Mr. Chips* for homework while in class we're reading the action/adventure novella *The Shepherd* by Frederick Forsyth. *The Shepherd* is a little known but wonderful holiday story in the Twilight Zone style, and the males generally love it.

One boy asks, Why don't we read more books like this? I respond, Because they haven't been written.

This is partly true. The bigger reason is that most of the good, hard hitting, contemporary world literature has objectionable parts for underclassmen in courses that are mandatory. We tried *Kaffir Boy* by Mark Mathabane years ago, but there's a child prostitution scene, and though nothing happens the words penis, anuses, and Vaseline are used together in the same sentence and the implication is adult/child sex, of course. A few parents raise hell, it makes the state media, and a panicky administrator suggests we black out the words or rip out the offending page in all the copies. No way, I say. Reading a book is an all or nothing proposition. I'd rather throw the book on the fire like the Nazis than censor one page. Might even be a copyright violation. Besides, I tell this honcho, imagine what the newspapers and tv stations would do if they ever found out we were using magic markers and scissors to modify our books. Headlines, lead off news features, satellite trucks, national wire services. Forget tiny print, page 10, late night news scroll. . . Dumb ass honcho.

Outcome: The English teachers agree to show up at the next board of education meet-ing to defend *Kaffir Boy*, but I'm the only one who does along with a few students, and the book gets canned as mandatory reading. We try it as optional African reading the next year opposite *Cry, the Beloved Country*, try it for another year as a senior project, but the third year it gets shelved permanently.

There are lots of lessons here: the public doesn't want the envelope pushed, boards of ed are conservative by nature, the squeaky parent gets the media, stick with the classics. But there's one lesson that stands out above all others for me.

Bewitched, Bothered, And Bewildered *– If you buck the system, plan on doing it alone. Most teachers will tell students to march to their own drummer, fight the good fight, stay the course. But most teachers wouldn't buck anything. Not a bronco. Not a lap dancer.*

It's A Paper World *– Think your school literature sucks the big one? Maybe it does. But don't think you don't like to read because of it. There are over 30-million books in the Library Of Congress. Odds are, you'll like a few. Maybe even a few without pictures.*

I was critical of my peers during the *Kaffir Boy* brouhaha, as were some of the students who showed up; yet, I understood then, even as I understand now, other factors come into play when walking into administrative headwinds. Nontenured teachers worry about their jobs. Tenured teachers worry about administrative retaliation, often with good reason. There are plenty of vindictive sons of bitches plotting in offices all over the globe. A big factor is that most teachers by nature are apolitical when it comes to school politics. They just want to be left alone to do what they were hired to do, i.e. teach in the classroom. Most teachers will teach an entire career and never appear before a board of education or talk privately to a chancellor/ superintendent of schools. The ones who do, the ones who are not intimidated and who are political often gravitate to union roles, and some eventually take the plunge and become administrators themselves. The biggest numbers come from P.E. and SPED.

The best stay in the classroom.

Reflection: The money is better in administration; the rewards are greater in the classroom. Where you wind up shows a lot about your own talents. And values.

Blood Brothers – *You will not always agree with your colleagues, but they are your colleagues, even the yellow twanging full-of-piss ones. In the end that should be enough.*

Walk The Line – *Sometimes your teachers do not agree with each other, but don't get in the middle, and never try to play one against the other. These aren't your parents..*

I get a poetry rejection back from the *New Yorker*. I never write poetry, can't write good poetry, but for some reason a few weeks back after a couple of gin martinis think I can write publishable poetry and five minutes later I email off a submission.

The Teacher
He stared, and they stared back.
He recited Marlowe and Frost and Bukowski.
They turned up their ipods.

I share the rejected piece with the English teachers, they smile, but that's about it. Still, I feel encouraged, and late that night after a couple more dry gins, I email off the sequel.

Teacher II
She got up and grabbed her pocketbook.
Can I go to the lav? she asked and added, I got the rag on.
No problem, he said, and clicked his pen. You may, if you can.

***Put It Out There** – It's important to actually practice your discipline. You can't teach what you don't know, haven't done. English teachers read, but they also need to write and write and write. Even if what comes out is drivel. Even if they'd flunk themselves royally.*

***It Never Was Never** – Sophocles said, One must learn by doing the thing. You don't get better at soccer by hitting baseballs, and you don't improve your academics by hanging out, shopping, e-gaming, watching tv, or praying at exam time – though maybe there's a piss-flap magnet/alternative school now that grades those things.*

In my life I've had a lot of newspaper work published and written several unpublished novels. None of this was/is of much consequence and I only mention it to make the point that it's important to practice what you preach, to grab your crouch and get to the front. You can't teach writing, if you don't write. Not well, anyway. Imagine hiring a coach who's never played the sport. You can't be a grazer in your content area: contentedly munching away, shitting in place, sleeping on your feet.

Mr. Bentley? the boney, long-faced boy asks while looking around to rally the Dead Zone.

- Yes?

- How about we change seats. We've been in the same ones all year.

I always assign seats Day 1 to underclassmen. I put them in alphabetical order alternating rows, boy-girl-boy-girl. Everything I see regarding them is alphabetical. I think alphabetically.

- Some of you already changed seats.

- Not many.

- OK, how many want to change seats?

A few hands go up. It's not close to a majority. The boy who asked is waving his hand.

- Come on! he calls out his buddies' names. They raise their hands, but it's still less than half.

- How many want to change seats? I ask one final time, and when no more hands are raised I say, Looks like you'll stay right where you are then, at least for the time being.

- How about letting just the ones who want to change?

The boy won't quit. It's a good question, a fair question, a logical question. But it's one I was hoping no one would ask. A fucking pox on his head. I hate to reshuffle the class and my seating chart for a few because change is not always so easy and some have already been reshuffled. Special needs students have legally mandated seating, e.g. must be in the front, good right ear must face the teacher, must be separated from so-and-so, etc. Students who prefer being fashionably late I like to seat near the door to cut down on distractions. Talkers and showboaters I scatter throughout the back.

- Not now, I finally say to the wannabe migrator. Let's finish the lesson.

- When?. . . He's not going to let it go.

- How about right after holiday break? We'll start the new year with new seating.

- That's a long ways off.

- It's only a few weeks. And we have to get going now. Be patient.

Of course I'm hoping he'll forget about it. And he does. I figure it's for the best. He'd probably only move closer to his friends, talk excessively, and get moved back with a detention to serve. That's how it usually plays out.

Tomorrow Might Never Come *– Mark Twain said, Never put off until tomorrow what you can do the day after tomorrow. There are times when it's OK, even desirable, to put things off. This is not OK for the business office and your pay.*

Squat Down Students *– Where you sit is important in concerts, movies, and sports, and it's important in class too. You have to be able to hear the teacher, see the teacher, and cheer for the teacher. Otherwise, a seat is just a seat is just a hard-assed piece of formica.*

Film projects are due today for the Film class, and the seniors are excited. They worked singularly or in groups to create an original film. Along with the film each group turns in a finished script, and each student turns in a detailed self evaluation and an evaluation of everyone else in the group. These are all confidential.

The films themselves generally last 5-15 minutes. Final grades are based on all this plus my own impressions and conclusions.

The noise in the room is high, but it's good noise. There's an administrator sitting in the back evaluating me. The presence doesn't bother me; I've been through too many of these and only find it incredible that after 32 years I'm still being observed and evaluated in essentially the same way.

I collect the DVD's, one vhs tape, finished scripts, and evaluations. Two students have their camcorders. Neither could transfer the digital signal to DVD for some unknown reason, so we're going to have to hook up the camcorders directly to my data projector and hope the movies play. It should be simple; sometimes it's not. One year a boy brought in his bulky desktop computer with monitor and speakers. It was the only way we could view his project.

Most students are prepared, several are not.

I ask one boy, Where's your self evaluation?

- Mr. Bentley, there was an ice storm this morning, he says.

- I know.

- Well, I crashed my car in the driveway.

- You did what?

- I crashed my car.

- So where's your self evaluation? I ask after the shock wears off, i.e. it's an excuse I've never heard before.

- It's in the car, he says getting exasperated fast.

- You didn't think to take it out?

- Mr. Bentley, he says fast, I was in a CAR CRASH!

He's red in the face and is obviously distraught and telling the truth. Others are nodding and silently covering his back. I pivot and say, My car slid down the driveway this morning too. I thought I was going into my neighbor's yard for sure, but I hit a storm drain that slowed me down. OK, give me the paperwork tomorrow. No loss of credit. . . I pause. I've created fictional stories in the past for various effects, but this anecdote really did just happen. It's my attempt at belated empathy. I feel badly I doubted the boy and gave him a hard time, but original excuses that are well acted out are not uncommon, and a teacher has to be fair to the ones who do the work, who meet the deadline, or homework's just a big gang bang for all.

Individuals and groups are volunteering and actually arguing over whose film is going first. I have a predetermined order based on when the group/ individual signed up, but I defer now to their working it out.

For the next two days we sit in semi-darkness and evaluate, applaud, and laugh. There's one called *Powderpuff Stories* on the all-girls' football game and another called *Real Men Dance* filmed at the school beefcake contest. We laugh at *Room Raiders*, *Weekend In the Hood*, and *Justin Timberlake Is Afraid Of Stairs*. One girl shows a classic Hitchcockian chase scene synchronized with appropriately eerie music; another girl gives us pause with a disturbing introspective called *My End*.

They've incorporated props, costumes, makeup, popups, background music, various types of fades and dissolves, slo-mo, out-of-sync audio, lip synching, shifting color and b&w, voiceovers, wit, humor, originality, et al.

At the end, spirits are high. Envelope, please. And the winner is. . . I hand out Oscars in the form of many A's.

Take A Bow – *Show them the best, teach them the way, generously bestow the rewards. This is how education is supposed to work. No bell curves. No lowered standards. Applause all around. Success in the house.*

Kudos Kiddo – *There's nothing like a job well done to give you a feeling of self worth. High self esteem through real accomplishment. Date this* ***A****. You'll like it and want to go steady.*

Of course it's a lot easier to interest students in a film project than in a project like a formal research paper, though I've found if I give enough latitude on choice of topics, even formal, stilted papers get better and more interesting. But nothing is foolproof, and there are troubles even with these film projects. One student cannot transfer the movie off his computer once he downloads it for editing, and I finally watch it on his laptop. We can't get sound from a highly worked DVD and have to switch playback units. One student is totally unprepared, never helped the group, and winds up getting assigned one week to do a singular project. It's happened before.

Another teacher warns me about one video she's already seen. What're your sexual standards? she asks and adds, I've seen this film and it seems mild to me, but may not be to you. . . Students are told to use their best common sense, I tell her. I tell the class I'm no prude, remind them that we did watch *The Deer Hunter*, but emphasize we are a public school. It'll be OK, she says. Your class is excited to see it. I hope she doesn't mean that literally.

I'm concerned and take the finished film home to preview it. The teacher is right. It is mild. Involves some cross dressing and some sexually suggestive moves, but for a class that's watched *The Graduate* and will see Spike Lee's *Do the Right Thing* it's not beyond their sophistication. Sidebar: Jack Nicholson said, If you suck on a tit, the movie gets an R rating. If you hack it off with an ax, it'll be PG. . . It's ironically true, but this student film is neither sexually explicit nor gruesomely violent. Make love, not war is not an issue.

Postscript: I show it on the second day, and it gets howls of laughter. Though it's not my sense of humor, it's hard to argue with a roomful of laughing people and impossible to slight it technically. Another faux-gold statuette.

A large male student is wearing his hat when the bell rings to start class. Why is it always the males? I have a no-hat policy, and this student has violated it nearly everyday this year. Classic Korsakov Syndrome, short term memory loss. I've already told him it's easier to house train a dog than to get him to take his hat off, already answered the question, Why can't we wear our hats in here? with bigger questions, i.e. Why *would* you wear a hat indoors? Is the sun in your eyes, is the roof leaking, do you have a degenerative scalp disease, is it a gang thing, having a bad hair day? Students will admit to a bad hair day in which case I tell them, I have the worst hair in here, we won't notice yours.

I motion for this student to bring the hat up and tap my desk indicating where I want it put.

- Why? I took it off, he argues.

- It's not enough. Put it on my desk.

- Mr. Bentley, it's hard to remember to take off a hat in here. You're like one of two teachers who doesn't allow them.

- That may be so, but I think after nearly a half year in here you ought to remember. Besides, you come in, sit down, look around, and no one else has a hat on. Doesn't that ring a bell? Give you a wake-up call?

- I got other things on my mind.

- Fine. I'm going to give you plenty of time to think about them without worrying about your hat.

- I don't worry about it.

- Come back in 3 hours, just before lunch and you can have it back.

I tap the desk again, and he dejectedly walks up, puts the one-size-fits-all chapeau down, and walks away, taking a quick look back to be sure it hasn't sprouted wings and taken off.

- I'm doing you a favor, I say eyeing it. This thing needs an oil change. And you look better without it. Besides, it's time to air out your head, let those hair follicles breath, prevent premature male pattern baldness.

- I'll give you a cookie for it. Right now.

- The offer takes me back. Bribes have been tried before, but not this year with a cookie. He reaches into his backpack and pulls out a small ziplock bag. He jingles it up and down. I can see there's a cookie in there.

- That must be some cookie to keep under wraps like that.

- It's peppermint chocolate chip.

My mouth starts to water. I love cookies, especially good ones, especially any cookie with chocolate. He might know this. I can't remember if I ever confessed to being a minor chocoholic, but I am. I summon my quickly fading will power.

- Can't do it. Not for one cookie. Would take a lot more than that after 70 days of reminding you to take your hat off.

- What about a pack of gum? a classmate asks from the opposite side of the room. I'll give you a pack of gum if you give me that hat.

- A whole pack?

- Yep.

It's tempting, the student obviously knows another one of my weaknesses. I go through a lot of gum in a day.

- Why would you want this hat?

- I'm going to give it back to him.

- Really? Let's see the pack.

He comes up to my desk and holds out a pack of gum a foot from my face. It's unopened, and though not the sugarless kind I chew, looks mighty inviting.

- Why would you do this? I ask.

- I feel sorry for him.

I can't tell if he's serious or fooling, but I wave him off. Once he's seated I say, I can't take bribes, payoffs, or boodle. Then I turn to the first boy.

- That was impressive, don't you think? He nods. You should give him your cookie.

- Why?

- Because that was a generous gesture.

- But I still don't have my hat.

- You should give him the cookie anyway.

He silent debates this, screwing up his features as if he's in a government think tank trying to solve the fossil fuel crisis. He doesn't move, doesn't talk. I finally say, Are you going to give him the cookie?

- No. He pats his smooshed down hair probably reminding himself that I'm the cause of this gruesome hirsute ordeal.

- You're sure?

- Yep.

- OK. . . and I let the moment expand. . . Too bad. Had you given him the cookie I would have given you your hat back. He rushes to say, I'll give it to him– But I cut him off. Too late, I say. Had you shown the same generosity that he showed, you'd have your hat now. Instead, I'll see you in 3 hours. He's crestfallen, so I add, Cheer up. You still have your cookie, so life isn't that bad.

Don't Blow Your Lid – *In the classroom pantheon, hats rank last, but this isn't true of all apparel. Pants are near the top, especially ones pulled high enough to cover that big ass crack.*

Say It With Style – *If you wear a greasy, tilted, two sizes too big baseball cap, this isn't a fashion statement, but does make you part-of-the-herd, which can be also accomplished by giving out a loud, Moooooo. Ditto on pulled down knit caps and bandannas, unless you're auditioning for the street or a pirate movie. Goddamn, arrrrgh!*

For most of my teaching years hats were never an issue. No one would think to wear a hat in class any more than they'd think to eat, drink, or cell phone. I don't know when things changed, but I knew change was here when a father showed up one year for a conference wearing a baseball cap. Our administration's always left it up to individual teachers whether or not to allow hats in the class. I've banned them from the first. Thirteen years ago I brought in a hammer and drove big spike-like nails through the wooden frame of the bulletin board by the door, called it a hatrack, and had students hang their lids there as they entered.

Sometimes a student will wear what I consider is a really cool cover like a fedora, and some sure-as-hell can pull off the Robert Mitchum film noir look. Still, don’t cut shit. No hats.

An emaciated dishwater blond sucks on a bottle of water. No drinks, no water, I remind her. Why not? she questions. Because drinks get spilled 10% of the time (a reasonably fictitious stat I make up), and then you have to find some way to clean it up which usually involves a time-out for lots of paper towels, or a phone call to the janitor. But, she says, I have a game today and the coach told us to hydrate. You're running a marathon? I ask. No, it's a basketball game. Didn't know you could lose that much water in so little time, I honestly say. You can, she assures me. I think to myself that hydrating is usually a very long procedure reserved for ultra athletes, but I wave for her to go ahead. If she psychologically believes it'll help her, maybe it will. If it doesn't, if she has a bad game, perhaps it's an argument against bloating yourself with water. It becomes an interesting test case. One thing for sure, she'll be asking to go to the bathroom soon.

Another girl has a pocketbook on her desk the size of a picnic basket. I don't think anything of it until I hear cellophane rustling, then it dawns on me I can't see her. I lean sideways for a better look and see she's all scrunched down, chin practically below desk level, mouth going, swallowing reflex working overtime. Whatcha eating this afternoon? I ask. She holds up a nearly empty package of cheese doodles. They look good, I say. Have enough for everyone? She shakes her head. Well, I say, you can't eat them in here unless we all get some. Put them away, and take that pocketbook off the desk. I smile and wonder what else she's got in her traveling pantry. How can you be hungry anyway? I ask her. Didn't you just eat lunch last period? It was a while ago, she says and wipes the orange residue off her mouth and fingers. All over the room classmates eye her vulture-like; they're always hungry, always thirsty. They'd trade their souls for a steady supply of junk food or whatever she's got in pocketbook #1. Cheese doodles – there's magic in those words.

Menu Please – *You see a classroom. Students see a dining room with separate tables and a BYOF policy.*

Eat, Drink, And Be Merry – *The surest way to eat and drink in class is to bring in a doctor's note. While you're at it, see if you can get the doctor to require smoking and drinking alcohol too. Nothing like a good cigar and a snifter of brandy to top off a snack.*

I'm on caf duty, the bell rings, and one table bolts leaving a mess. Teachers are assigned different areas, and we're supposed to monitor our area and have the students clear as they finish eating. It's not always easy, some eat right up to the bell, others argue that the mess isn't theirs even when it's right in front of them. The sneaky make a mess and change tables forcing you to play detective. Anything small: peanuts, raisins, croutons, grape tomatoes, grapes, corn, peas, etc. they like to throw at each other. Teachers on duty are expected to clean up any mess left behind in their area before the next lunch wave comes in. No administrator ever said we *had* to clean it up. But there are veiled looks that say, Hey! Pick up the mess or you'll be back on caf duty next semester too!

If a table leaves a mess and you know who, the office will call the pig-ster(s) out of class to clean up. Students who leave messes generally do not mind getting called out of class. Most love it. They wander the halls, eventually wander down to the caf, push a sponge or broom around for a minute or two, then go back to wandering the halls. The poor classroom teacher has to deal with the disruptions then try to get them up to speed.

I point out to a boss that it's crazy not to impose additional penalties like restricted seating. Total food deprivation is out, though some would certainly benefit from a prolonged diet of raw vegetables and water.

Boss tells me it's human nature to leave a mess. As a matter of fact, Boss says, the teachers left a mess last night after the faculty meeting. Really? I ask. Yes, Boss says, it's human nature. I find it hard to believe the teachers left a mess, I say. And isn't there a big difference between a few handouts scattered on tabletops, and smashed grapes and slippery slides of mozzarella on the floor? And isn't it also human nature to eat food, and not launch it?

Our conversation is interrupted when I spot a girl throwing food for the second time. I mosey over and ask, What do you think you're doing? Without blinking an eye she answers, Just playing basketball.

Strike three! *– If boss tells you it's human nature to throw food, your problem isn't with the students or with the airborne edibles. You need to reduce the administrative footprint in your school. It's human nature to throw bosses.*

Guess What Students *– Throwing food is fun. Don't let anyone tell you differently. Food fight, food fight, food fight! Just wait till you have an* *administrator or two as targets, then zero in. And don't worry. They'll understand.*

I have nothing against administrators, not even the bad ones. This too shall pass, has a lot of validity and comfort. Administrators come-and-go, and I've outlasted more than I can remember. Administrators are dated people. They're of-the-moment. Blink, and most are moving on, usually in 2-5 years, sometimes sooner. Their names are forgotten, and if any mark is left, it's usually in some passing trend that goes shortly after them. They love trends. They repackage them, rename them, call in experts to validate them. Any teacher or committee that opposes the trend du jour is branded as being against the best interests of students. Because so few administrators ever actually taught for any length of time in a mainstream academic classroom, they tend to trust methodology and people skills over straight academics. They play politics and feel they are very strong in people skills, even if they're not. The worst are cocky in the same superior way some cops are. Many were C/B students themselves, few were excellent. They would never say academics are an anathema, but the worst spiritually feel it. Most can order supplies, cancel school in blizzards, bounce the disorderly, oversee a meeting, release a press statement, and hire replacements, though even some of these simple things prove challenging for the worst. . . The worst and best alike refer to their time in the classroom as an easier time, one they would gladly go back to though few ever do because most are smart enough to realize that this is just PR and borderline delusional. The classroom isn't easier at all, and they could never go back to being on-the-clock. . . The worst make the classroom teacher's life tougher. The worst wreck morale and esprit de corps right down to the student body. The worst trust and admire no one but the ones above them in rank and salary. Their legacies are writ in biodegradable chalk dust.

Dilbert: Leadership is nature's way of removing morons from the productive flow.

In my 32 years I've worked for many many bosses. One was horrific, several were bad, most were average, a few were good. None were above good, in my opinion. The worst tend to follow Murphy's Law and step a rung or two above their abilities. One of the worst ever says to me, The students in this school aren't the problem, the teachers are. Turns out this poobah's the problem but is myopic and can't see it.

Best selling business author Guy Kawasaki in his book *Reality Check* talks about how to determine if your boss is a jerk. I have my own ways, and though a bit smart-assed there's some truth here.

Ten Ways To Tell If Your School Bosses Are Jerks

10. Their phone numbers aren't listed, they have p.o. boxes.
9. They wait for the halls to clear before taking a walk.
8. They say, Oh what I wouldn't give to be back in the classroom. and expect you to believe it.
7. Secretaries and janitors don't like them.
6. Kneeling in their presence may not be required, but don't contradict or upstage them either.
5. They bring air-popped butterless popcorn for meetings, or nothing; they're not corner bakery/nonfranchise pizza types when it comes to staff.
4. There's no suggestion box. If there was there'd be no slot or it'd be electrified.
3. The nicest thing you can say about them is that they don't have a

prison record and/or they're are not registered sex offenders.

2. People from their past laugh or go purple/red when you mention their names.
1. They're here long-term because no one else wants them.

Numero Uno – *If you have good bosses/administrators, rejoice. If you don't, try getting them to wear one of those doggie collars that gives a shock whenever the bastard attempts to leave home.*

Super Student Secret – *At home, you're tops; in school, you're not. Pretty much everyone's your boss. On the other hand without you, no one else has a job. Just don't get all pop-top bloated about it.*

Bottom Line: If a boss cares more about style without class, authority without compromise, power without compassion, prestige without merit, salary without work, mandates without consensus, communication without listening, respect without feeling, leadership by proxy/in absentia, this is an administrator who's confusing being an educational leader with being a third world potentate. You want someone who believes, like D.H. Lawrence, in a good heart, a lively intelligence, and the courage to say shit in front of anyone. No sieg heils, in any case.

Seasonal Snippets: There's a near blizzard, school isn't cancelled, I barely make it in, and then school gets cancelled. It's just moi and a couple of administrators who want to know why I'm here. I tell them I'm contractually obligated to work 185 days, and that it's easier to get the days in when the students aren't around. There are no ho-ho-ho's.

An English teacher covering Dickens' *A Christmas Carol* has a student refer to Jacob Marley as Bob Marley.

A neighboring social studies teacher covering the ancient Middle East has a student talk about the *whaling* wall and another gives Jesus Christ's timeline as, Born: 27 BC; Died: 14 AD; Reborn 17 AD; Crucified 1456-1459.

I'm at my computer, one class is leaving, the next pushing in, and I hear one LL Bean fashion plate say in a hurt tone, You didn't invite me. Her friend says matter-of-factly, It was only family.

Must be a holiday party.

I push my computer chair back and swivel around. The girls are close, and I say, Want to hear a quick party story?

They look at each other, eyes go way up like he's-down-the-fucking-rabbit-hole-again. I say, Years ago there's this girl who doesn't like me, I don't know why, just one of those gut things. It's the end of the year and she's having a pool party. I find an invitation on the floor. Next day I leave it out on my desk and go into the hall as the class enters. When the bell rings, I come in and make a big deal out of finding it on my desk. I say, Meredith, this is so thoughtful. You're inviting me to your pool party. I thought you didn't like me, but this just shows you how wrong a teacher can be. Mr. Bentley, she says totally unfazed, I don't like you, and that invitation isn't for you. But it was right here on my desk, I protest. I don't know how it got there, she says suspiciously, but it's not for you. You mean, I'm not invited? I ask. That's right, she says, and holds out her hand for the invitation. I'm crushed, I say and turn it over. I doubt that, she counters and pockets the envelope. . . She graduates, moves out of the area, and I never see her again. Years later I get a promotional flyer in the mail for some publication that names all-star teachers. Seems that Meredith entered me as a teacher who greatly influenced her. *Shut the fuck up!*

The girls' looks change from tolerance to relief the story is over. I add, You just never know about invitations.

Ain't No Way – *Don't make yourself a part of your students' partying scene, even if you're a young teacher, even if you think you'll never see them again. Marshall McLuhan said, The past went that-a-way. Don't try to follow it.*

Growing Pains – *Teachers can party, love to party, but not with you. They also can't share their experiences with booze or drugs, or teach you the kama sutra, or show you the way to San Jose. These are tough life lessons you'll have to learn on your own.*

I have plenty of fine students this year: solid academically and very likable. They just don't make as good copy as the turd birds. Some of my favorites are the ones who give a great effort, the ones who are friendly and talk and participate, the ones who have a spark of genius/talent, the gentle souls, the generous spirits, the happy people. They're easy to like, and it's no great stretch of a teacher's emotional range. Yet I'm also drawn to the rebels, the bohemians, the Age Of Aquarius types who, if they were of my generation, would have been marching on Washington, grooving to Leonard Cohen and Judy Collins in the Village, or camping out at Woodstock, chasing butterflies, looking for meaning in Jimi Hendrix and Janis Joplin.

In past Decembers I put a small festive tree on my desk, plug in a bubbling candle, hang a large 2-sheet poster of Santa, and hand out hard candy as a bonus. I wear holiday themed ties to include a Santa bolo, and shirts and sportcoats of red and green. Over the years I assign O. Henry's The Gift Of the Magi and Langston Hughes' One Christmas Eve; the famous 1897 New York Sun column Yes, Virginia, There Is A Santa Claus; Robert Frost's Christmas Trees, Dickens' *A Christmas Carol*, Truman Capote's A Christmas Memory, and several of my own true life holiday columns. I show the Twilight Zone episode Night Of the Meek and offer extra credit to anyone who can memorize Clement Moore's 1849 classic A Visit From St. Nicholas.

Most of my Christmas assignments get tossed when teaming comes in. It's around the same time the word *holiday* replaces Christmas, and St. Nick is judged an intrusion of Christian symbolism into education. Jay Leno: The Supreme Court has ruled that they cannot have a nativity scene in Washington DC. This wasn't for any religious reasons. They couldn't find 3 wise men and a virgin. . .

Christmas has shrunk like a cold weiner.

As the holiday break gets close we English teachers exchange presents. I get a home-made peach pie, a scratch off lottery ticket that doesn't hit, chocolate covered expresso coffee beans, a coffee house gift certificate, and a plate of cookies. I give small bottles of homemade kahlua and my own blended Irish cream, both vodka based and odorless. Years ago I watch as two teachers top off their coffee mugs with a healthy dose of the kahlua and spend the morning smiling and the afternoon thirsty.

I throw a party for the English Department and friends. Six hours later some are still tossing down glassfuls and one is playing the piano. Back in the 70's and 80's the last day was always a half day, and as soon as the students left, we started a party in the library complete with a full buffet, a liquor raffle, and more than one bottle's opened before dessert. One year the girls' basketball coach wins a large bottle of wine, but he's at practice so we crack the sweet vino and toast the his memory. Merry Christmas. Joy to the world and eggnog dreams.

Outside, December gets close to 20 inches of snow which is close to the total for all of last year. Inside, my Drama class brings in decks of cards and I teach them how to play gin rummy in preparation for reading *The Gin Game* over the holiday. A few already know the game, or variations of it; the rest catch on fast. I have to stop them short of playing for money.

In the last period of the last day before the break I offer a 9th grade study hall the day's newspaper, unopened and unread.

- What's in it? a rock concert t-shirted freshman in the back asks.

- It's a newspaper, I say stressing *news*.

- So what kind of stuff is in it?

- Today's news. *News!* His friends are laughing, and the young cretin's looking puzzled. Stupidity on steroids. He'd probably be OK with the e-version. Maybe. Maybe it needs holiday wrapping. I'm tempted to stand up like Dick Diver at the ending of Fitzgerald's *Tender Is the Night*, raise my right hand and give them a papal blessing, God bless you all, everyone, and any teacher who expects you whacko prodigies to remember anything come January. Out with the old, in with the new, get off, get on, get out – but not until the bell.

Eyes watch the clock. . . 5-4-3-2-1- Brrrrringgggggggg!!!!! Holiday break! The school empties amidst whooping and hollering and the surge pushes through the doors and towards the busses and that wondrous of all holidays, Christmas!!!!!!!!

I heard the bells on Christmas Day,
Their old, familiar carols play,
And wild and sweet the words repeat
Of peace on earth, good-will to men.
-Henry Wadsworth Longfellow-

JANUARY – The Emperor's New Clothes

We come back on January 2, which is a Wednesday, which is good. Nothing like starting the new year off in the middle of the week, and I need the short week. I was sick for 9 of the 11 days, I'm still coughing up phlegm, and I'm sleepy because of the antihistamine/nasal decongestant I'm popping.

I cough and sneeze and blow my nose. There's not a single, Bless you, but that's understandable. They're recovering themselves from the shock of being back.

- Oh my gosh, are you sick, Mr Bentley? a red-headed girl finally asks while contemplating her nails.

- Sure sounds it, I smile weakly, unless one of you is a ventriloquist.

- I thought you said you're never sick?

The question comes from a boy who remembers just about everything I tell him, except anything dealing with English. His question is a change from the one I usually get: Why were you out yesterday? To that question I usually rebut, You can ask me that when I can ask you why *you* were out. I believe in telling students some personal things, but hardly everything, and hardly things such as sometimes when I'm out I'm not really that sick.

I look at the boy through watery eyes.

- My younger son came home for Christmas and gave it to me. He seldom comes home so I'm seldom sick. I got his cold, he got my genes. I don't blame him if he's angry. . . I smile weakly again, and the matter's dropped.

A few days later I'm still feeling crummy, and I call in sick. The day I return I run into one of the bosses right off and boss asks, Are you feeling better? I hold my hand up in a stop motion, reach into my pocket and hand boss a folded piece of paper. Boss opens it and reads, I'm fine. Thank you for asking. And you? Below that is a large stick figure jumping up clicking his heels. Boss is puzzled then laughs. How did you know I was going to– I cut him off. Because you always ask, I say and think, *and it never sounds sincere.* I smile, take the paper back, and I'm reloaded.

Some retired teachers tell me I should take all 15 of my sick days my last year. One says it's his only regret about his own final year. It's a thought, I mean, there's sick and there's sick, and who doesn't get sick of the daily grind, sick of meaningless arbitrary mandates, sick of spaceship school?

***Ye Olde Work Ethic** – The world won't end because you're out and neither will your classes. As a rule of thumb, try to be in more than you're out.*

***Love Your Teacher** – If you're truly concerned, send flowers or chicken soup. Candygrams and moneygrams work well too.*

I'm working at my desk between classes and a boss comes in. I look up, feign interest, and say, Yes? Boss comes right to the point.

- Unless you can get 6 people signed up for African American Literature and Film, the course will be cancelled, one of the larger electives will be split and you'll be given that.

Boss is talking about second semester which is a few weeks off. My Drama course ends and I'm scheduled to begin my new African American course. For the last 4 months there've been only 2 students signed up, but I was told the course was going to run regardless of numbers so this is a major change in the 11th hour.

I'm not happy about it. Actually I'm silently p.o.'ed, and that makes me resolute. I wonder if this is some new game of theirs. Are they smart enough to have a game? Are they trying to make retirement so attractive I announce early? I feel like saying, Hey! How about a break? Don't you think I deserve one after more than three decades of dealing with large numbers of students, three academic preps, pulling all sorts of extraneous duties, coaching, etc.?

But I say none of it. I know from past experience teachers are not cut a break, whether it's their first or last year, though many administrations like to finish off their own careers with some cushiony, high paying, central office sinecure. But it doesn't work that way for teachers. Teachers battle in the tiled trenches right to the end.

I put on my best blank expression. It's time for Sun Tze and *The Art Of War*.

- Do what you want, I say as unemotionally as I can. . . Sun Tze: All warfare is based on deception.

- Boss is surprised.

- You don't care?

- You're the boss. Make the call. I'm on the slide to retirement. I'll teach any course you give me. . . Sun Tzu: Do not besiege walled cities if it can be avoided.

This is an exaggeration. WTF. Of course I care. I've spent days/ weeks, and it's no exaggeration to say *years* of my own time, energy, and passion putting this course together, and I'm excited to teach it. There's a lot more work ahead, but any course that'd be split is a lot of work too, and most likely I get either Advanced Composition or Creative Composition and I've taught them both enough times to know I don't want piles of compositions all the time.

But I don't want boss to know that.

- OK, boss says, hesitates, then walks out dodging the incoming sophomores.

The next day I see boss sitting alone and go into the room. Boss looks up surprised, and it's my turn to come right to the point.

- If the African American course is cancelled, I'm going to call in the NAACP and the press. . . I say it matter-of-factly like I'm ordering a chef's salad at the caf.

- For what? Boss's face is barely controlled, voice is pinched, emotion is revving. Bosses hate negative press. Nothing ruins their day like negative press.

- Because it's the only minority course offered in the school, and there are precedents for running courses with low enrollments, such as 2 or 3.

- Are you talking about AP?

- Yeah, but what's the difference? Different needs have to be meant. We need to acknowledge diversity.

I sound really, really p.c.. Boss says nothing, I say nothing, and *diversity* becomes my exit word. It's a good goddamn calling card to leave behind.

Calling in the press has a mixed history in this system. In a case of reverse discrimination several boys are denied a cheerleading tryout. They call in the local news channels and the dailies, and voila! they're on the team. All quit soon after practices start.

Press coverage during the *Kaffir Boy* brouhaha doesn't accomplish much, though it does for the *A Day No Pigs Would Die* brouhaha. I don't know what the outcome will be now if I call in the NAACP and the press corps, but in any case it'll be a lengthy battle. Sun Tze: In war let your great objective be victory, not lengthy campaigns.

I know even as I threaten to wave in the reporters that I'm probably not going to do it. Not that I mind a public battle or fear retaliation. There's little they can do to me at this stage. It's more that by the time of the final Armageddon, the year'll be over, I might be retired, and all my work up to this point will have been for nothing. Still, the threat is a good temporary diversion, it'll get them thinking/worrying, and it's weirdly entertaining to me. Reverse the roles for once. Let *me* bring the heat to them, let *them* fucking sweat.

- I need four students or more to go down to guidance right now and sign up for my African American Literature and Film course.

I'm talking to my regular Film course – euphemistically called Interpreting Film In A Modern Society, but no one moves. Most aren't giving me any more attention than they give morning announcements. This group won't really come alive until I start our current film *Crash*, which they think is awesome. I try again.

- How many of you need to take an English course next semester to graduate? I ask. Most hands go up. Well then, I say, do you really think you're going to like Mythology? Advanced Comp? Women In Literature? Remember my course is called African American Literature and Film. **FILM!** Of course if you want a lot of reading and writing your last semester in high school those other courses will probably fit your needs better.

- But Mr. Bentley, your course has literature too, doesn't it? a sharp-eared girl asks.

- That's true, I say. But so does this course, and how many of you have been doing the reading? Don't bother to answer that, I know. Practically no one. And yet, how many of you are failing? No one. And that's because your grade is also tied into your critical viewing of our daily film. And it's going to be that way in the new course. **FILM!** You can't go wrong. Do yourselves a favor and sign up, right now. I'll write anyone a pass to guidance who wants one. You can go this period with no loss of points. Tell your counselor you want to add African American Lit and **Film**!

Four students come right up and ten minutes later three are signed up, the fourth can't get a schedule change. The word gets out quickly and by the end of the day there're 14 students signed up, and the course is a lock. Other teachers are happy for me. Sun Tzu: If you fight and conquer, the whole Empire will say, Well done!

True, I didn't appeal to anything noble: the students' multicultural social sense, their higher thinking skills, their theoretical curiosity and addiction to learning. But I learned early on that many second semester seniors are lame ducks, made practically catatonic after college applications go out. They won't work a lot, some won't work at all, some don't even need to pass a course to graduate. They only need to register for *a* course and to take a minimum number of credits. They don't really care what course they sign up for as long as they perceive it's going to be easy and not too early in the day. Seniors without classes can arrive late.

Dance A Little Sidestep *– Robert Frost said, Two roads diverged in a wood. Frost's narrator took the one less travelled, I took the one of least resistance. Frost's was the high road and led to fame and glory. Mine will lead to a new course in the twilight of my teaching days, and to retirement and a pension. These are not bad things.*

Student No Brainer Advice *– Sure you'll sign up for film. Everyone loves* ***film****. And some of you want a career in film and are already tearing ticket stubs, pouring butter over popcorn, and running the new digital projectors. It's a start. It'd be a better start if your backwoods parents were the Spielbergs, Hanks, or the Will Smiths. But it's a start.*

Postscript: In reality there'll be literature in the new course, nightly assignments that have to be read if a student expects to get anything higher than a D-, so maybe I did sucker the new 12 into signing up. On the other hand they will see a lot of film, no one will likely flunk, and anything they learn about African Americans in literature and film will be prodigious compared to what they know now, which is little/nothing.

I see this as a victory of sorts for everyone including the administration who'll get expanded course offerings and improved diversity to take credit for in their own resumes/portfolios. Makes me wonder in retrospect if the course was ever in real danger of being scrapped. **Conspiracy Theory**: Perhaps I was set up. Told in the 11th hour merely to put the pressure on. Applied Stress, the name of admin's game. Psychic thumbscrews. Payback for a thousand bustings in 32 years. Incentive to take a permanent hike after June. . . Did I get played? Did Oswald act alone? Am I paranoid? Does it fucking matter?

The class is quietly working when the cute but ditzy girl's cell phone goes off. She's embarrassed just a smidge, the class is amused, I'm patient. She smiles, I smile back, and she wordlessly fumbles through her pocketbook to shut it off. When the music stops I say, No problem, but if it goes off again I take it for the rest of the day and give it to the main office. School Policy: I'm supposed to take it now and turn it into the office so they can check to see if this is a reoccurring motif. It seems harsh, but makes sense, and it's necessary. Cell phones, cell phones, cell phones. Students with unlimited minutes would spend all day calling each other if they could. The worst would call friends seated right next to them. It was never a problem before; the school had no reception. Then last year one of the tele-giants erected a tower across the road from the school, and that started it. The cell phone chitchat circuit, the cell connected day, cellonomics.

Some of the teachers are no better than the students. I watch one teacher phone his son who's matriculated at the middle school next door. Isn't your son in class now? I ask. He checks his watch while he presses the phone to his ear. No, they just got out. Whew, I think, heaven forbid you should miss connecting with bambino the second he's free. Bet the little bastard loves that.

I see a dark-eyed girl with her top pulled down over one shoulder revealing her bra strap standing in the hall keying her cell. This particular girl's given me a hard time more than once and I'm not inclined to cut her any shit. Attention Students: As you cut slack, so shall it be cut in return. I delicately slide through the crush of moving bodies. She sees me coming, snaps the cover shut and drops it back into her handbag. Unfazed I move closer and say, Excuse me. I hold out my hand. What? she says aggressively. I'll take that phone, I say. You know the rules. I have to call my mother, she says. I need to get picked up after school. You can call her from the office, I say, but I'll take the phone. My hand is still out there like I want her to slap me five, and the hand is still empty. The girl doesn't move, doesn't say anything, so I ask, Are you going to give me the phone or not? I told you, she says even more defiantly with a crossed arms attitude, I have to call my mother. This is your last chance, I respond. If you don't give me that phone I'm going to write you up for using it, and for insubordination. You can get expelled for insubordination. She's angry but not intimidated. She slams a locker door, turns away, and joins the flow of students moving to class. I watch her long enough to be sure she's not coming back and head off myself. I'm calm. I learned long ago not to get worked up over these tête-à-têtes. You wind up either saying something you regret, or carrying it with you the rest of the day, simmering on low, getting your ass in an internal uproar while the student has long gotten past it. I write her up, and she gets a detention. Not much, but it's something. Wonder if she ever got through to mom?

A teacher not even in my department and on the other side of the building comes in between classes. Would you give this to Missy Sue? she asks and hands me a cell phone. She's in your last period study hall, she adds. Oh, OK, sure, why not, I say while thinking, *And now I'm the fucking FedEx delivery man?* Then I remind myself, *Colleague, colleague, colleague, be nice. At least she's not asking you to deliver a baby.*

I see a boy working his hand in his pocket. In the old days this would mean a game of pocket pool. In today's world it means texting without looking. I smile at him, glance down at the pocket, and he stops. Of course it could be texting *and* pocket pool, i.e. getting a dual connection. Whatever, a disconnect is required.

I'm walking down the hall behind two MTV hep girls. Girl 1: Text me. Girl 2: I can't, I'm going to class. Girl 1: So go to class, then go to the lav. . . I think, Daaaahhh. . .

The best cell phone story didn't happen to me, I got it secondhand. Student comes into class with a cell pressed to her ear, hands it to the teacher, and says, Can you please talk to my mother? She wants to know why I got B- on my last project.

Cell phones can be a damn distraction, and no cell phones during school hours is a school rule I enforce. I don't enforce every rule. You can't or you'd be spending all day nitpicking and playing cop. The rule used to say no gum chewing, but my caveat was I don't care if you chew as long as you don't blow bubbles, snap it, leave it lying around, or choke on it. There was a time backpacks were banned from hallways and class, but I didn't enforce it and had a complaint lodged from other teachers that some of us weren't enforcing the no-backpack ordinance. I've also overlooked 3 minutes only on a lav/ locker pass, no going to locker during study hall, no Walkmans or Ipods *ever* to include study halls and lunch.

Be Sure To Wear Some Flowers In Your Hair – *All teachers enforce some rules and overlook others. This will never change. Hopefully the ones you enforce someone else overlooks, and vica versa. This leads to just about everything being enforced, and just about everything being overlooked, and how much more damn consistency can there be?*

Student Wink – *Right action leads to right results, wrong action leads to wrong results. Teachers expect you to do right, and to do wrong. No big deal. Just try to do more right than wrong, and try not to complain when the shit hits the fan. No one likes a crybaby. Don't be a whimporexic.*

Teachers get an email announcing some sort of farewell soiree for a big departing honcho. No way I'm going, no sense in being a hypocrite. I don't like honcho, and many of the teachers I talk to feel the same way. Goodbye and keep cold – it's the farewell Robert Frost gives an orchard as he leaves for the winter. I'd give the same farewell to honcho but leave out the goodbye, that is if I had anything at all to say, which I don't. Mini Lesson: If you have nothing to say, it's best not to fucking say it.

- Mr. Bentley, we're getting a new honcho, aren't we?

Of course the fishing student doesn't say honcho, but it's as good a word as any. More importantly I'm surprised the student knows about this personnel change and even more surprised that it's brought up. Big honchos don't dwell at this level.

- That's right.

- What's the new honcho do?

- I don't know.

- What do you mean?

- I mean, there are a lot of big honchos. I don't know what this particular honcho does. I don't know what's left to do. . . Sidebar: If it sounds sarcastic or naive, it's not. It's honest. I don't know, not totally anyway. Trying to figure out the job behind the title isn't always an easy thing. In literary terms it's a Gordian knot, Cretan labyrinth, and the riddle of the Theban Sphinx all rolled into one. More astute taxpayers than I have questioned and failed to unravel our Rubrik's Cube bureaucracy, and our honchos are undefeated in fighting off a number of attempts to shrink their numbers through budget referendums.

- Won't the new honcho be the one to cancel school when it snows? . . . The student still wants some sort of answer.

- A honcho, or two, or three. There's talk and the bus company has a lot of say. . . I try to keep it vague.

- Will our new honcho make a lot of money?

- Two-and-a-half times my salary when every thing's considered. . . Of course, they don't know what I make and I doubt any could do the math if they did know. Taking out their calculators would be too much work.

The student understands that there's a multiple involved and that means the salary has got to be big. The entire class looks impressed. Money, and the phrase, There'll be no school today are at the top of their comprehension list.

Loose Lips Sink Careers *– Students will occasionally bring up the subject of top honchos. Talk or don't talk, but if you talk, say nothing. Students are A/V equipment who record everything of interest, and play back at supper or to the honchos themselves. The reruns generally do not go your way.*

Student Shoutout *– Big honchos are not of your world. The gods on Olympus do not follow the comings and goings of you one cell amoebae. Keep your curiosity, respect, and kind words for the ones who care the most about you: your parents, teachers, and armed forces recruiter.*

Student/Teacher/Honcho Interface: Years ago I have a Valley Girl convertible type who gets a 78% on a literature test. The test is a combination objective and subjective questions. The student loses 22 points on the objective portion, but writes superb essays. I decide that despite the objective point loss, the test is worth an 80%, a holistic B- because of the excellent essays, and that's the grade I put on it. We go over the test, and the student finds an objective mistake I made. Took 2 points off an answer that's right. Student wants the 2 points back and an 82%. But I already gave you 2 points, I say. I thought your test was worth a B-, even if I had to give you 2 imaginary points to reach it. I'm not giving you 2 more now. The original

80% was a gift, now you have it legitimately. . . Student is very upset. We discuss it more but get nowhere.

Student goes to see a honcho. I get called into a conference with them. As soon as I enter I see student's been crying, which elicits bafflement, pity, and annoyance from me in quick succession. I've never seen tears over 2 points, and don't understand it. I reiterate my position and logic and say in conclusion, The 2 points may seem like a lot to you now, but it's only 2 points and even with the 2 points you want, it's still a B-. There's no letter difference between an 80% and an 82%, and 2 points will be meaningless when I calculate the marking period grade, and less than nothing in the final year's calculations.

Student is sniffling and adamant, and honcho takes student's side. Give her the 2 points, honcho orders. NFW, I think and I look at the girl. You sure you want to do this? I ask. I'm telling you, you don't want to do this. Turns out student does want to do this, so I go back and change the grade. I'm not happy with the girl and even less pleased with honcho who should have never taken sides. Barring extreme abuse, grading is a teacher's prerogative.

Aftermath: For the rest of the marking period I occasionally grab a point off an essay here, a point off an essay there, and get the 2 points back quickly, and then some. I'm careful not to overdo it, and at the end of the marking period/year the points mean nothing, as predicted. Her average is solidly in the middle. I do not feel wrong for doing this, and my cosmic sense of proportion and rightness is restabilized.

When You're Right You're Right – *Be fair, be consistent with your grading, and don't let outside influences shake you. There are times your honchos are more clueless than the students, and with less excuse. Damn bunch of fart twangers.*

Ain't It Obvious *– Don't go over your teacher's head for the trivial. Even if you win, you lose. And never ever cry over anything less than a teacher or administrator beating you with an iron mace or electric cattle prong.*

Postscript: The girl graduates, years pass, and out of nowhere honcho tells me they're in contact and she now admits she should have never gotten the extra 2 points. In that admission her own sense of cosmic proportion and rightness is restabilized, and I feel good for her. Honcho still does not admit any wrong doing and remains a clueless dimwitty morph.

Midterm Exams are approaching. In the past this would mean detailed preview sheets, note taking, and lots of pressure for my classes. Not this year for the sophomores. The department's decided to go with an all essay exam that closely models the statewide test all 10th graders take in the spring. Read an article, respond to it in four essays. Has almost nothing to do with the literature we've read this semester, but it is the kind of writing they've done, and all our school's sophomores will take the exact same exam which is a big deal from the admin's vantage.

One of my classes starts the exam. They're reading a short selection from *Angela's Ashes* before responding to it. Five minutes in one of my barbarians at the gate drops his pen on the desk. Not one of those light plastic Bics, but a heavy metal howitzer that hits with a goddamn BANG! I ignore him, and a minute later it happens again, BANG! I stare at him, and he smiles back. Two minutes later, BANG! again. This time heads jerk up, and I realize I need to do something. This urinal cake is disrupting the exam. If another student bombs it, any distraction becomes an excuse. It's happened before, and I'm not about to explain to angry parent why I was deaf, dumb, and mute.

I walk over to him, and he looks up faux-puzzled.

I understand you're nervous, I say, and that your palms and fingers are sweating which makes it hard to hold a pen. But I'm sure you understand you're disrupting the others, and I can't let that happen. If your pen drops again, I'm dismissing you, sending you to the nurse's office for everyone's good, including your own since you're obviously nervous and may be sick. You can come back tomorrow during the early morning makeup period when you'll be less nervous with everyone gone and after a good night's sleep.

My voice is soothing honey, and my expression one of beatific benevolence. He gets the point, and the fucking pen doesn't drop again.

Reflection: In 1940's parlance some students are punks, the type that a steely-eyed Bogie would've gladly grabbed by the lapels and bitch-slapped silly. This particular student is what I call a Second Tier Weisenheimer. Not the in-your-face, openly defiant kind. Not even the if-wits-were-dynamite-couldn't-give-himself-a-headache type. Rather the sneaky, laugh-and-talk-whenever-you-turn-your-head, behaviorally oppressed type that smirks and dares you to catch him and say something. Never does anything big, anything traumatic. Just pesky, drop-the-pen, roll-the-pen, noisily break the pencil stuff. Passive-aggressive, definitely weird. The type who waits till your back's turned then it's slam the book, drop the notebook, pull hair, pinch, sneeze/cough/burp, crack knuckles, throw things, etc. I've had lots of them over the years, every teacher has, and I have a number this year.

An Eye For An Eye – *You have to be careful with this kind of student, or you wind up looking like an idiot when administration says, You kicked him out* *for coughing? Because you thought it was forced? To such weasels cut no break, but don't say that. Weasels expect, and demand, to be treated like everyone else. Moreover they don't like to be called weasels. You can't even call them skulky little rodent shits. So give the semblance of treating them the same, smile when they smile, and bide your time.*

Watching Your Back 24/7 *– Think you're putting one over on the teacher? You're not, you're only fooling yourself. The gotcha day always comes and delivery is free. You won't even have to sign for your kick-in-the-academic ass.*

Midterm exams for the sophomores, and final exams for the seniors in Drama and Film come-and-go. The sophomore grades are high, as expected, but at 10% it doesn't matter. Ten percent is scarcely a breeze and averages are mighty sequoias. It takes more than 10% to move them. With the seniors it's different. Exams are 20% of the semester/course grade, and that kind of percentage is a tsunami that sweeps averages out to sea, or to higher ground.

Exams in English are a dichotomy for me. On one hand I don't believe in them and question their relevance. We assign substantial reading and writing in the course of a semester/year that amount to many hours of homework, so where's a 100 minute test fit in? On the other hand I believe there can be good exams in English, but I don't believe any exam should count 20%. It's too much out of proportion to the great amount of classwork that's already been done. On the other hand if it counts less than 20% what's the point, as *less* affects little/nothing.

Einstein: Not everything that counts can be counted and not everything that can be counted counts.

Some teachers argue exams are good practice for college exams down the road, but I counter that I'm not a surrogate professor. Let the profs do their own prep work. Boola, boola.

Past Exams, **Snippet 1**: The long-haired, watery-eyed student's sitting in the second seat middle row directly in front of me. I shouldn't see him, heads are supposed to line up like cemetery markers at Arlington, but he has a rubber neck and keeps stretching up or sideways to see the exam in front of him. They're taking the first part, quote identification, and cheating is easy. He stretches again, I make eye contact, and he settles back down. A minute later his body's elevated again, eyes are roaming, and I say, Excuse me, concentrate on your own paper. It's blunt and terse, which is usually enough. A few minutes later he's sneaking peeks again, so I ratchet it up and say, If you do that one more time your exam's over and it's a zero. The class, of course, has been warned about this, but I guess he figures he's going to flunk anyway so what the haydeehayhay fuckfuckfuck is there to lose, which isn't true because in his case there's a big difference between flunking with a 50% and flunking with a zero. In any case, he locks onto the exam in front of him again, I get up, walk over, take his blue book, and that's the end of it. Nothing said, no histrionics. I don't feel good about it, but the snot drip seems fine and puts his head down for a snooze.

Woody Allen: I was thrown out of college for cheating on the metaphysics exam. I looked into the soul of another boy.

Snippet 2: Way back Big Cheese wants a new exam for all sophomores. We brainstorm, write and rewrite, but Big Cheese keeps changing the requirements and retracting approval. Big Cheese is the type of administrator who goes to a restaurant and tells the waiter/waitress, Bring me food. Not sure what I want, but bring me something. When the dish finally comes it's, No, this isn't quite it. Bring me something else. I finally tell Big Cheese to write the exam himself and submit it to us teachers for approval. And that's when the exam draft gets approved.

Snippet 3: Student's been an A- student through 2 marking periods, works to his full potential, has extensive notes for this exam, but is just not good at test taking. I give him extra time, but it's still not enough and his exam's a D which pulls his A- average down to B. What!? NFW. I go over the exam again, cut slack here, cut slack there, and get the grade high enough that he won't loss his A- for the mid-term. I do this many times over the years, and I always feel good about it. Students who deserve a break, get one. Hard work does pay off, semester grade mirrors what the student's achieved, knows, and deserves. I wonder, *Do other teachers do this too? On the QT?*

A Bladeless Guillotine *– It would not be a bad thing to abolish exams, at least in English. There's a time when less is more, and this might be one of them.*

Cast A Giant Shadow *– If your school has exams and believes that more is more, what can you do other than prepare diligently and do your best. Believe me, effort and preparation go a long way, and sometimes there are unseen mysterious forces at work.*

The semester ends, it's the official halfway mark in the year. It hasn't been an easy year so far with all the meetings, parent queries, misbehaving and failing, and new mandates such as a homeroom period every two weeks and the expectation that we're supposed to lead students we barely know in discussions on subjects we're not certified to deal with. The one saving grace has been I don't have big numbers of students – 83 total this year, down from the usual 100-123. And now it's the halfway mark, and while the end of the year's not yet in sight, it's imaginable somewhere off in the misty mist and the dusky dusk. Fuck yeah.

Sophomores started *Macbeth* before exams. We didn't finish it and now have to pick up with Act 3. I hate going around the marking period corner like this and would've fought like hell to avoid it had the exam been literature based. As it is, I hope they remember the name of the main character and haven't lost their books. These are reasonable expectations.

As if *Macbeth* isn't tough enough, we issue an unabridged cheap copy with few footnotes. Students have the options of buying the book for $1 and writing in it, or not buying it and not writing in it, or just using their own copy. Owning the book and writing in it is good practice for post high school, and that's our rationale for this el cheap-o version. The thrifty write in pencil and erase before turning it in – a buck is a buck. Some use sticky notes. Quite a few don't write in the book, don't read the book, don't even open the book, which is *also* good practice for some forms of post high school life.

We're two days into *Macbeth* when a tall skinny Olive Oyl type who is normally very extroverted is just quietly sitting there like she's pondering the possibilities of an expanding universe.

- Is something wrong? I ask her.

- This book isn't fair, she says and releases all the pent up energy of a stuck geological fault. I mean like who can understand this? Why does he write like this? Why doesn't he just write so people can understand him?

She's angry and doesn't look around to see who agrees with her. She doesn't care. The book's in a foreign language, it's unfair, and I must be a fucking madman to assign it. The outburst surprises me. I've had many students not happy with Shakespeare, but never any this passionate.

- Didn't you read *Romeo and Juliet* last year? I ask. You must've. All freshmen read it. How did you understand that? It's the same author, you know.

- I didn't understand it.

- Look, I say and hold up a handout they got a couple days ago. This is a strategy sheet for reading Shakespeare. We went over it. I modeled some of the strategies. Lots of good pointers here. . . The girl looks disinterested in strategies, but she's a powerful enough personality that if I don't pursue this she could initiate an open rebellion. Many feel the same way. At the least she'll totally shut down and wreck her average, which will bring mom into the picture. I don't know mom but judging by daughter she's probably one tough bitch à la Grendel's mother, Madame Defarge, or Lady Macbeth – all PMS queens. I just don't need the hassle.

I wave the strategy sheet.

- How many of these have you tried? Did you read a summary of Act 1 before starting? Read out loud, reread sections, look up key words in a dictionary, rent the movie, check out a line-by-line translation? Translations are all over the internet.

- No.

- Shakespeare is manageable, but you have to try. Takes a little effort on your part.

- It's not fair.

- What? Expecting effort, or reading this play?

- The play.

- Every high school in the country reads *Macbeth.*

- Who cares about them?

- Look, come back after school if you need extra help. Come in before first period in the morning, but do something.

I'm not without sympathy, it is a tough read. But four hundred years of readers have gotten through it, many have enjoyed it, and I tell the class now it's your turn. I also tell them that if Shakespeare had a computer and could word process instead of scratching with a quill and dipping in ink every few words maybe he'd have edited more and made the language easier. On the other hand, I say, if you can dunk a basketball why not dunk it? Shakespeare had the vocabulary and such a mastery of our language that why should he be expected to do a simple layup off the glass like any 5-foot nothing? He was capable of a 360 spin, flip, bounce the ball off the rafters, slam-a-jam, and that's exactly what he did. Think of *Macbeth* as a #1 ESPN Sports Center highlight.

All this is amusing to me, not to them. The students still feel *Macbeth* is a rotten joke.

***Shit Or Get Off The Pot** – Sometimes, might is right. You have the power and the obligation to assign challenging course material. Assign it. You also have the power and obligation to make it fun, relevant, and lively. Do your best.*

***Double Double Toil And Trouble** – The night is long that never finds the day, is a line from Macbeth. But night always does find the day, and everything ends including Shakespearean plays. What's 5 acts anyway? You have cold sores and hickeys that last longer.*

Mainstream Flashback: There's a student in class who's mentally challenged. One of the nicest, sweetest, hardest working students I've ever had. Her notes on *Macbeth* are longer than the play itself. She comes back after school nearly everyday to go over the reading. We're going over some particularly tough lines and I say, Of course you don't have to understand every word, every phrase, every line, to understand what's going on. She looks at me very intently and says, It's very important to me, Mr. Bentley, to understand this play. I understand what she's saying and we go back to translating and analyzing. It's this kind of effort I think of when I get fair/ good students who just quit when they hit Shakespeare. If they only knew.

I tell the class to get ready for a surprise tomorrow, which of course is oxymoronic since how can you get ready for a surprise?

- I know what the surprise is. The lip-glossed brunette is waving her hand like she's welcoming the fleet in.

- How?

- My sister told me.

- What are you talking about?

- She told me what you do near the end of *Macbeth*.

- That's not the surprise.

- Want to bet?

- Sure. How about 3 chocolate chip cookies from the caf?

- OK.

- What's the surprise?

- We're not doing the rest of the play.

- You think I'm dropping the last 3 acts to start the next book?

- Yep.

- Your sister doesn't remember correctly. I make the test on Act 5 optional and extra credit. That's the usual *Macbeth* surprise. I can show you my past grade books if you don't believe me. It just so happens it isn't the surprise this year, but in any case, you lose.

- We didn't shake.

- You don't have to shake. A person's word is her word. And you are a person, aren't you? . . . The class ohhhs and ahhs.

- You do to have to shake.

- Where's that rule written?

- Everyone just knows it.

The girl's quick – you go girrrrl! – and making it up as she goes along, but so am I. This is one of those rare back-and-forths I haven't had before, i.e. there's no ingrained script.

- When you bet with the bookie you don't shake, and try not paying off, I say.

- Maybe, but you upfront the money.

The girl's quick and won't back down. I'm legitimately impressed. If only she put this much effort into her studies she'd be acing World Lit instead of barely getting by.

- No, I say, you don't upfront the money. Listen, I don't want the cookies. It was just a point I was making, that you can't always second guess me and expect to be right. Not always.

She starts to protest more, and I signal for her to zip it. A little repartee is good for whetting the wit, but this one's gone far enough, and *Macbeth* is waiting. Let 'em run, reel 'em, it's good sport if you can do it. Rookies probably shouldn't try. In the back of my mind I wonder if she'll give me the cookies anyway. It’s been sort-of fucking earned.

Sidebar: A short time ago a teacher in Massachusetts was fired for allegedly duct-taping a 12-year-old girl's mouth shut. This is not an approved version of the let 'em run, reel 'em in technique.

Transporter Beam Off *– Sometimes wasting time isn't wasting time. Sometimes it's just warmup.*

Out, Out, Brief Candle *– You have to read Shakespeare to be fully educated, and not 2 acts out of 5. Don't want to do that? Then you're an obstinate mule, a tongueless block, a dumb show. Sorry, but those are Shakespeare's words not mine.*

Quicky *Macbeth* Anecdotes: Talking about Macduff not being born of woman, one of my students writes, His mother gave birth to him in a sea section. Another writes, Macduff was taken from his mother's stomach. A third pens the thought, Macduff was in udder discomfort. . . I get observed years ago during *Macbeth*. I'm pacing and lecturing, working the room, working the crowd, reading, analyzing, zinging, questioning, and we're all into it, students psyched. Big Cheese says after that it's the best class she's ever seen. She doesn't credit the author, but great material does help. For fucketh sure. . . I'm showing the opening scenes of the Japanese movie version of *Macbeth* called *Throne Of Blood*, which is b&w and subtitled. It's as alien to them as *Macbeth* itself until I start talking, explaining, pointing out, and paralleling. I'm a voiceover as the movie runs, and they soon stop mimicking the guttural dialect and laughing at the over-animated acting. They become attentive and ask if we can go beyond the opening scenes and finish it. . . Students have memorized lines and scenes, some are in costume, most have props. They're performing final *Macbeth* projects on stage in the auditorium. I'm filming and will evaluate later at home during the playback. A group of girls is performing the witches' cauldron scene, and it appears to go well, though one says to me later she's unhappy with her performance. I never acted before, she says, and I know I was pretty bad. But it's made me appreciate just how tough it is, and I have a new respect for anyone who does it well, even the ones who just try. I tell her, You weren't bad at all; you're being too hard on yourself. She says, I was bad, and she gives me a look that ends the conversation and consoling, and I realize that my own acting is pretty damn bad too.

For the first time in nearly 40 years a course in African American Literature starts. I wasn't here when the last one ran, no one remembers it, and the only reminder that it ever existed are stacks of yellowed, dried out paperbacks in the book room: *Nigger* by Dick Gregory, *Go Tell It on the Mountain* by James Baldwin, *To Be Young, Gifted, and Black* by Lorraine Hansberry, et al. I started reading them a dozen years ago and wound up devouring them all and buying more on my own. Four or five years ago it dawned on me that there was no African American course at our school.

It was a fight to get this course approved long before the enrollment issue. Took two detailed proposals, an uphill battle when money became tight even when I showed them I could make do nicely with the yellowed paperbacks we already had, and eight curriculum documents spanning many hours and pages of research and regurgitated redundancy. At the end of it all, a top banana says to me, Bet you're happy, looks like your course will be approved after all. Says it like I'm supposed to be appreciative of the bananas approving a course they should have had all along. A course they should've been kissing my ass to put together instead of laying down a gauntlet of banana-made obstacles. I reply to banana, You can go with the course or not, it's out of my hands. If you do, great: if you don't, that's fine too. Banana asks, What's gotten into you? You're so calm. I tell banana, My doctor has me on Prozac, and it gets a laugh. I opt for weak humor and keeping banana in the dark.

The day the course starts another banana pops in and says, Bet you're excited you're finally going to be teaching this course. Banana implies a question, so I reply simply, No, not really, and I shake my head for added effect. You're not? banana says incredulously. After all you went through? No, not really, and I continue deadpanning and shaking my head.

Of course I'm happy and excited, but banana was part of the problem, not part of the solution. I'm openly smiling and upbeat when the new class comes in.

American Gothic – *You are under no obligation to share true emotions with bananas. Not even to send them email emoticons. But whether you do or don't, enjoy your own day. You deserve that much and more.*

Go Figure – *Who knows why your teacher is happy, but bask in the glow. Now might be a good time to borrow lunch money, take an extended lav break, or openly text.*

First Day: African Americans In Literature and Film. It doesn't matter how long you've been teaching or how well prepared you are. In the initial stages of a new course you're excited and nervous, or at least a bit apprehensive. How much can they absorb? Are there better materials to be using? Do I really know this material well enough to be teaching it? It's like being a new teacher all over again with the adrenaline rush but without the hassle of worrying about failure = poor evaluation = dismissal/non-renewal.

I have a ton of books and film to choose from. Half were here, half I got approved and ordered. It's overkill, enough material to run 3 or 4 different courses, but I like having choice/options. And it's always good to spend available money while it's available. Why not? School systems are black holes – money in, darkness out.

I decide on *Roots* to start the course. I tell them we won't be doing the whole thing, but will do most of it. The book's as thick as a dictionary and as the students thumb through while filling out book receipts, one student comes up and drops it back on my desk. Can I have a pass to guidance? he asks standing there with his backpack slung over one shoulder. I want to drop the course. No problem whatsoever, I tell him while adding, do you understand we won't be reading all of it? He shrugs as if to say, Any part of this thing is still too much chicken shit. I hand him a pass, wish him luck, and speaking louder say, Anyone else want to drop the course? Now's the time. No one does, and the course is off-and-fucking-running.

Winter Brevity: One of my wife's kindergartners is looking upset. She asks if anything's wrong. He doesn't answer at first, then says, I'm mad at my mother. He explains that mom put heavy pants on him that morning with buttons on the front instead of a zipper. He's upset that he can only get 2 unbuttoned, and says that it's not easy to get his penis out the small space.

A middle school staffer comes into our faculty room every morning to do the Word Jumble in our newspaper. One cold January morning I glance at the Word Jumble before handing him the paper and tell him the first word. Oh no, he says, don't do that! He's crestfallen like I just revealed there's no Bigfoot. A few days later the scene replays, and this time it's like I've pinpointed the final resting place of Amelia Earhart.

The next morning I get in earlier than usual, open the newspaper in my room, and stare at the first jumble. It dawns on me that words generally end in standard patterns: ed, ing, th, etc. I try getting the ending first and reverse engineering the word. It works and in five minutes I have all four and the riddle. I ink in the blanks.

In the faculty room I leave the paper neatly folded as if no one's read it yet, then leave. I'm not in my room five minutes when another veteran teacher comes in. You're so funny, he says. Tells me the man was just in his room complaining, That damn Bentley! He doesn't care at all about the Word Jumble; he's just doing this so I can't! The veteran tells me he pretended sympathy while cracking up inside.

The next day I do it again though it's not really fun. I'd never do it except for the reaction, he’s right about that. I keep doing it, and over time he complains to different teachers and in the course of a week I have multiple teachers laughing.

Finally, he stops coming into our building. Time goes by. On a hunch I ask the librarian if he's coming in early to look at their newspaper. He is, the media specialist says. I get there ahead of him the next morning and again fill it out in ink. The next day his ass is in an uproar. He’s really jumbled, because the Word Jumble isn’t.

Then I cease and desist. It's gone far enough, joke's over. I don't want to be responsible if he does anything radical over a broken a.m. paradigm.

Epilogue: Weeks go by. When the staffer finally comes back into our faculty room, I explain that the faculty newspapers are purchased from our Sunshine Fund and that all teachers contribute $10. I tell him that even though he's not a teacher, not even a sub in our school, that if he kicks in I won't write in the paper because then it'd be as much his as mine. Offer to pro-rate it since half the year is over. Five bucks, c'mon, it's cheap. He nods but is grim. If this were Greek theatre he'd be wearing a tragic mask and the chorus would be chanting a solemn dirge. Sunshine fund never sees the five dollars or five cents, but I stop filling out the Word Jumble anyway. It never was any fun to do, though the joke did delight a peripheral faculty audience.

Channeling Jack Lemmon – *It's a long winter, break it up. The Grumpy Old Men tried ice fishing, practical jokes, chasing women, drinking beer, even chess. Lots of fun things. But no Word Jumble.*

Baby It's Cold Outside – *It's a long winter, don't let school get to you. If you start to develop cabin fever, do something, but don't let a lack of sun and warmth beat you. Try tanning salons, saunas, hot tubs, long weekends in Cancun, or if money's an issue, hot steaming baths/showers at home. Lots of fun multiple realities. But Word Jumble? Sthi.*

Once Upon A Shower: A retired teacher lets himself into school on Sunday mornings in the dead of winter, turns on all the showers in the boys' locker room, then works out in the gym. After 90+ minutes he returns to an improvised steam room, undresses, and sits on a chair in the middle of the still running showers. His pale body in the thick fog appears and disappears like a ghostly image on a weak picture tube, while hundreds of gallons of scalding water pour down the drain. Not exactly energy efficient, but warm and relaxing and a pleasant way to get through the winter. . . The school disagrees and changes the outside locks.

Cold as a brass toilet seat: My room is cold and wicked drafty. I've complained and complained, the students have complained and complained, and the only thing that changes is that I don't need to refrigerate my lunch.

Many sit here wearing coats or heavyweight sweatshirts. There's sneezing, coughing, and sniffling, and I keep a box of Kleenex on the front of my desk. When that's gone, I put out a roll of toilet paper and encourage the students to take all they need. They sometimes get embarrassed but I point out it beats using a shirt sleeve or hand. The t.p. never runs out.

I tell students to stop sucking water, to gain weight, to imitate the polar bear and build up a thick layer of subcutaneous fat for insulation. I'm only half fucking kidding.

Girls are draped in fur necked sweaters, one comes wrapped in a blanket. I wear woolen turtlenecks and sometimes bring in a small ceramic space heater. I used to have a very small Allen wrench that fit the thermostat cover and I'd adjust the temp myself. Now it's controlled from a central panel in some unknown cold dark corner, and there's little I can do aside from keeping the blinds closed and moving the students away from the windows and air handler.

In the worst cold spells I wear a flannel lined pair of pants with an inner layer and outer shell, and a pair of navy surplus gloves, thin enough to allow me to write. I keep the gloves in my briefcase and in the closet I've got a pair of warmup pants big enough to fit over my regular pants. I prefer looking like a dorky dingbat to being cold.

The teacher in the room next to me last year had a student do a wind chill test in her room and it registered in the mid-50's. She moved to a different room this year, one with more sun and a different air handler. Me, I'm not moving. Conceptual art piece for a snowman. Bottom Line: If I get sick, I'm out, and I'm out until I'm not sick, which might be awhile. Whatareyagointado? Teachers, and students, have an obligation not to drag unwanted germs and viruses into the building. There are enough runny shit contagious life forms here now.

January ends with a rain, sleet, and wintery mix forecast for February 1. I'm not a big fan of snow days because we have to make them up in June which shortens the summer and with no a/c, but this one I'm ready for. And I'm thinking if we get one it might be a sign I should retire, i.e. retirement would make a shortened summer moot, i.e. life would become an endless summer.

The school goes to sleep with dreams of staying at home tomorrow, warm and buried under the covers.

FEBRUARY – Red, Red Whine

The wintery mix hits, school gets cancelled, and we all roll over, turn off the lights, and don't reset the alarm. All around the state cars are sliding off the roads, emergency crews are out, distant sirens wail, motorists are being advised not to travel unless it's necessary. I vow not to travel farther than the bathroom and kitchen.

The break's only a day, clearing weather's forecast, but a day, is a day, is a damn blessing. Many would've taken a virus in the laptop for time off. Though it's only been a month since holiday break, winter's taking its usual toll. Go to work in the dark, freeze in school, go home in the dark for those many who stay late.

The new teachers I talk to are really dragging. They're exhausted and spiritually blue. They need mental recuperation and catch-up-with-paperwork time. Since September they've asked me many times: how have you managed to grade papers for so many years? Are there tricks, easier ways, does it ever get easier?

These are FAQ's with this generation. I hate to break the ass-busting paperwork news to them, i.e. the reality of teacher-by-day, corrector-by-night/weekends, but they might as well learn now how it's going to be and accept it if they're going to stand a chance of sticking and licking it.

- Look, I say in scattered conversations, the paperwork never goes away. It's like unwanted hair. Shave it, wax it, pluck it – it's coming back. There's no laser treatment that'll keep your briefcase light, and your nights and weekends free, though there are ways.

- What ways? they all want to know.

- Once you get tenure you can assign a bit fewer compositions, quizzes, tests, etc. Even now you can take students to the computer room for composition and work with them on the rough drafts. A lot. That way when you get the finished comp it's really finished and you can breeze through it in less time. . . You can assign oral presentations and evaluate with checklists and brief comments while they're speaking. . . You can assign non-written projects. Let them self evaluate and evaluate each other, it's not much to read. . . You can have them present compositions orally and require that they hand you a duplicate copy beforehand. As they read, you correct. If they talk too fast, you tell them to slow down or interrupt with questions. They finish reading, you finish grading about the same time.

The nontenured teachers like what they hear, but they want more. Want to hear there's a day coming when they can slip into auto-teacher and let the computer grade all the paperwork, especially the compositions. Logic: It's already doing the grammar and spell checks.

That kind of hope I can't give; there is no robo-corrector, no teacher-bot on the horizon, but I try to break the reality as gently as possible.

- You'll always have composition and paperwork. We deal with the written word, and there's no way around that ultimately. But it's also what makes us special. We read what they write, and what they write is them.

Still, life could be better and I don't ignore that in these mentor/paternalistic conversations.

- The school could give us fewer students, fewer department meetings, fewer observations, and lay readers. Maybe if you love education you should consider getting out of the classroom altogether and getting certified in library science or guidance. These are routes other English teachers have taken before you. Have you considered another school system? It's a cliché to say the grass's greener, but maybe it is. Greenbacks. How'd you'd like to make more money with less hassle. Plenty of better paying systems in the state would kiss ass to hire an experienced teacher near the bottom of the pay scale. And that's what you all are. Experienced and cheap, ain't the truth a bitch.

God Willing And The Creek Don't Rise – *It's OK to whine, it's cathartic. But if you want to do more than just get it out, if you actually want action, Number 1: Don't get your hopes up. Number 2: Talk to administration. Number 3: Talk to the union. Number 4: Talk to a lawyer. Number 5: Same as Number 1.*

Action Figures Aren't All Plastic – *If you hear your teacher carping and bitching it just means teacher's letting it all out. Better this than teacher cracking up and pulling out a fully automatic short barreled 12-gauge with a hair-trigger.*

Literary Parallel: In *Crime and Punishment* Raskolnikov has a nightmare that the townspeople load up a wagon then beat the horse to death because he can't pull it. It's a good story and moral for all teachers.

I get a rejection from the *New Yorker* for my Teacher II poem. I immediately email off the next in my series.

Teacher III

They bend over the test scribbling furiously,
pens bobbing like buoy towers in a rough sea.
But some look around the room and yawn and roll pens.
Others read and reread the essay questions as if it's 1900,

and they're archaeologists breaking into the pyramids,
discovering hieroglyphics.

I don't have big hopes for Teacher III, but it is mildly amusing, and any diversion this time of year that lightens the day and shortens the long winter night is better than just sitting around with a stack of comps and a lonesome woodie.

I'm walking down the hall before first period: slapping fives, poking my head into rooms, and squeezing through bottlenecks of humpbacked students with low riding backpacks. I walk-and-talk, stroke and joke, stop by my door to pick up some litter and check to see if it's a note before chucking it.

Text messaging and email have cut down on the number of notes I find, no doubt about it. But I still get some. The latest one goes: 2 day was a typical day. LOL OMG. My hair straightener broke in the morning and I was like OMG ugh! My BF called me in the morning and he was like totally flippin out. Wow! I'm not sure if he loves me 4 my bod. IDK I'm just so stressed. Ya know it's the time of the month for me, and I'm so sad b/c my idol Paris is in jail. OMGGG I just hate life. I just broke a nail. WTF This girl just put naughty comments on my myspace and she wants to have a catfight. OMG This chick is such a bee-o-tch. Wow. Ugh. She thinks I'm fat like WTF. I hate her totally. I G2G. I mean bye.

A good note. Energetic, with lots of the latest teen-ology. Most notes are along the lines: i love him, i hate her, this class sucks, bentley sucks, this school sucks, what are you doing tonight? One of my favorites to this day is one I found my first year.

Note #1 1970's: I like you a little bit you got a nice ass and body to. W/B/S

Analysis – It's direct and sincere, if only sincerely horny.

The following are unedited and uncensored. They represent a small portion of the notes I've found and show a side of school life many adults are only vaguely aware of.

Note #2 1970's: Q: What base have you gone to with a boy? A: that's disgusting!!! Q: Will you tell me if I tell you? A: no way Q: Did you go to 2nd? I did. I think thats as far as I'll ever go. 1st = kissing or making out. 2nd = feeling 3rd = B.J. Home = Fucking A: I wouldn't mind going to Home but I would skip 3rd. It's disgusting. Q: I know. Would you go to Home before you got married? I wouldn't. A: Neither would I unless I was going to just get married and I'm 17 or 18 yrs old. Let's change the subject.

Sexxx and self, life and love are the favorite topics, and students will write often and passionately about these. Teen viewpoint: Anything else is boring. Might as well write a school composition.

Note 1980's: your the most beautiful girl in the whole school. I like the way you look, you have a nice personality, and I love your long hair. I'm not saying you have to go out with me just get a chance to know me and maybe we could be friends. I'm nice, very funny, smart, and very mature for my age. Don't judge me by my appearance. I'm all right looking but just a little different. I'm not going to tell you who I am right away. XXX P.S. Don't go by what your friends say.

Analysis – This 1980's young man is obviously in love and it's probably going unrequited. There's a kind of innocent naiveté to this bumbling teen, a throwback to a hand-holding era at the Main Street Soda Shoppe. Oversexed, under fucked. For the teacher who finds these notes there's no third party consulting, no eHarmony matchmaking. Read 'em, laugh, weep, whatever. Or just remember how it used to be, and still is occasionally, i.e. a bit of sweetness to young love.

Note 1990's: your the biggest Dickhead That ever lived on the face of this Earth you thought you could get away with it but I am not that Fucking Dumb you Cocksucker The Only reason I went out with you was because it was a Dare. You can go fuck yourself for all I care Because at least I fucked someone. Even a hog wouldn't kiss you. Bye. P.S. Take a shower.

Analysis – Some might judge this 1990's writer to be a student slut: a foul mouthed, girl-woman, soon-to-have-one-in-the-oven types who will never amount to anything. Seinfeld: Not that there's anything wrong with that. Me: I teach English, and leave the rest to guidance. And the school nurse. And sex-ed. But I still read the notes.

Note 21st century: Q: do u swallow everytime? A: yeah, but i don't like it Q: yeah doesn't it make you gag A: yup and I almost throw up Q: I heard you were having oral sex in the back seat when u were driving around A: no we just were making out, not the right atmosphere, ya know? Q: yup giving head in the back seat isn't the most comfy position. . . its to cramped A: i know but we still had a bunch of fun Q: has he done anything to u like eat u out? A: no but man do we have good sex. I won't let him eat me out Q: why no? A: because i've only had it done 2 times and once the guy bit me Q: oh yeah u told me about that. im sure he wont bite you. isnt sex great A: yeah u gotta hook me up w/some condoms I'll pay ya. just tell me when Q: OK. you should come over today, can u? A: not today. Why, what r u doing? A: getting bored

I've wondered for years if parents really know what their hormonal creations are up to and the language and acts they're practicing. I wonder if there are any studies that show females write more notes than boys, write more sexually explicit notes, write more openly than Anais Nin or the old *Playgirl* Advisor? It's been my experience that where notes are concerned, it's Girls Gone Wild – no cobwebs on those vaginas. Far-out Thought: Could these sexual ramblings be flights of fantasy, fictional worlds created by young writers looking to experience in print what they haven't known in life? Notes = Cheap vicarious thrills?. . . Actually no. To believe *that* would be a flight of fantasy.

Most notes I find on the floor, occasionally I intercept one being passed. Sometimes I take it, sometimes I don't, depends on my mood and the student. Only once did a student refuse to hand over a note and I sent her to the office, though I doubt the office ever saw the note either. Might make an interesting assignment in Creative Writing, i.e. write a lengthy note that you'd rather take a detention for than turn in. Of course, then they'd have to turn it in for grading, so it'd be a self-defeating exercise.

Twice in 32 years I find notes talking about suicide. These I turn immediately over to the main office. I also turn over a note I find lambasting an assistant principal in totally gross sexual terms (think of the classic Aristocrats joke). . . Years ago I turn in both a girl and her notebook, though a notebook really isn't a note. I'm walking the aisles checking work and someone innocently says, Mr Bentley, why don't you check Penelope's notebook? I think nothing of it and say to Penelope, Do you want me to check your notebook? I don't care, she says. You're sure? I ask. Go ahead, she says. I check it, and very quickly come across a series of very unflattering, very obscene sketches of me as the naked porno star. Ultimate Outcome:

She's unapologetic and a big cheese tells me I was wrong to check the notebook. Tells me I had no business checking one notebook if I wasn't checking them all. Tells me notebooks are private. Tells me it's pretty much a case of I got what I deserved, or at least asked for.

Sleaze On The Bun – *It's not being nosy to read notes. Feel free to read minds too.*

Diddly Ditty – *Don't leave notes lying around. Flush them, burn 'em, swallow 'em, or write in code or some obscure foreign language (English for some of you students).*

I don't make an appointment to see a kahuna. It's easier to just drop by and chance an opening. Some might call what I'm doing whistle blowing, being a rat fink, getting above himself, etc. I prefer to think of it as being proactive, championing doing the right thing, or at least pointing out what the right thing is. Can't always depend on the union.

Kahuna gets up to greet me. I explain I'm here mainly to bitch but also to offer insight and suggestions. We take seats and get right to it. I'm supportive for the nontenured teachers. Explain the concerns they have, that the department teachers have, that many have. Predict that unless changes are made the English Department will lose as many as 4, maybe 5, of the 8 teachers. I show this kahuna an easy way to save $40,000 with no loss of personnel. I take a student's side in a dispute, and I criticize behavior and policies of other kahunas.

Our 45-minute chat's friendly, respectful, but 90% one-sided. There's laughter, some grimness, but usually we're in sync, no need for the Teacher/ Kahuna Handbook. Still, I leave feeling as if I've been in a Pilates class, i.e.

worked like hell but gone nowhere. Master kahunas, like veteran politicians, know the fine art of head bobbin' and shuckin' and jivin'. Ain't no way, no how, they commit easily to a position or action. But I knew that going in and my expectations were thisclose to zero.

On A Clear Day You Can Kiss Off – *Kahunas giveth shit, and kahunas taketh away shit. And the giveths are always a lot more than the taketh aways.*

Grab Hold – *As Tom Hanks points out in Saving Private Ryan, bitchin' always goes up the chain of command. You just need some fire and guts, some big open air huevos/cojones.*

Philosophical Difference: Many kahunas want to harness teachers like mules. I've always believed we should be given more open range like thoroughbreds, along with shared responsibilities and shared decision making, neither of which happens much in many systems. Personal Introspection: I am a nonconformist by nature, a rebel with a built-in suspicion of authority. Like Chicken Little I figure not much good's coming from above. It's ironic that I chose to go into a field that has so many authority figures, but there's not much I'm going to do about it now except stay pigheaded and try to keep my fine madness low key – a tweak here, a tweak there, but no kicks to the administrative ass or groin. And I try not to let any of it distract from my teaching, the lessons must go on. Perpetual academic motion.

Modern Kahuna Sidebar: I'm passing a kahuna in the main office, and kahuna asks. When are you retiring? I retired years ago, I reply. I just keep coming in. Kahuna laughs and points his finger at me as if to say, Oh you. A few days later I run into same kahuna in same exact spot and kahuna smilingly asks me again, When are you retiring? Not soon, I say, I'm in the zone of invulnerability. What do you mean zone of invulnerability? Kahuna's smile is gone. It takes 3 years of bad evaluations to get rid of me, I say, and I'm within 3 years of retirement, so there's nothing you can do to me. I'm invulnerable. This time kahuna doesn't laugh, doesn't point, and never asks again. Of course, I'd never play the invulnerability card, never take a three year hiatus. I gave them the best years of my life, and I'll give them what's left. I honestly don't know where that stands on the worst-worse-bad-good-better-best scale, but it's not at either extreme. I don't think.

Mr. B, do you round grades? the army-booted student asks even though we've barely begun 3rd marking period.

- The computer does. I can undo that feature, but I won't.

- Suppose someone has a 59? Would you give them the 60 to pass?

- Well, first off, it might have been a 58.5 that the computer rounded to 59.

- It could have been a 59.4 that was rounded down.

- True.

- So would you pass a 59?

- Probably not.

- I know someone that you failed with a 59.

- To begin with I never fail a student; students fail themselves. Secondly, the highest average is always above 100 because I give extra credit, so a 59 isn't even out of 100, but more like 101, 102, 103. I also look to see why it's a 59. Did the student fail at first, then improve? Or did they start off fine and go downhill? Maybe it was a 59 because they failed to turn in a major project or blew off an exam. No show, no go. . . Anyone remember what Robert De Niro said in *The Deer Hunter*? He held up a bullet and said, This isn't something else, this is this. It is what it is. A 59 is a 59, it isn't a 60. Understand?. . . Heads nod, though faces aren't happy.

In reality, I've both passed and failed students with 59's. Just depends. One year a big wheel comes into my room just after we hand mark report cards. What was Roscoe's final average? he wants to know. Roscoe is arguably the #1 trouble maker in the school, a kid who in the old days would've been taken out to the woodshed for a good old fashioned ass whooping. He got a 59.44%, I say. You're not going to round it? wheel asks incredibly like he's the prison warden holding the gate wide open while I'm staking Roscoe down. I did round it, I say. A 59.44 rounds to a 59. Suppose it was 59.45? he asks suspiciously. . . I see where he's going and I say, It wasn't. But look, I wouldn't round a 59.999 for Roscoe. I told him he needed to do all the work the last month and he didn't. He doesn't deserve a break and I'm not giving him one. Do you want want him back here next year? big wheel asks in a conciliatory tone. No, not really, I say, but I'm not passing him on either. Look, I say, you have the power to override any grade I put on a report card. I'm doing what I have to do, you do what you have to do. . . Note: This is back in an era when a failed student might be assigned the same teacher again the next year. It'd never happen now, but it did then and more than once to me. Record would have been 3 times: same student, same class, but the third year the student mercifully moved. And now it's potentially Roscoe, le infant terrible. If there was a song Horse's Ass you'd think of this kid every time it played. But the repeat's not to be. My F gets overridden, Roscoe gets passed on.

Don't Sweat The Small Shit – *You probably already know this, but you do not have the final say in the school, not even in your own classroom. Positive Spin: You do not have to take the blame for ultra-final decisions. There's always someone else to blame. Like bitches, blame goes up the chain.*

Is It Good For You – *You students can suck your thumbs and hope to catch a break now-and-then. Or, you can stick your thumbs up your asses and get working. Probably less painful to just do the work.*

I'm assigning a new student to your Film class, the guidance counselor tells me.

- You're kidding, I say. We're three-and-a-half weeks into the course.

- It can't be helped.

- Oh sure it can. We're way past the deadline for adds and drops.

- The boy just realized he needs another English course to graduate. Thought a theatre course he took met the English requirement.

- Why would he think that?

- He claims I told him.

- Did you?

- I don't remember. I don't think so.

- And you're his counselor?

- Yes.

- Then, why didn't *you* realize he needed an English course when he registered?

- I missed it. Sorry.

- I don't understand. You're sorry, and he and I have to do all the back work. Three-and-a-half weeks is a lot to catch up. And all while keeping up.

- I know.

- How about if he just keeps up from this point on. I'll exempt him on the earlier assignments.

- No, he has to do them all.

- Why?

- He's in this fix because he messed up. He has to do all the course work.

- Really? Listen, you haven't heard the end of this.

I email a top fry, relate the conversation, and suggest the boy be given an independent study with the counselor as mentor. Then I meet with a couple of top fry and get tag-teamed. They tell me I'm not being co-operative. I tell them flexibility is my middle name and tell them the school's not being flexible. They tell me everyone makes mistakes, and don't I? I tell them sure I make mistakes, but my mistakes never cause additional work for anyone but me. What about just grandfathering the boy on the theatre course he took? I ask. Why should he be punished for the counselor's mistake? Or, what about an independent study? I name a top fry who's certified in English. This counselor's caused me additional work before, I tell the fries, and it's happening again. The fries tell me they'll look into what the counselor told the boy.

Later in the day the boy shows up for Film class, and he stays for the rest of the semester. Some of the missed work gets made up, most doesn't, and no one seems very concerned about any of it except me.

Bite Me – *Guidance counselors do not exist to make your life easier; sometimes they don't even exist to counsel. They move in mysterious fucking ways and you cannot hope to understand all they do. Hopefully someone does.*

Student Daze *– Guidance is a great place to hang out, read college catalogues, talk about the future, ignore the present, delete the past. But when it comes down to signing forms, counsel yourself. You're responsible in the end anyway.*

Grade 0 Anecdotes: My wife takes her kindergartners to a local theatre in the dead of February to see the live 45 minute play *School House Rocks*. Halfway through she asks one of her boys how he's enjoying it. It's OK, he says, but when's the movie start?

A 5-year-old comes over to my wife and complains that another little boy is making noise in their reading group. Wife calls the boy over and asks, Are you bothering the others? He says, I'm just singing Twinkle, Twinkle Little Star.

Valentine's Day arrives accompanied by 3 cards from fellow teachers, a paste on tattoo, and a chocolate chip cookie from a student who has a bucket of them and is generously doling them out. One of my students is sitting in class smiling quietly and holding a huge bouquet of flowers. Some wear red, but there are no candy or flower grams like in past years and the day overall is a red, red whine.

The week following Valentine's Day we have a 2 day February break. It's not much, but hopefully it'll be enough that no one, especially our rookies, returns with PTSD. The Japanese call working yourself to death *karoshi*, i.e. a heart attack or stroke brought on by stress. I call the same affliction, BOAJ, i.e. Brains Of A Jackass. There's no honor in it, or bonus. We're not working to rebuild bombed out WWII Japanese cities. There aren't even hurricanes, floods, or earthquakes affecting this area. Time to come down off the cross and relax.

I tell a senior boy, You owe me a composition. It's late and if I don't have it soon it's a zero.

I don't always remind students who owe me work, but this is a major grade and this student has been fairly conscientious all year

- I turned it in.

- Sorry, but you didn't.

- I did. Look for it! He's instant flare-up.

- I don't have it.

- Look for it!

- I don't have to, I already did. You didn't turn it in.

- I was missing a literary connection, remember? This is bullshit!.

He gets up and storms out. It's so sudden and violent I'm taken back for a few seconds. Then I ask the class, What did he say was missing? Literary connection, comes back. I pick up an earlier stack of compositions, find his, and call up one of my dependables. Go find him, I say. Check the lavs, nurse's office, guidance. And give this to him. I hand the messenger the last composition the boy turned in which, in fact, *is* missing a literary connection.

The period eventually ends, class leaves, and boy comes back to get his things.

- You confused the compositions, I say calmly.

- Don't talk to me.

- You still owe me a composition, and other makeup work.

- DON'T TALK TO ME!!

He storms out again, and I make a mental note not to talk to him again about it, but to just fill in zeros when the makeup deadline comes and goes.

In hindsight I probably should not have reminded him of the work he owed in front of the class, but 99.9% of these reminders are a simple, You owe ____, followed by, OK. I should now call the parents, or at least his counselor, but I'm not in the mood. We've had other run-ins, and some students just wear you down.

In The Beginning: It's the 1970's and I'm recording grades of the first research paper I ever assign. I finish and I notice a blank space after one boy's name. *Did I skip over his paper?* I don't remember reading it. I go back through the pile and his paper's not there. I tear my briefcase apart, then the room. I look under the couch, pull out the cushions, mentally and physically backtrack everywhere I've been. I search and search and it's nowhere, I figure he didn't turn it in. The next day I look at him sitting in the back and tell him he owes me a research paper. I turned it in, he says. When? I ask. When the rest of the class did. Not before or after? No, when you collected them. He's straight faced and seems upset. Tells me he won't write another paper, doesn't even know where his rough draft and notes are. I probably threw them away, he says. . . I tear apart my school desk, file cabinet, and classroom; go home; upheave everything again including my car and garage. The paper's nowhere. I don't know what to do.

The next day I'm standing meekly in front of the class, it's a zone of silence, and I tell him, I can't find your paper. I'm about to say, I'm giving you a bye on redoing it, when a lightbulb comes on, and I say to the boy ahead of him, Did Phineas ever pass his research paper forward to you? No, the boy says without hesitation. Quickly I ask everyone in Phineas' row and they all respond, No. I look at Phineas and he knows he's done for. Ratted out by his own rowmates. I'd like to give him a zero for lying and all the trouble he's caused me, but instead I give him a 10 pt/day deduction. He never does turn it in.

Liar, Liar *– Students both forget and lie, they're human. Some lie very convincingly, some forget very frequently. For some this will metastasize into doing hard time; others will straddle a pole and have dollar bills stuffed down their panties. But give them a break when you can. You never know.*

I get an email from a mother saying her daughter is baby sitting after school in addition to working part-time at a restaurant and has been sick and rundown. Wants to know how she's doing, why she's failing, what I can do about it. This has happened before, i.e. working teen increases work hours, grades drop, teen gets stressed and strained, and parent wants to know what teacher can do. You just want to grab the parent/guardian/caregiver by her iceberg lettuce head and say, SHUT THE FUCK UP! What ass-patting world do you live in? Do you think we cut slack just because your daughter can find the room everyday? Maybe you need to cut back the outside work or pump this sleeping pillow so full of caffeine, ginseng, high energy drinks that she's got enough umphh to claw her way up to the bottom. Stir some cognitive action. Stop short of a stake through the heart, perhaps a sixties amphetamine or old fashioned smelling salts. But it's on you.

I calm down, make recommendations, nothing changes. Arnold Schwarzenegger calls this doing the kabuki, i.e. doing a song and dance when you know regardless of what you do the outcome will be the same. Girl continues to work outside school, sleep in class, and fail. I think of a long gone guidance counselor telling me, Don't worry too much over the unmotivated students. You'll only make your own life hell.

Snippet: One of the teachers is having a mouse problem in her closet. Furry little critters seeking warmth from winter's icy winds. Several years ago they infest my closet during a cold snap. They eat through my granola box, gnaw crackers, and leave little tiny turd pellets. I finally bring in a spring trap and post a scoreboard on the inside of the door. Everyday my first period class is on cardio-watch to see if I got a new one. It ends after I clean out the food. Final Score: Bentley – 3, Mice – 0.

I redo the seating chart of my worst behaved class. It's the kind of class you dread before they arrive, and exhale after they leave. As they enter I direct them to their new desks, which spreads them out like inmates in solitary. I tell them if anyone turns around it's an automatic detention: no warnings. It's harsh, but for once they're quiet. Temporarily. A top fry once suggested that I give badly behaved classes lots of silent reading and writing, emphasis on *silent*. Busy work. I occasionally do it and it does work up to a point. But some of these students do not read or write well, and learning goes out about the time frustration kicks in, i.e. about the time it takes me to record and send in attendance.

News Item: It's reported that a Connecticut high school student has been expelled for allegedly lighting her science teacher's hair on fire during class. Purportedly the girl ignited the ponytail of her teacher with a lighter. Hair was singed. Girl was charged with reckless endangerment, 3rd degree assault, and breach of peace. I read this and think, Thank god I'm bald. I also start thinking that maybe, just maybe the class with the changed seats isn't so bad after all. Fucking angels. Mental Gaming: There's a psychological theory called depressive realism that holds people with the most accurate view of the world are more inclined to get clinically depressed. Helps to delude yourself, put on the rose colored glasses, see the world without a lot of reflection. Swell fucking kids.

A senior girl with the energy of a proton collider and the personality of live sunshine says, Mr. Bentley would you write me a college recommendation? You know I'm you're favorite student. I say, You are indeed a FOB, but even Friends Of Bentley need to sweeten the deal. You need to bake me something. Some homemade chocolate chip cookies would be nice. She smiles and says, Recommendation first. I shake my head. She pleads, then is gone.

I don't ask for homemade goodies from all students for writing recommendations and I write 3 freebies by year's end, but I do from most. I wasn't always like this, the change occurred gradually. For years I wrote lengthy detailed letters late at night after finishing class work and got thank you's from around 50% to include the popular monosyllabic, *Tanks*. I was getting more-and-more disenchanted with student manners, when 8 years ago the thank you's sunk to a record low of around 30%. That killed the golden goose, busted my ass. Want a golden recommendation nowadays: #1. You have to be the kind of student I'd write a recommendation for, i.e. you cannot buy a Bentley letter. #2. You have to bake me something upfront. Cookies baked from frozen supermarket dough are fine. The point isn't the cost, it's the effort, any effort that says, Thank you. Can't afford the ingredients, you can clean desk tops in my room, scrub my wet-erase board, carry me out to my car, etc. It may be mercenary, but quid pro quo is not a bad lesson to teach.

Looking For An Echo *– You are a professional and are contractually obligated to teach academics. Manners, one would think, are taught at home, but when they're not, feel free to teach these too. And get some cookies.*

Bow, Curtsy *– Thank you is a really good phrase. It honors both the giver and the receiver. You cannot say it often enough. Practice.*

Recommendation Protocol: A handwritten thank you is best; it's not really a lost art, times are not that different. And use a dictionary. One brief note I got had three misspelled words. Mailing a note elevates it, though there's nothing wrong with posting it in the school mailbox or personally handing it to the teacher. I can still remember students who took the time to do this. It may not mean much in the grand scheme, but it has plenty of meaning in the personal.

As far as actually writing the recommendation letter goes, teachers need to give the college admissions officer insight that he/she can't get from the student's transcript. You cannot lie nor should you engage in hyperbole. If you can't be honest and write an overall positive letter, you shouldn't write one at all. This is not payback time, and it's good student strategy to always ask the potential recommender what he/she'll write. There's nothing wrong with covering your ass. I recommend it.

Mr. B, can I make up that vocabulary quiz I owe later today?

- How about before class tomorrow?
- I'll forget.
- Write it down.
- I won't look at it.
- Write it in your school agenda.
- I won't remember to look at it. Wait, I'll put it in my phone.

- Your phone? How do you do that?

- I'll put it in the calendar and an alarm will go off to remind me.

- You type it in?

- Of course.

- A message?

- Yes.

- How do you type letters? I mean, doesn't a number on the phone represent more than one letter?

The class is looking at me like maybe I've just thawed out from Paleozoic times. And they're smiling at this techno-retard in front of them. I don't mind that it makes them feel superior and hence good about themselves. Gorgeous George the old time wrestler was a certified psychiatrist who felt he was treating more people in the ring by letting them scream at him than he ever could in private practice. He played the villain so others could play the good guy. I'm playing the stooge so my class can play the enlightened.

Except I'm not playing. It's not a dumb-ass act. I really don't understand using a phone for anything other than talking.

Dueling Banjos – *When you tell your students there's no such thing as a stupid question, be ready to demonstrate with real life questions/curiosity. Be a risk taker, leave that comfort zone, jump out of that skin. Sure you'll look like an idiot, but that's how some of them feel everyday in your class.*

Go To The Head Of The Class – *Be prepared to educate your teacher politely, respectfully. The child really is the father of the man. Be a kind and gentle parent/teacher. Be the one you were waiting for.*

I'm sitting in one of our three weekly department meetings remembering back when teachers were independent shop keepers and no one interfered with the way business was run. Department meetings were 10 minutes a month, observations 15 minutes once a year, and evaluations were a few short sentences and a checklist. Teachers were the epicenter of the school and no one messed. I remember in the way-way-back when one of our math teachers locked out the curriculum director when he saw her approaching and there were no repercussions because we were considered top shelf teachers and who did not need our molecules shaken or stirred.

Something in today's meeting is being said about wanting volunteers to serve on a committee to revise something or other. How many volunteers do you need? I casually ask, and I barely hear the answer. I'm remembering when a former top pickle asked me to volunteer for a report card committee. I replied by asking her, If you were the track coach and wanted to win the high jump, would you want 6 jumpers who could all clear 1 foot, or one person who could clear 6 feet? Top Pickle looked puzzled, so I closed the thought with, You'd want one person who could high jump 6 feet. I can high jump six feet. Make me a one-person committee, give me the power to make the decision, and guarantee that my decision will be followed, and I'll volunteer right now to be the committee. We can't do that, T.P. predictably said. Well then, I closed, good luck.

And this is pretty much the way department meetings have gone for me this year. I doodle, daydream, let the hamsters run like hell on the treadmill, and every once in a while inject a sagacious observation from my fail-safe position. In a phrase, these department meetings are nothing more than talking yeast infections.

Wally In Dilbert: Nothing I say in meetings actually means anything. . . I tried listening once. It was awful.

Puff The Magic Dragon: My first department chairman was a ball of fire I'll call Mike. I'm a few minutes late to one of my first ever department meetings and Mike goes up one side of me and down the other. Who the hell do you think you are, he asks, to keep us waiting? He's red-in-the-face with almost visible steam. We've got important things to do, he says. Don't you ever be late again! Ever! Then without missing a beat the thin angular bearded man who looks a lot like Pete Seeger segues right into the month's business. . . I'm never late again. He's right, I take no offense.

Mike was an authority figure but because he also teaches a full load, he's one of us too and a great, great teacher. He uses folk and rock lyrics as part of his poetry units, signs out film from a distant library in the days of celluloid and projectors, attends summer writing workshops at Bread Loaf, and organizes various field trips. Out of school he bartends at Mory's, the Yale eating club, and later starts a bank cleaning business that he runs after school to midnight. He's an accomplished woodworker and uses the school's wood shop at odd hours.

I have the honors 7th graders and he has the honors 8th graders. We assign a lot of grammar, spelling, vocabulary, composition, and reading. At one point the boarding school alma mater of Jackie Onassis, Miss Porter's, sends a rep to interview and observe us. We're told that year-in-and-year-out we give them the best prepared students they get, and they want to see how we're doing it. Then one year the junior high becomes a middle school, teaming is added, and classroom teachers are no longer fine craftsmen, but team players, consensus builders. We're told to stop teaching the fundamentals and to grade holistically. Honors groups are eliminated, classes are heterogeneously grouped. The absolutely worst students in the school get grouped with the absolutely best. Knowledge of English goes downhill, grades go up. In the midst of all this stands Mike: a superlative teacher, coordinator, and man. He tells me he's been made to feel he doesn't know how to teach anymore and he retires without a word to anyone. He goes to work for a construction firm and eventually becomes a foreman. At one point he tells me, I like what I'm doing, but I'm not kidding myself that it's as important as teaching. Several years pass, and 65-year-old Mike falls off a second story ladder and dies. It's the end of an era and man.

John Henry Was A Steel Driving Man – *No teacher, administrator, or person can consciously instill love and respect. All's you can do is to lead by example, and be the kind of boss you yourself would like to have.*

The Dolly Clone – *We all need role models, there are good ones all around you. Pick one and emulate the traits you don't have and be validated in the ones that you do. You have worth now, but you can be better. Like Frank Sinatra sang, You could be swinging on a star.*

I'm reading Howie's analysis of a chapter in *Cry, the Beloved Country* and finding some facts that aren't in his section and some phrases that seem beyond his abilities. I Google key words and wind up at sparknotes.com. It doesn't take long and I find the same out-of-order facts and the same word perfect phrases in the on-line analysis. It's not a lot, but it's more than enough to give Howie a zero for plagiarizing. I decide to hit him with a ten point deduction, and a stern warning that next time. . .

Cheating is a big deal, and I catch bunches every year. One of the first ever involves homework answers. I take the girls into the hall and say, You two have several phrases that are exactly the same that are not in the book, and also several identical misspellings. They both protest and swear they did not copy or work together, but I give them both zeroes anyway. It's my version of tough-love. One mother immediately calls and protests, but she might as well be tossing both ends of a rope to her drowning daughter. I don't budge. Later the other girl approaches me privately and admits, Yes, we cheated, but Agatha is angry because others in the class did too and you only caught us. I tell the girl, I appreciate your honesty and wish I caught the others too, but their day will come. Would you care to give me names? She declines. Five years later I run into Agatha in the high school hall and stop her. You know Agatha, I say, I still see your mother every now-and-then, and she's still giving me dirty looks. Why don't you do us both a favor and confess to her that you and Ginger did, in fact, cheat. It's never too late. Agatha gives me an are-you-fucking-crazy look, and I know she's too far down the Mariana Trench to resurface now.

Accusing a student of cheating is nothing I do lightly. Of course you have to teach what constitutes plagiarism, e.g. even many high schoolers don't understand that using someone else's original ideas, even reworded, is cheating though I've never yet called a student on this subtlety unless they borrow the words too.

Most cheaters are not subtle. They sit in the hall before first period copying someone else's homework. They sit in classrooms, the library, or the caf and copy. They print out multiple copies of their answers/notes and distribute them. There have been some funny ones. I'm giving a quiz once and a boy is wading through a pile of papers. Even though I allow personal notes on literature quizzes, I go over for a look. He sees me coming and shoves them into his binder. What are those? I ask pointing to the floppy ends of the papers. Let me see. He sheepishly pulls out a wad of old quizzes, tests, notes, compositions, etc. from his 2 older brothers and sister, all of whom I had. It's so Mr. Bean clueless I have to laugh. . . A girl copies approximately half of her research paper from various sources, and I cite the sources and pages and give her a zero. Mom protests that half was original and the girl should get some credit for that 50% or so. . . A boy turns in a research project with quotation marks at the beginning and at the end. His paper is one huge quote two pages long with one source. When I ask about it he says, You told us if we wanted to copy, it was OK as long as we used quotation marks. . . A boy goes into his sister's computer when she's not around and they wind up turning in the exact same paper without her knowledge. She nearly breaks down when I confront her before brother finally confesses. He does the exact same thing a week later. . . A boy comes into my room before first period and slips the homework out of a girl's binder while she's in the hall and I'm not around. The girl can't understand how they can be turning in the same answers. The boy finally confesses.

Boys are generally more honest than girls when it comes to admitting to cheating. I ask a female teacher about this and she says that it's her impression too and speculates that boys are taught from an early age that it's OK to be upfront with emotions: wrestle, punch, don't hold back, live in the skin. Girls, on the other hand, are taught to repress true feelings and that it's not ladylike, or the mores of American society, to be in the moment, let it all hang out. Repress, repress, repress. This might be a dated theory. The last physical fight in our school was between two girls, and it's mostly girls who get the restraining orders i.e. keep so-and-so away from so-and-so.

Top Of The World *– The world is full of people who will lie, cheat, plagiarize, and act as pure as newly fallen snow about it. Though it's a pain, and a bit hypocritical since you yourself have cheated, you have to call them on it. And then flunk their sorry asses.*

Silent Student Shoutout *– Diogenes walked the ancient world with a lamp looking for an honest person. It sounds corny and pretty fucking hopeless. Try at least to be mostly-honest; halos aren't easy to keep on.*

Near the end of the month we have an in-service day. In-service days are great cons foisted on the American taxpayer by well meaning school systems. If only board of ed members sat through one, or asked the teachers what they thought. . . Mark Twain: In the first place God made idiots; that was for practice; then he made school boards. Essentially you sit around in groups of other somnambulant teachers trying their best to stay awake while overpriced, overdegreed, faux experts lecture on matters they've theorized on for years. Older teachers laugh, joke, and gossip – sometimes outright, and everyone tries to sneak in some grading time.

In this district we have 5 of these a year, i.e. students come in for 180 days, teachers 185. Districts could save money by simply doing the in-service on half days, as in days of yore. Cutting back on in-service days could also put money in the taxpayer pocket, i.e. districts could freeze teacher pay and cut the days progressively back over time. A win-win, i.e. taxpayers wouldn't be burdened with annual pay increases, and teachers would get their raises, i.e. the same money for less days is a de facto raise.

This particular in-service starts with a 2 hour workshop on Teaching With Style. How many of these have I attended? A dozen? You fill out a worksheet on teaching styles, chart them, get together with teachers of similar style, fill out posters, and finally report strengths and weaknesses to the assemblage. It's not a bad workshop to do one time, but I filled that quota long ago and I know my style. I blow it off and take the time to fill out a lengthy survey that I got from the State Department of Ed. Near the end it asks: 1. Is your level of enthusiasm for teaching the same now as when you started? 2. If you had it to do all over again would you still become a teacher?

Is it? Would I?

I look around at the room. It's past workshops like this that have laid the educational buzzwords of the day on us: Madeline Hunter, John Collins Writing Program, synetics, CRISS Learning Strategies, Kansas Learning Strategies, Understanding By Design, Literature Circles, Portfolios, Whole Language, Big Questions, Programmed Texts, Co-operative Learning, Anderson's Revised Taxonomy, Through the Eyes Of the Learner, Learner Centered Education, Vocational Teaching, etc. etc. I don't even remember what half of them are anymore. WTF

I answer, No and No on the State Department survey, which are actually false negatives, i.e. the answers aren't that simple, but there're no bubbles for 1. Half The Time, 2. Only With A Return To Fundamentals.

Rip Van Winkle – *You might learn something helpful during an in-service workshop, you might not. In any case don't knock yourself out, you need to be fresh for class tomorrow. Enjoy the peace and quiet of this adult-only world, the coffee and pastry, and go out for lunch. This is how the rest of the working world functions everyday.*

Laying The Line – *Is your teacher trying some new techniques that appear confusing and pointless? Are you using magic markers, large sheets of paper,* *and working in groups? Is teacher acting unsure and very formal as if there's an administrator present? Don't worry, it'll pass. There was a in-service.*

The month of February ends. There are 73 school days left. Winter's pushing past, spring's ahead. I'm trying to stay positive, trying hard to enjoy my last year, if indeed this is it. I'm going to have a good time if it fucking kills me.

MARCH – In Like A Lion, Out Like A Lamb

March 1 there's a big snow storm, but it's Saturday so F it. Two days later it's 50 degrees. Freeze, thaw, snow, rain. March is the month of endless possibilities: the month of rebirth, the ides of March, St. Patrick's Day, the month I came home from Vietnam in 1970 and set the tombstone on my father's grave. It's also my birth month, and it's strange to think that soon I'll have lived longer than my father did.

I'm walking down the hall before first period and this older boy and girl are going at it pressed up against a support beam that frames a plate glass wall. It's a powerful two-way A/C current. He's leaning back into the support and she's leaning into him, pressed tighter than a spray-on condom. These two are in this exact same spot everyday, at this exact same time, in this exact same position. I always just walk past and ignore them as do the rest of the passersby in this central artery.

This morning I stop.

They don't break apart but slowly turn their heads sideways to look at me. Good morning, I say and I smile. They smile back and I say, You two go at it every day in this same spot, this same time. I'm informing you that what you're doing bothers me. Sorry, but it does. Now that you know you're bothering me, if you continue it's a form of sexual harassment. Sexual harassment, *you* harassing me. I smile, pause, they say nothing, and I end with, The law sure is a funny thing. And I walk away.

As I'm walking towards my room it occurs to me I forgot to point out to them that if their dry humping gets any more energetic, they could roll sideways, crash through the glass, and wind up in the center courtyard and wouldn't that be a shattering experience?

Will they be back tomorrow? What will I do if they are? A teacher friend of mine was told when he tried to break up an ass grabbing, lip-locking couple that he was just jealous. Am I jealous? Would I trade 59 for 17, and reading the morning newspaper for a good ole fashioned public ass grab? Yeah, sure, abso-sucking-lutely. But that's not my motivation this morning. I honestly don't know what is.

Flashback: A 14-year-old couple are going at it daily between periods in front of her locker just across from my door. I warn them to break it up several different times, but you might as well hope to find a rotisserie chicken without the legs spread. Next day they're still catching some trim, so I go, Woof, woof, woof, woof. They break apart, and the girl asks through slitted eyes, Are you saying I look like a dog? No, I say, just getting your attention. I'm telling you for the last time to knock it off and to get going. Later that day one of our suits calls me in. Did you say Pearl looks like a dog? suit asks. Absolutely not, I say. I just went, Woof, woof. I meant she followed her boyfriend Earl, like a dog wrapped around his leg. Suit says, You're sexually harassing her and you'll be in trouble if you don't stop. Me in trouble? I ask. Didn't you pay attention at our last sexual harassment workshop? I've warned these two before, told them their behavior is bothering me, so it's *they* who're harassing me. Suit has no response, and Pearl and Earl take their act somewhere where the teachers don't shine.

Sex in school, signs of affection in school, the mating rituals of scholastic cave people post-Flintstone pre-Morlocks/Barbarella. I usually let it go unless hands are doing exploratory surgery. Sometimes I announce, Group hug! and I embrace them both. Sometimes when I'm on hall duty, I just announce quite loudly with an Italian accent, I lubba you, I lubba you!

followed by kissing/puckering sounds. It usually gets a laugh which usually breaks up the moment. . . I don't allow sitting on laps in study hall or touchy-feelly grabby-gropey fooling around/horseplay. I keep the door open if I'm alone with a female student, step back if one violates my sense of space, and never touch or hug any female teen. I try to enforce the dress code, e.g. no exposed midriffs. Many a girl's come up to my desk with blouse riding high, and I simply say, I can see your bellybutton. If that gets no tugging down of material I add, Want to see mine? *That* usually gets an, Ugh or Eeechh. Only once did a girl say, Sure. It threw me for a few seconds before I recovered and said, I don't think so. It ain't a pretty sight.

Roger Rabbit – *School might be Animal Planet, but there can't be mating out of season, in public view, or on the grounds. Sex-ed does not have a lab component.*

The Laying On Of Hands – *I know most want to help propagate the species, but school isn't the place. If it were, how would students feel about viewing the older teachers doing it? Ugh, eeechh? Enough said.*

There are three possible combinations of sexual trysts in a school: student-student, student-teacher, teacher-teacher. It's gone on ever since I started, in pretty much every district, I believe. A quick sampling: A maintenance men catches a girl giving a boy a BJ on stage in the darkened auditorium. . . A not-of-age male's caught screwing a not-of-age girl on the tiled floor in the lav. Statutory rape. . . A male teacher gets it on with a female teacher in a closet in the auditorium area. There are callbacks. . . A pickup truck in the parking lot puts its heavy duty suspension system to the test nightly. Chevy – built to last. . . A teacher and a senior girl get voted Most Promising Couple in the class superlatives, but the yearbook advisor refuses to acknowledge the vote count. Love and democracy lose out. . . A principal tells me he'd love to catch a rumored teacher and his student girlfriend but doesn't know how. I tell him, Hire a private eye. He doesn't, the girl graduates, they marry, eventually divorce, and leave behind a living reminder. . . A car's running on a winter night next to an industrial arts wing. The windows are fogged, the car body's bouncing up-and-down. A maintenance man takes a bag of nails and feeds them into the vacuum unit which empties into a 50 gallon drum right next to the car. The nails hit the metal drum with the speed and loudness of a RAT-TAT-TAT machine gun. The car zooms off and never returns. . . The school puts an achievement flag on the front flagpole whenever a student does something exceptional. One early morning a bra and panties are flying below the American and state flags right where the achievement flag belongs. The flag detail's reluctant to take them down saying, Now *that's* achievement.

How old are you, Mr. B? the girl asks.

- I'm 60, or I will be in a few weeks.

- You look 35. She smiles.

- Thanks.

- I mean it.

- Thanks again. Actually, counting the 9 months in the womb I'm 60 now, almost 61.

- Huh?

- I was alive for 9 months in the womb. Why shouldn't that count, especially if you believe life begins at conception.

There's puzzlement. Some heads nod in agreement.

- Then when is your real birthday?

- My birthday is in a few weeks. You asked me how old I was. To know that, add 9 months to my birthday – I believe I went full term – and that's how old I am. Almost 61.

- So you can't know your real birthday?

- Birthday, yes. How old gets a little tricky.

- Can you know it exactly?

- Not unless your parents kept a diary. I smile and think, *And then only if they weren't doing it 24/7 like a pair of oversexed gerbils.*

Old Yeller – *Your birthday's about as far into sex-ed as you want to venture. Anything beyond that they can tutor you on.*

16+ Candles – *Asking your teacher's age or birthday is not too personal. And remember the banana rule, i.e. people like bananas generally don't get better with age. They get spotty and mooshy.*

Monday morning I tell a class, Please stop your talking. Get your pen and book out, open up your notebook and let's continue to work on last week's unit. The weekend party's over.

I wait. They don't settle down, heads are still turned around, few classroom materials are showing. I'm not surprised. It's Monday selective hearing. What they might've caught was: <u>Please</u> blah blah <u>talk</u>. Blah blah blah blah blah blah. <u>Open up</u> blah blah blah blah <u>continue to</u> blah blah blah blah blah blah blah <u>party</u> blah blah. . . But who knows for sure what really got through or if they heard anything at all. SOP: Usually one or two hear, start following directions, then it's follow-the-leader with the brakes on.

Today it takes several reminders, a raised voice, and finally The Big Bang, a slammed hand on my metal podium to bring order out of the shit storm. It's no way to start the week, but I tell myself: breath calmly, chew some gum, have a sip of diet cola. Another week is off and crawling.

Four months ago the parents gained access for the first time ever to our on-line gradebooks, i.e. they no longer have to phone, email, or come into the sandbox to find out how the nob gobblers are doing. A few clicks, a pin number, and voila! they're inside our gradebooks.

Public exposure and technology now drive grades and curriculum for some. Some teachers I talk to tell me they record fewer grades, are more cautious about the ones they do record, grade on the high side, and play semantic games, e.g. instead of recording in-class assessments based on homework as quizzes, which might imply the student just isn't good at quiz/ test taking, the assessment is recorded as homework even though it's done in-class and is nothing more than an old fashioned quiz. Parents viewing poor homework grades from the comfort of their PC tend to put the blame squarely on their womb popouts where it belongs, and belay the email and/or phone call.

Phone calls and emails decrease, but don't vanish totally. I get an email from a mother upset over zeroes she's seeing on the computer for work her daughter missed and never made up. It's your daughter's responsibility, iTeacher zips back, to get a makeup sheet when she's out and to make up the work. Your daughter never even asked what she missed, never showed any sign she's even been out. I don't mention that daughter is a pain in school, a pain in class, a pain in the neck, and a pain in the ass – a polyfecta of pain. Needs a whole life suppository. It's *unfair*, mom accuses, and we're locked in the classic *unfair* pas de deux, a dance parents and students love.

The Classic Unfair Pas De Deux: Mr. Bentley, here's my late work. You're two days past the deadline. But you let her turn it in. She's never been late before, you're always late and I told you the last time, No more. *It's not fair*. . . Mr. Bentley, may I go to the lav? You're on the restricted list. But I really have to go, it's an emergency. I'll have to call the office and have them send down an escort. There's not time. Sure there is. No there's not. I'll do what I have to do and call the office, you do what you have to do. *It's not fair*. . . Mr. Bentley, can I go to the lav. Sure, get your passbook out. I lost it. Can't let you go then. You could handwrite me a pass. Why should I? Because I have to go. You go everyday during this period. I can't help it. You just came from lunch, why didn't you go then? I had to wait in the lunch line, there wasn't time. Teachers eat lunch, check mailboxes at the office, shoot out emails, and still have time to go. Then teachers must be fast. We are. So can I go? Only if you have your passbook. But I told you I don't. That's not my problem. *It's not fair*. . . Mr. B, I can't take this vocabulary quiz. Why not? I don't have the definitions, when did you do it? Monday. I was out Monday. But it's Friday, you've been in school all week, knew we did the vocabulary on Monday and should have gotten the definitions. So I have to take the quiz? That's right. *It's not fair*. . . Mr. Bentley, may I go to the nurse? Sure, but turn in the homework first. I don't have it. Then it's a zero. I was sick last night so I didn't think I'd be in school today. But you're here. I know. So let's have the homework. But I just told you why I don't have it. Fine. So is it a zero? Yes. *It's not fair*. . . Mr. Bentley, how am I doing in this course? I pass back all the papers. I know. You can figure your own average. But don't you have it, it's on the computer, can't you look it up? Not now, I'm in a different program. When? You know you can look it up yourself on-line. I don't know how to do that yet so can't you just tell me? Later. When later? After school or tomorrow. But I can't wait. That's your problem. *It's not fair*. . . Mr.

Bentley, would you write me a letter of recommendation for college? I'd rather not. Why not? Well, because I haven't had you for two years, and when I did you nearly failed the course. But I'm a good kid. Yes, you are. And you don't have to mention the grades. I don't, but you were also lazy and unmotivated. Can't you just talk about the good things. I could, but I'd have to mention the others too. So you really won't write me a letter? Get a teacher you did better with. But your class was one of my best classes. Sorry to hear that. So, will you write the letter? No. What if I brought you in some homemade cookies? It'd be nice, but I still won't give you a recommendation. Really? Really. *It's not fair.*

Drive The Chevy To The Levy – *You can cave in when badgered, be as hard as woodpecker lips, or fall somewhere in-between. Regardless, get ready to hear the word unfair a lot. You'll be tempted to say, That's unfair, but don't fall into the trap.*

Tuck It Between Your Legs – *You can call your teacher unfair, but wax on, wax off – what's it mean? Sand the floor, paint the fence, it's still Miyagi's class. And it's plenty fair. You haven't lived long enough or experienced enough yet to know really unfair.*

It's not fair/It's not my fault gets compounded when the parents get involved. This particular emailing parent is nothing new. Still I think, Damn on-line gradebook. I should've just left the missed grades blank for a few more weeks, waited even more beyond the makeup limit than I did before filling in the zeros. Nothing still would have gotten made up, but at least I could have said, And what did you think all those blank spots in my gradebook were for all those weeks – abstract whole numbers? Mom's confusing unfair with unfortunate, and I tell her that.

Mumbo Jumbo: Every teacher gets notes from home along the lines, Please excuse Ursula for not doing last night's homework but <u>fill in the blank</u>. Possibilities: She wasn't feeling well, we had a family crisis, there was a power outage, the computer crashed, the printer ran out of toner, the dog is teething and ate it, we used it mistakingly to mop up a spill, her book was stolen, it's a religious holiday, she tried but needs more time, she left her backpack in school, she didn't understand the assignment/the reading, etc. . . Sometimes I grant an extension, usually not. When I don't the student invariably says, But it's a note from my mother! as if the pantheon is God, mom, me. Sometimes the student adds, Call her if you don't believe me. Standard Bentley: I believe you, but why's it matter? Implication: Who's the teacher? As a postscript I usually close with, And how long did you have to do this assignment? I gave it out a week ago, but you chose to wait till the last minute. I'm sorry things fell apart at the last minute, but the world isn't flat. Plan ahead. Personal Disclaimer: I'm not a heartless monster, breaks are given on a per diem, per student/FOB basis. I'm also excellent at redeeming IOU's, but there aren't many of those out there.

I ask a picky bonus question on a homework reading check for African American Lit and Film and have most scratching their heads. I collect the papers and I'm going over the answers.

- I know the answer to the bonus.

I'm surprised at the hand waving in front of me and the proud assertion. The student is not a reader, has not been keeping up, generally cannot even give me a plot summary much less a tiny, inconsequential detail. But it just goes to show you.

- What is it?

- I wrote it down.

- So what did you write down?

- I did the reading.

- You wrote that you did the reading?

- No. I'm saying I did the reading.

- Great. And you know the bonus?

- That's right.

- What is it?

- I forget. But I know it.

I glance quickly through the pile of papers, and her bonus is wrong. Not even close. I sigh and wonder if maybe I'm developing cataracts and ear wax. Something's wrong. Farout Possibility: Maybe this student's had some recent transcranial magnetic stimulation which shut down her short term memory. More Likely Possibility: She just enjoys verbal spamming. Gambling Advice: Never bet on any animal that can talk.

- OK, can anyone else tell me the answer to the bonus?

Several hands go up, and they all know it with slight variations. The girl is telling those around her, That's it.

The African American course is going well. We're still reading *Roots*, but students have also done mini-presentations on 98 famous African Americans covering all eras and all walks of life. Presentations were spaced out over 2 days, students had to take notes, and now over the remainder of the course I'll have them identify individuals for daily bonus questions. Very soon they'll have to choose one name from that list for a biographical project, start independent research, and write a major paper due in June. Students are also compiling a dictionary of dialect and slang from *Roots*, and at the end of the novel will write an original *Roots* scene with the appropriate dialect and slang. I'm anticipating great results, they're anticipating graduation.

We start CAPT testing. This is a state mandated test for all 10th graders that takes about 2 hours a day, 6 days to administer. Poor students, it's always some standardized test staring them down, ripping their asses.

Is it true Mr. Bentley, the students ask as I pass out materials, that this test really *is* important? Yes, I want to say, and if you fail you *will* develop uncontrollable hormonal flashes, post menstrual and sinus drip, premature sagging boobs, a hairy back, and *will* be damned to endless dreams of Number 2 pencils (George Carlin: If the #2 pencil is the most popular why's it still #2?). I want to say it, but I don't. I just smile, give a little shake of the head. I don't want to be part of the snow job, but I don't feel like getting called in by the big chieftains either. The students get my point.

I've Never Been To Me – *How did you score yourself on state and national tests? Exactly. So go easy on the students. There's a big life waiting beyond this test.*

In school we teach the lessons first, then comes the test. In living people experience life's tests first, then draw their own lessons. Is that an important difference? Should education mirror life or just continue on as usual? I don't know. I do know there's an on-line website called Students Against Testing and that in a Time/CNN survey among the rich and famous most declined to give their SAT scores. Students don't want the testing, adults are haunted by it, but education = standardized testing = big business = stuck like a wart.

Our girls' basketball team gets knocked out of the state tournament.

- What happened? I ask one of the players.

- They had a deaf girl and a big black center.

- I don't understand. A deaf girl?

- That's right.

- Why would being deaf matter? You mean she could block out the crowd noise?

- I'd jump and yell right in her face when she was shooting and it didn't bother her at all.

- And they had a big black center?

- That's right.

- Why not just say they had a big center? Or a tall center? Or whatever it was you meant that related to basketball? How is black relevant?

The girl looks puzzled, as do many of the students. Then she sees my point.

- Black players are better.

- Are they?

- Most professionals are black.

- In the WNBA? Are you sure?

- Pretty sure.

- OK, if that's your point and your point's a fact, though I'm not really sure it is. I just don't want to see anyone, any group stereotyped. And none of you should either. It's a good deal what school is about, i.e. learning to see people as people, and not as types or colors.

I don't believe the girl's attitude for a second is racism as much as it's suburban naiveté i.e. there's this tiny corner of our tiny state, then there's the rest of the world. I don't know if, in fact, black females are better basketball players but I hope the class thinks twice in the future about qualifying anyone as black, or white, or yellow, or red as if they think that in itself says something.

Somewhere Over The Rainbow – *Eugene Bullard, America's first black aviator, had the motto: All blood runs red, painted on his WWI fighter. There's not a better way to say it, or a more important thought to live.*

Mary Sunshine – *You may hang in cliques broken along color/race lines, and maybe you're not prejudice, just more comfortable with your own kind. That's exactly how many of your bigoted ancestors felt too. Thought: Perhaps your own kind is the human race, and that alone.*

Snippets: Elwood, you're going all-ghetto today, his friend says and points at Elwood's hat, shirt, sneakers. Elwood shrugs. I don't know if Elwood sees it as a compliment or if it's meant to be one. Neither student is a GQ type.

A student writes, It was an angle from God. This is putting someone not so realistic to the future tense. . . I'm guessing angle should be *angel*, but I have no idea what the rest of it means. It's not unusual for students to write nonsensical passages when they're trying to say something with depth. It makes me laugh and I put a **?** next to it. I can't always translate student.

Student-to-me: Mr. Bentley, my so-called friends pushed me down the bleachers last night. They said they were going to do it every time I crossed my legs and leaned back. I was lucky I had my shin guards on. . . Student doesn't really seem upset. At this age assault = inclusion = friendship.

How'd you like to do a favor for me? the poobah asks.

- Not really, I say honestly.

- No?

- No.

There's a tight smiling between us while poobah figures out what to say next. It's not my move. Finally poobah lays it down.

- I'd like you to read the science portion of the CAPT to one of our ESL students.

- If you're asking me to volunteer, the answer is no. A science teacher should read it. If you're ordering me, I'm not going to say *no* because that would be insubordination. Are you ordering me?

- Let's say I'll expect you to be there.

- Then it's an order, and I guess I'll have to be there.

At a meeting later in the day poobah keeps smiling at me as if to say, We're still friends aren't we? WTF. Let poobah read the science portion, or any of the myriad of staff we have that's free during that time period and are not up to their armpits in compositions. Some of these poobahs want to kneecap you good, and then have you smile and say, I was hoping you'd do that. Once more, please.

MacArthur Park Is Melting In The Dark – *It's true: Never volunteer for anything that comes from the top-down unless it translates into retirement points, money, or getting out of work/class early. Exception: You're lobbying for Educator/Student-Of-The-Year.*

Many yearbooks ago due to a last minute shift in staff we have an extra English class without a teacher and a poobah asks me to volunteer to take it. I can't make you take it, he honestly says. It'll be a sixth class for you, and that's beyond contract limits. However, I've talked to the union about it, and they'll let you volunteer. I just can't mandate it. . . Is there additional pay? I ask. Well no, poobah laments with crocodile empathy, but I will remember I owe you, and next year I'll take care of you. OK, I say with scarcely a thought. As long as you take care of me next year.

Next year comes, and I learn the first day back that I have more students than ever before including many of the worst in the school. I storm into the office and corner poobah. I thought you were going to take care of me this year? I rage. Couldn't help it, he says. We had a last minute increase in enrollment and there weren't monies in the budget for even a part-time teacher. But I have more students than any other English teacher, I protest. The increase in enrollment isn't even spread out equally. Sorry, he says. Sorry? I say. Look, don't ever ask me for another favor, you won't get it. Now he gets mad and says, You know where the door is if you don't like it here. And just like that I'm dismissed like a fucking unwanted telemarketer.

It's a lesson in volunteering I never forget.

Walk Away Renee – *Volunteering is sometimes a trade off: that instead of this; sometimes it's taking more on: that in addition to this. You know what this is, just be sure what that is and it wouldn't hurt to get it in writing. Principals aren't always principled.*

Trouble In Paradise – *Only you can say whether or not some particular enterprise is worth volunteering for or not, but remember. If you're going to be a volunteer, be an enthusiastic one, or keep your fucking hand down and enjoy your own company.*

Certainly volunteering can be a generous noble thing whether it's just you or a well organized effort. Winston Churchill said, You make a living by what you get. You make a life by what you give. I agree, but I would add that the very nature of teaching is a life of giving. You give of yourself far beyond any compensation for it. You need to be gentle with yourself too. Mink glove every molecule.

It's mid-March, the end of winter sports, and our winter coaches are starting to smile again and look more laid back. Spring sports are gearing up. We're almost at the vernal equinox and spring's official start. Days are lengthening, there's no doubt winter's hold is easing up. Spring is in the air.

I get an email from one of my many commanding officers. When's a good time to meet? You can bring a union rep. This regards a negative comment you made.

Negative comment? I think. Which one? I make 'em everyday, so do other teachers. Administrators like this game. Like to keep you off balance. I email back that I'd prefer early morning before first period, but that I can't meet today or the rest of the week. This is to show Colonel Klink that the possibility of waiting doesn't bother me. I've been written up before by Klink for making a negative comment when I was overheard saying, Some teachers in this school have it made. Sometimes when you get written up it's not about the actual cited offense but about something you did that isn't citeable. In this case it could be payback for calling in sick one day during CAPT, or recently siding with a student against a poobah, or doing personal writing during PLC time, or sitting alone in the balcony at the last assembly, or the time I carped to another commissioned officer. Who knows which tweak it really is.

Klink never responds back: not this week, not for the rest of the year. We eventually stop talking altogether other than the perfunctory hi-hi, and our relationship goes down for the 10 count. At first I feel pugnacious and combative, but I quickly move to a neutral corner and change nothing other than not going near Klink's office as often. I sleep well at night, my appetite's robust, and I put no moratorium on my sardonic comments. My closest teaching colleagues side with me, and Team Bentley grows in strength. ADMIN 101: The threat alone of punishment alone is enough to silence most teachers. Most, but not all. TEACHER 101: The irreverent Susan Sontag said: Don't let the bastards get the best of you. Right on! So don't. It's unfortunate if education becomes an adversarial us-them standoff, but as long as the students remain unaffected I'm not gonna act like some whimp-ass extinct dodo.

I have for some time been cleaning out my file cabinets, sorting through boxes of thematic material, and taking down posters I want to keep. Over weeks I take home personal items: my model sailing ship, a basketball hoop, and dozens of college pennants that were hanging from the ceiling. I've already given away some pennants and posters, and on my last day I'll probably bequeath the rest of the flotsam and jetsam to faculty: my large storage cabinet, my electric homemade applause sign, 5 artificial floor plants, and my black metal podium adorned with various stickers. I return stacks of books to the book room as we finish them, weed through the bric-a-brac in the drawers, and don't disturb my bulletin boards.

I've always believed it was important to decorate a room in an educational and visually pleasing way. Elementary teachers do this intuitively, many high school teachers do not. I'm careful not to sterilize it and still leave enough so that academics aren't affected and that I like what I see. Not exactly eye bling, and people do comment that my room is looking emptier, it's certainly dustier. But it's still a decent home-away-from-home and much better creatively than many other rooms. I confess to being proud of that, though it's not competition.

It's been my goal this last month to be able to walk out the front door anytime after my 60th birthday carrying only my briefcase and one box of personal items. That's the way Lennie Briscoe a.k.a. Jerry Orbach did it on *Law and Order*, and I thought it had style/class. Here today, gone tomorrow, retired, not looking back. I'm not going to walk pre-June if they live and let live, but if they bust and nag and piss on my leg, I'm shaking it out of here.

An anonymous morning email says simply, Those Douche Bag Drinkers In Central Office. I realize instantly this relates to an ongoing lawsuit. The facts are lengthy, testimony conflicting, but the gist is that a student thinks a concert called Jamfest is cancelled by the big wheels, and she goes home and posts on her internet blog, Jamfest is cancelled due to douche bags in central office. She also encourages people to email and phone the administration.

The girl ultimately shows the blog to her mother, removes the posting, apologizes in writing, but regardless is not allowed to run for a class office she's held in the past. She winds up winning anyway due to write-ins but is not allowed to take office.

The incident makes national news and lawyers line up to take the case. A lawsuit's filed. The girl sues on freedom of speech principles, loses, and is now awaiting the verdict on her appeal. She was a fine student for me last year: smart, hard working, an irrepressible crusader with an easy exterior and a steel core. The type of student that in my era could have been leading the SDS or working in the Peace Corps. She's everything I want my students to be.

I personally do not feel it's anyone's business what a student writes off campus in the privacy of her home, even if it results in phone calls/emails that disrupt the school day a bit, and I let that opinion be known. More importantly I don't feel getting called a douche bag is any big deal.

Etymologically the word's come to mean a jerk, and not necessarily the sanitary product an older generation associates with it. Many of us have been called far worse over the years and with far less consequence, if indeed any consequence at all.

Flashback: A boy calls me an asshole then gets in a fighting stance and wants to mix it up. I'm livid when he gets a verbal warning not to do it again so I have him called back down to the office the next day, and with the head of discipline present I tell him, I can't threaten you, you can't threaten me, and that's how education works. If it happens again I'm *not* sending you to the office. I'm calling the state police, charging you with breach of peace by threat, and you're getting hauled out of here in handcuffs. He never calls me asshole again or wants to mix it up.

There are more recent cases of in-school verbal bashing, not even counting what's written on desks and lav walls. Students tell me to check out ratemyteacher.com, but I reply why would I want to read nasty comments by anonymous voices and have to boot up and log on to do it? It's all just specious ranting with a cyber bullhorn. I tell students we teachers are perfectly capable of making our own tastelessly specious comments, but only a coward anonymously sucker punches. If you have something to say to me, say it to my face, and if you can't be civil then let it out, take your chances, and don't complain if there *are* consequences. There's a certain honesty to an upfront in-your-face, and while I don't like the negative vibes, I respect it more than permanent magic marker in a lav stall.

Make Love Not War – *Evaluating is not a one-way street that's confined to school. Students are rating, making remarks, praising and dissing teachers* *on-line. Sure you can read it, but what's the point? There's no appeal and no consequences. We're not the great and powerful Oz.*

Milk A Pig *– Don't get paranoid about your online blogs. Unless you're plotting to overthrow the government, hack into the NSA, hit the school website with a virus, repeat Columbine, or YouTubing the locker room, no one's much interested.*

My birthday arrives and from my teaching compadres I get a few gifts: a tuna casserole, a book on Army vs Navy football, a chocolate cake.

I'm 60, older than my father lived to be. That in itself is strange, but what's even stranger is that I don't feel older or wiser. I guess I expected some sort of airbag impact moment, but aside from the presents, it's just another day, another year. I'm not ready to carve the tombstone yet, but I am starting to think that I really don't want to teach another year. Too many changes, too many young administrators, the day's too long, the students too student. I'm not at the stage of being a misanthrope, but I'm not getting any more Mr. Roger-ish either. Bottom Line: I've seen too many good teachers hang on too long, grow too bitter, and leave disenchanted. They have a decent/good year, decide they can do one more, the next year's a living hell, and just like that a grumpy old person's born.

Dead Man Walking *– Get out while it's still fun and leave a shining legacy. Let them remember your smile and being as good a teacher as a teacher can be.*

Kissing George Washington *– Go easy on your teachers, especially the grandparent aged ones. Some, like me, will haunt you with a poltergeist shit storm if you don't. Promise.*

There's a faculty meeting with a guest speaker from the state department of ed. The topic's special education, classroom accommodations, and the guy's really going off on it like we teachers never heard of SPED before or don't follow state mandated guidelines. He tells us he once threatened to sue a teacher for not meeting accommodations. The nabob's way over the top – a living, breathing air horn, and way out of line acting like we're guilty of not caring until he exonerates us. Trouble is the state tends to lay the problems of the worst schools in the state on everyone as if we're all swimming in the same urinal.

SPED Accommodations: Depending on the student, teachers may have to give extra time on all written work, allow for access to a computer, supply large print text, dismiss to an alternative test site, rephrase test questions/ directions, provide notes/outlines, check work in progress, allow extra time between classes, dismiss to the nurse as needed, assign preferential seating, allow a water bottle, provide a word bank and test study guide, give daily feedback and positive reinforcement, cue expected behavior, modify tests/ quizzes, limit multiple choice, eliminate deductions for spelling, etc.

How all this plays out in the actual classroom varies and is a study in eras and personalities. Example: A SPED teacher assigned to a couple of my classes once tells me I have to start modifying tests/quizzes for a select few. I tell her, You're the expert and you've only got a few students. So how about if I give you the tests/quizzes/composition assignments ahead of time, you do the modifications, then you grade those papers since you know your standards better than I do. I'll record whatever grades you give me. She does this for a couple of weeks, then stops and just takes the students out of the room with the same tests/quizzes/assignments everyone else is doing. I don't know what happens once they leave my room. I only know the students turn in great work.

SPED in actual practice is pretty much a case of everyone just trying to get by, live and let live, CYA, avoid failures, get results commensurate with effort, keep parents happy, head off lawsuits, keep students in-house and avoid costly outplacements. A SPED teacher once told me I already run my Level 2 classes like a giant SPED accommodation. I don't know if it's intended as a compliment, or even if it's totally true, but the SPED students I have who give any sort of effort usually do very well.

Casper The Unfriendly Ghost – *There's a Speed, but no SPED Channel on cable, but that doesn't make it any less real. It's real, as you'll find out if you ignore it.*

The Aurora Borealis – *Need extra time for the biggies like the SAT's and final exams? You need to get a SPED accommodation. Just be aware that post-school, the world will not bend over backwards for you and unlike Forrest Gump you probably won't fall into a shrimping fleet.*

My sophomores are finishing *Cry, the Beloved Country*. They used to hate this book because all we had were ugly hand-me-down yellowed copies and they'd go, So like how old is this book Mr B, do we really have to read it? Hey, this is my uncle's name in this cover. Oh my god this book is soooo old!. . . Now we have glossy Perma-Bound copies with a picture of James Earl Jones and Richard Harris on the front.

Give Em The Old Razzle Dazzle *– When was the last time you yourself were handed a coffee stained, creased, ripped, piece of shit, and told to read it? Exactly. No one likes books that look as if they've been through ground zero. Cardinal Rule: As far as books go, it's a beauty contest with swimsuit first, talent last.*

Book Snippets: Years ago I push for Perma-Bound copies and it becomes SOP for books that get high usage. The initial cost is greater, but they last and look good much longer than the softcover ones. Sort of like you vs. a mummy.

My honors 7th grade in the way way back wanted to read *The Hobbit*. I ask the principal about it but he says there's no money for new books. I go back and tell the class, Have your parents phone him and the superintendent. A day later principal tells me, Thanks a lot. You're getting your books. I say, You're welcome. But they're not my books, they're the students' books. And isn't it all about the students?

End of Month Snippets: The teacher is laughing so hard I walk in to see what's up. The room's empty and she hands me a diagram of the male body that students had to label. One girl drew a line to the genitalia area with the heading, Cerebral Cortex.

A guidance counselor comes in and talks to the sophomores about signing up for the ASVAB, the armed services vocational aptitude battery. Students are assured there's no military obligation to the test, but only two are interested until it's mentioned that it'll get them out of 3 hours of classes, including mine. Then three-quarters sign up.

One of our English teachers reiterates the modern comma policy: When in doubt, leave it out. One of her brighter students asks, But if you're sure it's safe, is it OK to stick it in?

My African American Lit class turns in *Roots* and one book has a big crease across the brand new cover. I smile but pretend to be annoyed with the student. How could this happen? I ask. It's the passion of reading, the girl says seriously. The what? I ask. The passion of reading, she repeats. Did you say the passion of reading? Yes, she says more emphatically and I think, Wow! and I'm not pretending either.

It's a good way to end the book and month.

APRIL – Switch To Vibrator Mode

It's spring and a new world's emerging. The snow's gone, the roads are margined with sand and old litter, and birds are migrating back and chirping in the trees. Edna St. Vincent Millay: April comes like an idiot, babbling and strewing flowers.

I'm standing outside my room between periods watching the passing hallscape. Students are a slow moving current in both directions. They're walking-the-walk with timeouts for hugging, high-fiving, darting into the lavs. I grab chop quotes here-and-there: call me when. . . my parents won't be. . . I'm going to kick her. . .

It’s good theatre and the body language is classic teen: keep your ass out of my damn way. Look at me the beauty/drama queen. Please can't you all just ignore me? Doncha just love love love my butt, boobs, biceps, sashaying, hair, jewelry, new clothes, four day growth!?

One thing I like to do out here is to read t-shirts. I scarcely notice the ones plugging brand names, teams, colleges, or rock groups. Vacation spots have some appeal: Cape Cod, Green Monster Fenway Park, Newport, Nova Scotia, but did you really go to Alcatraz, Havana, Fort Jackson, or Italia? The tees with philosophical statements/witticisms/sarcasm pique my interest the most, and I laugh and point and give thumbs up to: Genius by birth, slacker by choice; Wii-tarded; Did you eat a bowl of stupid for breakfast?; Good girls go to heaven, bad girls go to Amsterdam; Don't believe everything you read unless it's on the internet; A wise man once said I don't know, ask a girl.

It's life boiled down to nifty one-liners, stunted thought, superficial slogans passing for the day's motto. And it's a never ending stream: Live your life; So I'm up and out of bed. What more do you want?; Loser – Anyone who would take the time to read someone else's t-shirt all the way to the end. This means you.

I flag down a student wearing a Save water, drink beer shirt and tell him to turn it inside out when he gets a chance, though it is sophomorically funny. I personally relate to, Sarcasm is just another free service I offer. . . A boy is wearing a faded green tee that says, I'm with stupid. There's an arrow under stupid that points at his girlfriend walking alongside him and I wonder, Am I really in the 21st century? Did this school miss the Age Of Enlightenment?

***And You'll Find That You're In The Rotogravure** – Oliver Wendell Holmes Jr. said he didn't care anything for fashion but he was happy others did. Clothes may not make the man or woman, but they certainly cover the man or woman and don't we all like nice gift wrapping.*

I have no big feelings about the way students dress unless it's utterly inappropriate. I will enforce the school dress policy that says no spaghetti straps, strapless tops, halter tops, one shoulder and low cut tops, exposed midriffs, sleeveless shirts, diaphanous/mesh fabric (those who live in glass blouses shouldn't), skirts shorter than your crotch, pants with Peeping Tom holes, clothing that reveals undergarments, clothing with obscenities or derogatory messages relating to race/religion/gender, or any advertisements promoting sex, drugs, high cholesterol diets, enemas, or binge studying (kidding on the latter 3). The school dress code doesn't mention upskirts, nipple slips, camel toes, or butt cleavage, but somethings you just know.

It can be a hassle , but if every teacher enforces his/her own little corner of the school it's pretty easy to keep in check. Most of it's common sense that doesn't make allowances for haute couture, sleaze couture, weather, MTV, or what's on sale at Abercrombie, Speedo, or Victoria's Secret.

Appropriate dress for school has been a battle since my first day teaching back when heavy metal groups ruled. One day I get really fed up with the depressing way my general English students dress, and I let them file in and settle down before I stand up. I'm dressed in their same regalia: black army boots, worn jeans, black studded belt, and black Ozzy Osbourne t-shirt with sleeves rolled up. For accouterments I have a long chain loping from my belt into my back pocket where my wallet is. I don't say a word, they stare at me, I stare at them, and finally one girl says, Are you making fun of us Mr. Bentley? Heck no, I say. It just dawned on me yesterday that you all dress alike everyday and that I'm out of uniform. Power to Black Sabbath. They're looking at me like, Hey man, you putting us on or what? and they look at each other hopelessly clued out. Finally a boy says, We're not dressed alike. Others nod. Close enough, I say, but hey, that doesn't mean you're not individuals, and I spin the chain. . . Nothing changes, they remain a really depressing group visually, but at least they know how I feel, and it turns out that some indeed wind up wearing uniforms for life: soldiers, waiters, waitresses, cops, nurses, firemen, delivery personnel, prisoners.

Back then we teachers are the best dressed profession for dollars earned. Dressing up is important and we dress to the nines. There isn't a male teacher in the building without a wardrobe of multi-color/seasonal sports jackets, suits, and ties. The really hip also stock leisure suits, wide bell bottoms, platform shoes, and may even have a leftover Nehru jacket or two. Most do not repeat an outfit very often. The worst are color blind, a decade+ out of fashion, and hopelessly mismatched. But even they look formal enough to step right into a prom, graduation, or casket.

Things now've changed. Dress down Friday's everyday, and though we still dress cleanly and neatly only one male teacher still wears a sports coat.

Most of our female teachers dress much better: resplendent, conservatively sartorial, at times chic. They could seamlessly grace a country club social or bridge club, though these days they're more likely to be at a job interview.

The Emperor's Clothes – *You're a teacher, dress the part. That doesn't mean you have to wear Valentino, Hugo Boss, Givenchy, or Ralph Lauren. But it also doesn't give you carte blanche to flashback to Woodstock, the mosh pit, or your grubby-ass grunge years.*

Space, The Final Frontier – *I know you don't want school uniforms so avoid anything that's micro, mini, skimpy, partial, string, or thong. And anything with writing that grandma wouldn't like. The clothes on your back are as important as the ones on your front.*

April 1's come-and-gone with a rare lack of even belated April foolery. What happened to giving Bentley a faux office memo stating his grades crashed and that every single mark has to be reentered? Or a faux warning that his grades are too low and that every parent of a C, D, F student has to be immediately phoned? I fall for 'em every time. . . What happened to students putting a tack on my seat, draping a fake rubber snake in my plants, handing me a can of peanuts with one of those coiled spring snakes inside, turning my desk and chair around, or mimicking me by wearing heavy sweaters, chewing gum and saying, That reminds me of a story?. . . I once asked a student sitting in front of me in the first row, How'd you like a surprise? I don't care, he says, Yes or no? I want you to be sure. Yeah sure, he shrugs. And without standing I raise a full can of silly string, his eyes go wide, and from 10 feet away I spiderweb him.

April 1 can be a lot of fun.

The senior motor-mouth keeps laughing and talking. I tell her a couple of times to quiet down and turn around, and she suspends her talking jag barely long enough for me to tell the class, Your *Roots* compositions were great! before she's practicing her own talking points again. Ms. White Noise.

- Merle, grab your things and sit here. I motion to a seat in the front row and wait. She protests briefly then grabs her monogrammed backpack and handbag, bids her friends farewell, and deposits herself heavily in front of me.

- You don't like me.

It comes out of nowhere just loud enough to get my attention. One of those unsolicited opinions/emotions that some students feel must be shared as soon as it's felt.

- Not when you're talking when I am . . . Sidebar: I'm honest without being brutal. I do not have big feelings about this student one way or the other, but it would be cruel to go downtown and say that. Fortunately she lets her psychobabble go and opts to get practical.

- Do I have to sit here?

- Yes.

- For how long?

- I don't know. The rest of the period anyway.

I resume the general comments about the compositions. When I get to the girl's row, she's turned around again talking to the boy behind her.

- Hey! Do you understand why I moved you here? I ask. . . I am seriously annoyed and sound it.

- I was only half turned around.

- You want to be able to turn all the way around? . . . She doesn't answer and I smile and repeat, Would you like to be able to turn all the way around?

- Why?

- Because I can put you in a seat where you can turn around all period. . . I point to the empty corner seat, the one with no neighbors.

- I'm OK.

- Keep talking and you won't be.

I'm overreacting, a bit too splenetic, but she's a bit too smug and graduation is still 55 school days away, too far for senioritis to fully blossom. If I let 'em go now, treat 'em like discarded stem cells, I might as well phone in the class. They'd like that.

She settles down and we go over the compositions. Students had to expand an existing *Roots* scene or create a new one utilizing the novel's facts and dialect. Some students share out loud, and when they're done I can't resist telling everyone, Excellent! though one of you is a little confused. On his fourth and final escape attempt you have Kinte Kunte make it north instead of getting his foot partially chopped off. If he makes it, that negates the rest of Haley's personal *Southern* story. Poof. You also have him run all the way to Connecticut about 800 miles without seeing anyone or stopping for food, water, or sleep. Kunte is an amazing man, but *that* amazing? Then when he gets here the first white man he meets speaks in a thick Southern accent, like maybe Kunte ran in a circle.

The class, including the now quiet motor-mouth, bursts out laughing, and the one laughing the most is the author.

The Human Cannonball – *Writers learn by analyzing both good and bad writing. Just be* ***very*** *careful about reading any bad student examples. If you want to play it safe, share your own writing and toss in some of those old* *high school and college papers. Get ready to join in the laughing and groaning.*

We come to closure on *Roots*, I pass out *The Autobiography Of Malcolm X*, give an introduction, and we start taking turns reading orally. Many of these students, including Merle, do not like to read out loud. Most consider it a dirty trick they're even getting another book.

Some don't like to read out loud because they'd rather watch the movie or be left alone to daydream about pre-prom life. Some in every class don't read well. I'm not a particularly good oral reader myself so at the beginning of each year I model and share a few simple strategies that work for me: take it slow, let your tongue linger briefly on one word at a time and draw out the final syllable while your eye takes in the next word. And above all, don't worry about it. They're aren't many blessed with the voice of James Earl Jones, Orson Welles, Glenn Close – just give it your best. I encourage the better readers to continue on beyond their fair share, we all like being read to especially when it's well done. Sidebar: In ancient Rome the notoriously poor entertainer Nero loved to perform and would go on-and-on for hours while the audience was forbidden to leave. It's said women gave birth during his one-man shows and people feigned death in order to get carried out. So far no one's done that here, not even the real academic dead asses.

Fight! the rally cry rings out in the hall and I react instinctively. I'm a fast mover bobbing and weaving past knots of students, eyes locked on a circle in the middle of an already crowded hall. I'm motoring and reminding myself, Be careful Bentley. Some of these kids are a lot bigger than you, and a lot crazier. Downright freak-o-nites.

I push into the center and it turns out that 2 girls are jawing at each other with all the class of 2 street walkers fighting over a corner. Break it up! I say loudly and step in closer. Get going. NOW! . . . I'm nervous. Getting between two catfighting girls is a risky thing for a male teacher. I'm not a Jerry Springer piece of meat. Sidebar: If you're going to go in harm's way do it with force and confidence. Stand tall, talk loud. Like snarling animals some of these hooligans can sense fear or indecision and would like nothing better than to sandwich you and sumo bump you into early retirement. My 5'9" 185 pounds is not what the state police call command stature, but when I stand on my huevos I'm bigger. I could also douse their super anger with super calm and hope that the two neutralize each other, i.e. the placid, if-hippies-ruled, sisterhood schtick.

But these two aren't Haight-Ashbury types and are more likely to whip me with a proffered flower than sniff it and move dreamily along. Moreover, the equation of calm over anger usually results in talk and more talk and I'm in a hurry so it's just easier to repeat, Let's move it, NOW!

Slowly the group disbands. Fight fans are letdown that today's featured event's been cancelled, or at least postponed. I don't know the two girls, probably should have gotten their names, but it ended without getting physical and that's enough for me. I'm relieved. Greatly. If the office asks I'll just ID one or two of the ringsiders, and the office can take it from there.

In our school the penalty for fighting's usually suspension and arrest. It's severe and it works. There're shouting matches but not many physical confrontations. And unlike Jerry Springer no one gets rewarded for revealing their breasts.

Rumble In The Jungle – *Large and violent forces of nature are difficult and dangerous to deal with. Perhaps the school should issue us tasers,* *tranquilizer guns, pepper spray, and body armor. At least squirt guns or silly string.*

Hard Wood Head *– I understand the physical urge to curl up your fingers and pop someone but you can't, pure and simple. There're no good reasons to fight other than defense, and even then you can usually walk away. Or get a really big bad-ass friend.*

Literary Parallels: Contemporary author Cormac McCarthy in *Blood Meridian* says that even before there was man war waited for him. It's the belief of man's innate violence. On the other hand Dante says, Think of the seed of your creation. You were not born to live as brutes but to follow virtue and knowledge. In school we believe people are innately good and we follow Dante because his truth is truer, or at least more conducive to our communal, cul-de-sac lives. Disclaimer: It's not always easy to follow Dante. Dante never matriculated in the public schools.

In the years before schools operated in a semi-lockdown mental state, I'm standing in my doorway between classes pretending to shoot students with a plastic toy gun that normally shoots ping pong balls but I don't have any so I just click-click here, click-click there. I get called down to the office the next day.

- Were you shooting students in the hall yesterday? big schmoozer wants to know.

- I just pretended to. I used one of my son's toy guns. I didn't even use the ammo.

- I have a complaint that you weren't shooting everyone.

- What do you mean?

- That you were singling out the troublemakers and poorer students. You know the ones.

- I guess I was. I also shot some good kids.

- You have to stop it. You're discriminating.

- Would it be OK if I pretended to shoot everyone?

- Just stop shooting students. There's no reason for it.

- I was just having some fun. Most of the students I shot laughed.

- Are you going to stop it?

- Of course. But it *was* funny.

Fast Eddie Shoots Pool – *Don't shoot students, or anyone. Don't even pretend to. Don't even shoot dirty looks.*

Game Ends At Tilt – *Don't shoot teachers, or anyone. Don't even pretend to. Keep the guns, crossbows, spears, knives, slingshots, blowguns, paintball guns, crowbars, tire irons, RPG's, chemical/biological agents, thermonuclear devices, and rubber bands at home. Someone could lose an eye.*

A class enters right after lunch and I get the smell of chocolate. I look around, but no one has anything out and I wonder if I'm imagining it. There are a lot of smells floating around on a typical day: over perfumed females, wet wool, dirty hair, b.o., minty breath, clinging cigarette smoke, fried food, and the subtle but powerful pheromones of teenagers in heat. I'm a bit of a scentophile and the typical classroom can be a goddamn sniffapalooza. But I do smell chocolate.

- I smell chocolate. . . I say it as an invitation to slip me some. Everyone looks around.

- I have s'mores. A boy pulls a ziplock bag out of his backpack and adds, They're for the baseball bus.

- No, I wouldn't smell them wrapped up like that.

We start a lesson on homonyms and out of the corner of my eye I catch a girl reaching into her open pocketbook and quickly stuffing something into her mouth. I look at her, she freezes her mouth.

- You know there's no eating in class, especially right after lunch. Unless of course you have enough for everyone.

- The part about having enough for everyone is rote reply, and no student in 32 years has had enough for everyone.

- Well, she says, I don't have enough chocolate cookies for everyone, but I have enough Saltines.

She pulls out a whole packet and I'm dumbfounded and laugh.

- You're willing to share those with the whole class?

- Yes.

- OK, pass 'em out.

She goes around the room handing out Saltines, offers me one and I decline but thank her for the offer. Everyone is chewing now and happy. Funny how a simple thing like a plain, salted, white-flour cracker can bring on a technicolor mood.

The Candyman Makes Everything He Bakes – *An unexpected gift brings a joy all its own. Your gift could be a smile, a compliment, a kind remark, canceling a quiz, bringing in a guest speaker, etc. But students would prefer food.*

No Gratuity Necessary – *If you want to eat, bring enough for everyone. It doesn't have to be much or fancy or even very good. Food that's trash canned in the caf becomes 5 star dining in the classroom.*

It's not like there hasn't been any food this year. As part of an autumn unit sophomores closed with an herbal research project and had the extra credit option to bring in food featuring their herb. One class brings in nothing and complains that the other sections are feasting on garlic bread, rosemary and mint cookies, ginseng and chamomile teas, pesto (basil) and crackers, dill pickles, pasta with oregano, etc. I tell the starving group, You missed the point that if you want to eat you have to bring it in. Did you think it was going to magically appear like Meals-On-Wheels? It's a group that's into research on bloodroot, foxglove, and jimsonweed, wanted to do poppy and marijuana, and then wonders why I don't want them cooking. Fucking cerebral hernias.

One of the veteran teachers in the department asks me to write a letter of recommendation for her. She's had it with this school system. I write what appears to be a finished copy but with some toss away lines, e.g. she loves vodka and will share, loves dogs more than people, etc. I give her a copy, she laughs and suggests a few deletions and additions. I edit as per her instructions and give her a laudatory finished copy. Sidebar: Allowing input into a recommendation is something I don't generally do. Back-and-forth rewrites get too time consuming and in worst case scenarios stir resentment and frustration. What! You don't like my letter? You want me to compare you to Madame Curie/Albert Schweitzer/Dr. Livingstone/Mary Magdalene?

This teacher recommendation is the second I write in less than a month. In March I wrote one for a nontenured, and I expect to get asked soon to write for another department member who's also had enough and is collecting applications. The exodus I predicted is underway, and admin's as clueless as the cinder block walls.

Snippets: Teachers get a magnetic business card for a Safety Telephone Line. We're suppose to use it to report any safety concerns but I don't think they want to hear about computer radiation, razor edged paper, or overly dense answers. I toss it.

A student asks if I watch reality shows. *Reality shows*, I think, *like I want more fucking reality?* I tell him I prefer fiction.

Wife Story: She asks her kindergartners to list things that appeal to the sense of smell and one boy writes, My cat poop (complete with picture), and Dad's colon (he means cologne).

I get a rejection from the New Yorker for my Teacher III poem, and again late at night submit my next.

Teacher IV

He remembers when they were just a few years younger,
And he thought one day they might become friends, even lovers.
But none ever did, the desk was too wide.
And slowly over the years the desk grew,
Expanding like The Great Wall of China,
Keeping the barbarians out and the civilized man in.

I'm sitting in the faculty room early morning reading the newspaper and talking to a couple of our regular subs. I have a lot of respect for subs. They don't make a lot of money and they go into some pretty bad classes and situations. One's telling me how he subbed the other day at a large city high school for an alternative ed class. When he tried to get them to settle down they told him, Most of us are on parole but we're not gonna make it. Implication: It's back to jail soon enough so just read your newspaper and don't bother us.

We have all sorts of people who sub: students right out of college, retired teachers, the unemployed, moonlighting professionals, workers from other fields, people who never worked full-time, parents who're curious about the school, grandparents – bless 'em all. They span the range from very bad, OMG! To in vitro, genetically engineered, fantasy, surrogates.

One sub says she can't find my lesson plans and wings her own which consist mainly of talking to the students and letting them talk. My plans are on the middle of my desk in a large manila envelope labeled in large letters **SUBSTITUTE TEACHER PLANS**. I complain, turns out other teachers have complained, and the recent university grad's never called again. Another sub finds my plans but announces to the class, I think I'll just give you a study hall. What's Bentley going to do anyway? The middle-aged man never gets an encore.

It's important for teachers to leave good plans that'll take up the period. I'm subbing in the years before I get a full-time position and a teacher tells me, You're in for my classes tomorrow. I'll leave reading and writing work, but Claude's skills are too low so I'm leaving him a model ship. Tell him to put it together. Should take him the whole day. Turns out the ship is a Spanish sailing galleon with masts, rigging, 3 tiers of cannons, and more detail than a NASA rocket. The directions are Britannica-like, and I'm wondering how in the world a remedial level kid's going to understand them.

Turns out he doesn't. Claude can't read well, but his mind is genius-like at translating pictures. He studies the one on the box, glances at the progression of diagrams in the directions, and before the period's over has the model fully assembled with no extra parts. The square-rigged ship needs only paint, which wasn't left. I'm amazed with Claude, but Claude is now bored, and it doesn't take long for him to start acting up.

Take No Prisoners – *Leave detailed meaningful plans whenever you're out. Overplanning is better than underplanning. Your sub's a natural student target and the one thing he/she doesn't need is empty time. Empty time sucks.*

The Golden Gate – *I understand that you students regard any day that teacher's out as a vacation day. So stay home. Substitute teachers are not tour guides, cruise directors, or playground monitors. I mean, do you see a goddamn whistle?*

Back when I started in education as a sub, the 70's were nutso times. A friend of mine's subbing, gets called a fucking asshole, and knocks the real asshole to the ground. Punches him right in the nose. Friend gets called into the superintendent who asks him if he's crazy. Super tells him, You can't hit students! Friend tells super, You put me back into that same class and the kid calls me a fucking asshole again, I'll knock him down again. Friend voluntarily quits, goes into business, and has been happily retired for a decade. I recall at least one teacher being assaulted, paper airplanes and rubber bands filling the air, a teacher's desk getting overturned, students wrestling, toilets blowing up, lavs being flooded, etc. The 70's were unsettled and tough. A half dozen+ teachers I know call it quits.

In the 1960's, back in my own 7-12 grade years, things are different. The staff follows the belief it's more blessed to give than to receive. One teacher routinely uses a large oak ruler across the knuckles – Whack! A principal uses his leather belt on bare bottoms of the worst recidivists – Whack! A coach uses his lanyard to whip the bare back of a unrepentant wiseguy – Whack! Then the parents step in – Whack! Whack! Whack! Philosophy: Corporal punishment's next to godliness. What's good for one generation is good for the next. Just don't leave scars.

Rose Colored Bifocals – *The good old days were some meaner, less sensitive times, for sure. Today it's an eggshell, hypersensitive, be-careful-of-everything-you-say-and-do world. Humpty Dumpty would have made it today.*

Literary Sidebar: George Orwell predicted the existence of thought police by 1984, i.e. you'd be held accountable for what you both did *and* thought. That level of accountability didn't make it into the real 1984 or into the new millennium, but don't count Orwell out just yet.

One of our many paper pushers flags me down in hall and comes right to the point.

- When are we getting your letter?
- What letter?
- Your retirement letter.
- Maybe I'm not retiring.
- If you are, we should have the letter soon.
- Why?
- It's best for the school and students.
- How do you figure that?

- If you don't let us know, we won't find out till August from the retirement board. Then it'll be too late to get the best applicants. And maybe you can get out of meetings.

- Why should I care about getting out of meetings now? There aren't many left. It would have meant something back in September when I raised the issue.

- It's just best for the kids.

- Don't worry. If I retire and you don't find out till August I'm sure you'll still be able to hire a good teacher. It's not like English teachers are an endangered species. Of course I'm not sure you always appreciate a good English teacher when you have one. Judging by the past.

I'm smiling as I talk creating a discrepancy between what paper pusher's seeing and hearing. Pusher's not sure what to say so it's segue into Response Program 2.0, i.e. when in doubt it's good to say little, even better to get gone.

- We'll talk later, paper pusher cleverly improvises and goes off in search of the next manufactured crisis.

This paper jockey thinks I'm giving the view from Google Earth but I'm not. There really are plenty of good potential hirees still available in August. Both my wife and I were hired in August. And I really don't know my future plans yet, not 100%.

Oh-blah-dee-oh-blah-daa, whopppeee! with a jump and a heel click. No rush.

The Film class is finishing *Breakfast At Tiffany's* and I'm watching the clock and DVD counter. Five minutes to go in the period, about 4 minutes left in the movie. Perfect. Audrey Hepburn and George Peppard are arguing in the cab. It pulls over, she tosses Cat out into the rain, and Peppard tells her she'll never be wild and free, she'll always live in the cage she's built for herself.

Tears. He leaves, music swells, she steps into the downpour and starts to scour a littered metro alley for Cat, and. . . The school P.A. comes on with a last minute unscheduled weather forecast and a revised after school schedule. Games are postponed till. . . Practices rearranged for. . .

By the time the announcements end, the bell rings, backpacks are grabbed, the room empties, and the class is gone. Ahhhhh!!!!! Close, so close to finishing the movie. Damn. Now I'll have to start tomorrow with the final one+ minute, but the magic's lost. Even Audrey Hepburn can't do much in a minute. I'll have to back it up, give another intro, and try to recapture the spell and pathos.

Rabbit-out-of-the-hat time.

The next day I try but they can't get into it, barely settle down, and the movie's over. Poof. But I'm not willing to let Audrey Hepburn finish like this. I do something I haven't done for a while.

Here, I say, read this. I pass out an article entitled, A Valentine For Audrey, My Huckleberry Friend. Page 1 is a reprint of a newspaper column I wrote for a long ago Valentine's Day asking Audrey Hepburn to be my Valentine. Page 2 is a photocopy of her reply on her own personalized stationery. The room grows quiet. I silently reread it myself for the hundredth time. The class remains quiet even as students finish.

- Mr. Bentley, how old were you when you wrote this? a girl finally asks.

- Forty-two.

- How old was she?

- Sixty-one. . . Eyes go up. . . Yes, I was in love with an older woman. Still am. But it’s OK, my wife isn't worried.

- Isn't received misspelled?

- It is. She was fluent in several languages so her minor slip in one is very understandable. But it's the thought in any case.

The class takes this in, and I can see that the Holly Golightly magic has been partly recaptured. This is good, and I'm happy about it. Life needs some sweet magic.

Moon River Wider Than A Mile – *If you're ever in doubt what to do in a situation just ask yourself, What would Audrey Hepburn do? There's not a better educational model or part-time conscience.*

Closure: There's a spring feeling to Audrey Hepburn, a sense that we're rotating into stronger sunshine. It's as if the noon sun's been arrested in its course and added real warmth to our lives, with the promise of even better days ahead. I keep the thought to myself. Teens will accept the personal, but the sappy ass maudlin would be pushing it.

I like this kind of test Mr. Bentley, says a perky-eyed girl in the front.

- What kind of test? I ask playing dumb.
- You know, this kind.
- And what kind's that?
- The kind that we don't have to read or write for.
- You mean a short answer, highly objective test?
- Yeah.
- I don't blame you for liking it. I did too when I was student. It used to be the main kind of test we took. I like it now for grading.
- So can we have more of them?
- Sure, maybe one or two more. Why not?

There are smiles all around, I'm not surprised. Students are boosting their averages and without hours of outside reading and writing. These 10th graders just took an old fashioned spelling/vocabulary test on Words Often

Confused, e.g. their, they're, there; affect, effect; etc. This student, and most of them, like anything with quick positive feedback/results, but it's precisely this kind of test and lessons that coordinators tell us not to give, i.e. ever since whole language, holistic grading it's a strict diet of read & write, read & write, with timeouts for more read & write.

Sidebar: Half a dozen years ago we have a highly qualified AP teacher who's taught all over the world. She takes a look at our curriculum and comments, This must be the only school system in the country that doesn't have a K-12 skills rubric and doesn't teach *any* grammar. She moves for other reasons after one year, but her wisdom stays with me and it's a comfort.

She has reaffirmed what most of us know, but I'm not in charge and there's only so much headbutting I want to do. Several coordinators back I'm ordered to stop teaching vocabulary. Students don't learn words by memorizing definitions, I'm told. Nonsense, I say, I know plenty of words because I memorized them, and I know how to spell a bunch more because I memorized them too. Memorize *and* use, memorize *and* use – do the two together and it works. If teachers of the past were guilty of teaching too much grammar, the modern 7-12 teaching generation is guilty of teaching too little, and not even knowing it themselves. We threw out the baby with the bath, made English education into a School Of Schlock.

A student emails me a composition because her printer is down. Nothing unusual. It's what they're supposed to do if their printer doesn't work. I also suggest they email it to their own school internet account and to bring it in on a CD or floppy just in case. They are told all this in writing back in September, and they're told to give it a practice run so there're no later surprises like the school computer can't read their disk. As a last resort, if they can't print or email, they're suppose to hand copy their paper off the monitor and turn in a neatly written paper. Most won't do this, they'd rather take a late penalty than duplicate their effort, i.e. I typed it once, now you expect me to freaking write it out? That's unfair. I understand their attitude, but it's still -10/day if late.

I grade the girl's composition and pass it back. She studies it long and hard like it's The Daily Racing Form, and she's overdue for a winner. She raises her hand.

- Cassandra?

- You took off because I don't have paragraphs?

- Do you have them?

- No, but my mother's email reformatted the text. Look!. . . She holds up a correctly formatted copy of the same composition.

- What's that?

- It's my original.

- Why didn't you turn in that copy?

- It's too light. You couldn't have read it.

- Looks fine to me from here. In any case you have to give me the copy you want graded. You sent me an emailed copy, that's what I graded.

- But it's not fair. Look. It should've had paragraphs.

- Fine. I'll change the grade in the computer and in my gradebook. You now have 5 more points.

She's still studying the graded comp and her hand is back in the air.

- Cassandra?

- And you took off 10 points because I didn't have 2 highlighted vocabulary words. Look. . . She holds up the original that I never saw until seconds ago and there's one word highlighted. . . I should have another 5 points, she says.

- Why?

- I have a highlighted word.

- Not on the copy I graded.

- But you can't highlight in an email.

- You can underline or italicize or make it bold. Something so the word stands out. Or you could have asked for the email, highlighted the word, and given it back to me. Or you could have emailed it to yourself, done the highlighting, then turned it in. How do I know you didn't just highlight it and are guilty of originally not following directions?

- There are ways to tell. This highlighting is old. . . And she scratches at it.

- I'm not interested. You're not getting the 5 points. If you want to talk more about it, I'll see you after class, or after school.

She starts muttering, It's not fair, and keeps it up. The class is smiling, laughing, egging her on. This is a classic example of the student belief that they should be listened to, not read.

Flying Coach *– As hard as you work to make directions clear and concise, someone will always muddle them up. You need to rework assignments every year and strive for the perfect directions, the perfect handouts. It's not going to happen, there are humans involved here. It'd be easier to teach sign language to primates.*

Say What? *– You foul up directions, teacher doesn't cut you any slack, what's* ***that*** *all about? I suspect the teacher really doesn't like you. Or that you're really a Class A fuck up.*

April break comes-and-goes. It was a beautiful week off with a 9 week run now to graduation. My first class back looks as dead as some of the characters in *All Quiet On the Western Front*, our current novel.

- So how was everyone's vacation? I ask.

No response.

- Anyone go anywhere exciting?

No response.

- See any interesting movies, plays, concerts, games?

No response.

- Have any memorable adventures?

No response.

- Wasn't there a brush fire in the area?

No response.

- So, you're well rested and itching to go?

No response. I sigh. Their verbal water hasn't broken yet, the thrill of education's still on April Break. The only happy ones are the parents. I tell a student to take off his hat, and I pass out a WWI reporting piece by Alexander Woollcott called, The Story Of Verdun Belle. It's a 90-year-old story about a mongrel and his Marine master that'll make a nice bit of supplemental reading with our war novel and just might wake up this group, i.e. who doesn't warm up to a good dog story, except a cat.

One of my sophomores is bouncing off the charts. Antsy to the max like maybe he's on drugs, or ingested too much sugar, or confusing spring break with World Lit. He's bouncing around in his seat and proclaiming, I'm a happy guy, and I'm a really good poet.

I've heard a lot of lines in my years but never this one and I can't resist.

- So let's hear a poem, I say.

- What?

- Let's hear a poem, I say serving up a raw challenge.

- I can make them up fast.

- So let's hear one.

He starts off singing, Mr. Bentley one day–

I cut him off with a, Get a different topic. U-turn please. This particular student would like nothing better than to use an improv piece as payback for past grades and detentions, but no way. As much as I believe in freedom in the arts, freedom does have restrictions in this class.

- I can do this, he says but he seems stymied.

I wait along with the rest of the class and finally say, Tell you what. Forget the poem, let's hear a rap like Eminem in *8 Mile*. *It's dated*, I think, but it's my rap base, some of the little I've ever listened to. The pause continues, he still isn't inspired, and someone else says, I'll give you a beat. The beat turns out to be a jerky spasmodic wheel with a chunk out of it: wop-wop, cho-cho-cho-ching, baa-bing-baa-wop-wop. . . But it works and the potential rapper's bouncing his head, and getting into it. Several in the class have taken up the beat, and the rapper's off and laying it down.

- There's a phone by the door, teacher's looking at me. There's another kid who went to school with the first kid. . .

I like *8 Mile*, but this is just terrible pathetic tripe of the highest order. I mean, I know he's limited here in school, i.e. no fuck/suck, can't gas about shooting cops/teachers, pimping his bitches, etc. But this rapper loses the rhythm, there's no rhyme. It's ametrical, arhythmical, a-mess. A free form, free verse, free floating, freestyle bunch of jive with no center and no heart. He's keeping it too loose, it ain't got no juice. It's not even good tripe. *Or* could it be it's so brilliant, so cutting edge, so far beyond established norms it's pushing new horizons for future artists? . . . Nahhhh, it sucks, in my limited rap opinion, though it *is* gutsy of him to try.

- OK, all right, I say and I start clapping and the class joins in. I'm going to encourage him.

Give 'Em The Clap *– Sure this self proclaimed artist's a terrible poet/ lyricist, but what's one more in the world? Thought: Hitler was a failed painter. Perhaps if his own people cheered on his painting the world could have skipped WWII.*

No Money Down *– You may think you lack natural rhyme and rhythm but look deeply within, it's all there: G-clef, G-spot, G-whiz.*

Rap = poetry, which I taught a lot of over a lot of years. I don't do much anymore and I don't know why other than maybe I've lost a little poetry in my own soul. Back in the day students read all kinds of poetry from all eras, compile their own original poetry into projects, memorize lengthy narratives like The Cremation Of Sam McGee, Casey At the Bat, The Raven, The Highwayman, etc. plus soliloquies and sonnets from Shakespeare, shorter poems from Frost, Emily Dickinson, Poe, Langston Hughes, et al. I memorize a lot of them myself to show it can be done. We study and analyze song lyrics like U2 and share personal favorites. Years later students tell me they still remember their memorized pieces.

At the end of the month teachers get input forms on National Honor Society applicants. This vote calls for judgments on a variety of things including attitude, personality, and pretty much any other subjective facets you want to comment on. If it were up to me it'd be a 95% matter of straight academics, i.e. the brainiest highest achievers in the toughest courses, the ones with the Hail Mary scores, the miracle of Lourdes GPA's are in. Being only a good or very good student wouldn't cut it even if the resume says captain of this, president of that, stellar personality, award winning glockenspiel player, etc.

Sometimes I feel like the dinosaur Dirty Harry trying to police a world he scarcely recognizes anymore. But what areyagonnado? I fill out the NHS form.

There are 36 school days left of increasingly warmer days, brighter sun, and happier people. It's not quite time to put the pedal-to-the-metal and shoot for the finish line. But it is the beginning of the end..

May – The Daisy Chain

Nothing says May like budding trees, high pollen, sneezing, coughing, and OuWaOuWaOuWa!!! a fire drill. First day of the month the alarm goes off and my class moves out in an orderly but excited manner. Everyone's smiling and talking i.e. the modern day version of frolicking naked around the May Pole except we're just standing around talking, wondering if maybe there's really a fire, or at least a bomb threat so we can stay out longer.

I direct my class to keep going till we're totally through the parking lot to the edge of the woods. We're farther away than any other class and the students love it. It'll delay us getting back in and on a day like this that's not a hardship.

An administrator's staring at me and I hold up a green card, Everything A.O.K. I fill out an abbreviated attendance memo, check off All Present, sign it, and send it over with a student. I have no idea if everyone's here, I'm half-assing, going through the motions, feeling the chances very slim that anyone's missing. At worst one of my students is with his/her butt squeeze in another class and the only things burning are their pants.

Fire drills are a good chance to socialize with other teachers, and there are bunches clustered together laughing, talking, just not taking this drill seriously. These drills can also be an excellent opportunity to speak privately with students which I sometimes do. Last fall during a fire drill I hear Cosgrove, one of my zero liners, bragging to his friends how he just flunked another quiz. He's talking loudly and surreptitiously glancing my way, one of those I-want-you-to-hear-this-but-I-don't-want-any-grief-over-it-since-I'm-technically-not-talking-to-you spiels. I should know better, but I can't resist. I motion Cosgrove over. He looks a couple of times, I nod, and when it's just the two of us I put on a bleaching light.

- You know, you should really consider dropping out of school. . . I stand so my back's to the sun and he's squinting to see me.

- What? Drop out?

He says it like he's never had the thought while fighting off the urge to raise his hand to shield the sun, which would not be a manly cool thing to do.

- Sure, drop out, why not? You're doing zero work, sleeping in class, and not learning a thing. Frank Zappa said, Want an education? Go to the library. Or you could look into home schooling, though I don't think that'd work for you. I recommend that you drop out and make your part-time job full-time. Make money, learn the trade better, maybe eventually start your own business. Get a GED one day if you feel you're missing it.

He ponders all this, and it takes a while for him to come up with his rejoinder.

- I don't really like my job that much.

I think to myself, *You're a poor lazy bastard, but a great idiot.* I keep the alfresco insult to myself and throw out the last of my pimping the jack counsel.

- Then how's 'bout transferring to a trade or technical school? Or enlist. You're wasting a year of your life here and you're not even making money doing it.

Cosgrove smiles a vacuous smile, and I know I might as well be lecturing the parked cars around us. I keep him squinting for a few more seconds before waving him off.

The next day in class I say to him, You're back. I guess our talk yesterday didn't sink in, huh? He says, What talk? I look into his eyes and see he's serious. The one in the parking lot, I say. Huh? he says honestly puzzled. Never mind, I say, forget it, though you apparently already have.

Pissing Into The Wind – *Though fire drills are an excellent time for straight talk, those with ears don't always hear, those with brains don't always think, i.e. this is primo territory for airheads to air out. Still, it isn't a total waste. There's sun, increased melatonin and Vitamin D production, and the chance the school really will burn or explode.*

Student Thought Virgin – *And how great is this crowded parking lot and the funny sound the fire alarm makes!? Awesome!*

Fire drills are usually routine, sometimes they're fun. There's a steep bank on the other side of the school and students with spring fever like to roll down it. Some like to break out farther and get onto the track. They'll walk laps for as long as time allows which is ironic since if it were mandated PE they'd prefer to sit. There's a hotdog vendor a quarter mile away but it's off school grounds and out of bounds physically, and nutritionally.

Writing Faux Pas: A student in analyzing *All Quiet On the Western Front* says, The author says something, then right after says what would happen if or if not it were to happen. It may sound confusing but Erich makes it easy to comprehen (sic) without getting confusing. . . Another student talking about the same novel says, The deaths Paul named were deadly and most times there is a chance that they will not make it home cured. . . A third student observes, His leg was cut up and was lying in his bed, awake, thinking.

It's Teacher Appreciation Week and I wonder what our reward will be this year. I already have thrown out 2 ballpoint pens and 2 small calculators (none of which worked after a few dormant years), 2 tote bags – all with the system's name, and a t-shirt with the school's name. The only thing I ever used, and still use, is one of the tote bags. Recently I put it over my head and masqueraded as the unknown teacher, but it was dated and the class didn't get it. Some years we have a generous luncheon set up by the parents' group, and 2 years running we got individual massages from a pro who worked on you in the faculty room with no threat of police arrest.

Monday of the week we get a small pen light that doesn't work. I unscrew the battery compartment and it's corroded. Nobody's works and we're told they'll be reordered. Tuesday we get another tote bag with the school name except this one's for a laptop which I don't have. There's no laptop Wednesday, there's nothing for the rest of the week, not even a continental breakfast, not even a pen. My wife's faculty on the other hand gets food all week including 2 hot meals.

Johnny Appleseed – *If you want gifts and continued appreciation become an elementary teacher. They really rake it in at Christmas, T.A. Week, and the end of the year. Hug a kid, and you hug the parent. Those little shits have power.*

Driving into work I hear a morning radio host ask, Who were the teachers who most influenced you? That's an easy one for me. Most of the teachers I had K-12 had no lasting impact, a bunch still serve to remind me of what *not* to do. Only one truly stands out and that's a man I'll call The Colonel, a great educator who I had for several courses in college when I first got out of the army. He's both a university director and part-time teacher. He's witty and insightful and can take the deadest material and breath life into it, e.g. he brings in fencing foils when we read *Hamlet* to demonstrate the switching of the blades. He's a retired army officer who fought in the Pacific and later taught at West Point. He's short and stocky – a powerful physique that matches his intellect. I'm blessed to have him, and I let him know by word and action that I appreciate him even though I'm in college and there's no official week for that.

Mr. B, the freshman girl in study hall says, do you know anything about the police being here today?

- I did hear something about it, but not much. What do you know?

- I heard a bunch of seniors were drinking at a UConn party.

- I heard the same thing.

Rumors are swirling around the school that a bunch of our seniors went to spring fling weekend at Storrs, there's alcohol present, the party gets raided, and our students are arrested for possession even though they aren't drinking. I'm not about to inflame or validate this unsubstantiated rumor, but I do add a closing thought.

- I don't know why if something's done off campus and on the seniors' own time the cops are in our building now, I say. It's a puzzle. Of course, if you bring drugs or alcohol into school, either internally or externally, the cops will definitely be escorting you out. That's as true now as it was when I went to high school.

- Mr. Bentley, the frosh pauses and says, you sound just like my grandfather.

What!? Grandfather? Grandfather, did she say? Sigh. *Bah-bing for her.*

If You Open Up Don't Drool – *It's called the generation gap and the longer you teach the greater it grows. In any case keep an eye out for drugs and alcohol. Your own: Flomax, Geritol, Dulcolax, Metamusial, Philip's Milk Of Magnesia, Glucosamine, Calcium Citrate, Preparation H, Fish Oil, etc. don't count.*

The rumor the freshman girl and I are discussing turns out to be slightly off. Turns out it was a local party with about 18 students and that the athletes get suspended for a couple of games. At least that's what one of the athletes tells me. The school never does give the faculty a heads-up, and the party itself never makes the press. Most of what happens in most schools involving drugs/alcohol, I believe, stays private. It's not quite hear-no-evil, see-no-evil, speak-no-evil, but it's certainly avoid publishing evil if at all possible. To some of the media monitoring public, our school's locked in the halcyon days of *Pleasantville*, *Lake Wobegon*, and *High School Musical.*

I know a lot more happens than makes the press, but just *how* much more happens only the students themselves know for sure. I *do* know that alcohol/drugs result in some interesting malaprops in student compositions. Just in the last month I get, They arrived at school and the kids *pilled* up outside the front entrance. . . The person on the bottom *bong* would sleep on the floor. . . Everyone knows what it is to be *exited*. . . I think the key words are supposed to be pulled, bunk, and excited, but who knows for sure?

Of course these lines in themselves don't prove the existence of alcohol/ drugs in students' lives any more than spacey, muddled, confused thoughts or behavior does. If a simple snapshot proved alcohol/drugs then I have a lot of students who ought to be in rehab/juvenile court. Examples: I watch a student walk into a door, and a few days later when he turns his head to talk and he walks into a wall. This student isn't high, he just can't walk and talk. They're out there. . . A student falls out of his chair like a kindergartner with burgeoning motor skills. He's not disoriented, just a clumsy, web-only type, whose brain is rewiring and pruning his cellular synapses for a future life of chairman of the chair.

None of this is proof of anything but being a teenager in the midst of hard wiring his/her motor development. Aristotle: The young are permanently in a state resembling intoxication; for youth is sweet and they are growing.

Flashback: I suspect a girl of being high almost everyday and relay her symptoms to one of our ruling dukes. Duke is hesitant to call in the parents, but another teacher backs me with the same observations, and dad's contacted and a conference set up. Dad's ex-military with closely cropped hair, beefy Popeye forearms, and he's ready to go after me for accusing the apple of his eye without hard proof. I'm nervous, out there, anticipating a slugfest in a closet-like office, worried too that dad won't buy into it and that the girl will only get worse. No one in the school's history up to this point's ever accused a student of being on drugs with only circumstantial evidence, and I'm visualizing the worst.

Dad comes in tense, only slightly under the boiling point. I preface my remarks with, I like your daughter, see a lot of potential in her, and I have no proof of anything, but let me tell you what I've observed, things she's said and done, and you can draw your own conclusions. As the minutes tick by dad's sour look changes to a grimace, then to a fluster, and winds up with a quiver and a nose wipe. He finally says, It's true, I know it, all of it. The problem's that I never had any money growing up myself, and now I do and I wanted my daughter to have everything I didn't have. I give her too much money. He tells us how much her weekly allowance is, money with no strings or accountability, and I'm amazed. It's like 5x my own mad money. The anticipated confrontation winds up positive and the girl's work does improve.

Don't Shoot The Arrow Then Paint The Target *– Trust your instincts, but back them up with hard data. Legally you're expected to act in place of a reasonable parent, in loco parentis. And while many parents are instinctive and emotional, just like you, most appreciate the truth, even the drug related ones.*

Up Down All Around *– One of the 7 Dwarfs was Dopey and he lived up to his name. If you act dopey too, just remember that school is an ongoing field sobriety test. Stay straight. The school doesn't look any better or the day get any shorter clogging up your liver, kidney, lungs, or nose.*

The office phones and wants Lyle sent down. Lyle's sitting in the next to last seat by the windows and is barely awake. Lyle, go to the office, I say. What's it about? he's suddenly all attentive. They didn't say, I tell him. . . I'm at the end of a lesson and I really want him and the disruption gone fast. I write out the pass and wave it at him. Lyle stands up, takes off his hooded sweatshirt that he's never without even on the hottest days, and hands it to the burned-out girl behind him. I think nothing of it. He leaves. Five minutes later the period ends, and I'm on hall watch. The Popeye Doyle who called walks by and I ask him what he wanted with Lyle. I heard he was using this morning, Doyle says, and in possession so I had him searched. But he was clean. . . I think for a minute and say, I think I smelled pot on him when he walked up to get his pass. Yeah, Doyle says, but Lyle says he smoked before school and off school grounds. We're still going to nail him for coming in high, but I really wanted him on the possession. Wait a minute, I say and tell narc-man about the sweatshirt. Doyle's off and running, but we both know it's too late. He finds the girl and the sweatshirt, but they're both clean.

It's the one time that I know I really blew a drug/alcohol bust. Can't catch them all, or even most. But when it intrudes on the class I'm willing to try.

The Nose Knows *– Red Skelton said, How can a kid ten years old find a dope pusher and the FBI can't? Keep your eyes, ears, and nose open. Pot and most liquors smell, users use and abuse. They're not all Stepford students.*

You Light Up Your Life *– There's nothing that blocks drugs: not Prohibition, DARE, Carrie Nation, the temperance movement, the President's War On Drugs, BATF, etc. There's only you, the student, and if you is not enough, get help. That's why we're here, sweetheart.*

I'm cleaning desktops one morning before school and I come across, Stevie Harvey still smokes pot. It's written neatly in ink and there's no missing it. Stevie Harvey? I think. The same Stevie Harvey I had 20 years ago? Is he attending night school in this classroom? Is he on the 3rd shift cleaning crew? I ask around, no staff member knows anything, so I ask my classes. Oh yeah, one boy says, I wrote it, Stevie Harvey told me to. How do you know Stevie Harvey? I ask. I work part-time with him at the restaurant, the boy says and adds, am I in trouble? No, I say, but Stevie Harvey is if he still smokes pot, brags about it, has a teen write about it, and wants to be remembered for it.

Maybe Stevie's not temporarily forgotten, but he sure is gone, gone, gone. I don't say anything more and the air clears of imagined smoke and bygone addled students.

For years I want *Reefer Madness*, *Lost Weekend*, or *Days Of Wine and Roses* in the Film course but somehow it never happens. Similarly we don't read anything in my courses that deals with alcohol/drugs. There's the drunk Porter in *Macbeth*, Martha and George in *Who's Afraid Of Virginia Woolf*, and a few more minor imbibing scenes/characters throughout our literature. But there could be a lot more. Rudyard Kipling said, Words are, of course, the most powerful drug used by mankind. Kipling's right, but it wouldn't hurt to have some drug centered stories too. Even if they turn out to be a waste. Even if it's only waste for the wasted.

Sky Pilot – *Books are the ultimate drug in the school environment, i.e. they bring you up, they bring you down, they distort reality, they validate reality. Books are a safe drug to push.*

Nowhere Is Too Far – *The surrealistic artist Salvador Dali said: Take me, I am the drug; take me, I am hallucinogenic. Dali didn't do drugs, he didn't need to. He was high enough on life, and himself. You need to be too.*

Teacher Warning Sidebar: None of you is a church certified saint and none should pretend to be. Students can spot a phony faster than you can transfer your retirement money to the Cayman Islands. On the other hand you're not an addict either; chances are you live a life of moderation with slips now-and-then. Don't be afraid to acknowledge your humanness. Students will want specifics, but just smile and tell them you'll talk when they're on the other side in the confessional.

I know firsthand of teachers having a drink on the clock (though not routinely), hear rumors of one habitual sneak drinker, read about female students soaking tampons in vodka, am told by an eyewitness of one public school administrator smoking weed during the workday, and then there's the legend of a head custodian who reportedly hides bottles all over the complex as evidenced by his crimson face and alky slanted eyes. We've lost too many fine students and recent graduates over the years to alcohol/drugs, and there's been a number of teachers in this area fired for drugs. Writer Aldous Huxley says that most of us live in a rather dull universe most of the time but that it's not the only universe and he talks about his own drug use. Sure as shit school can be a dull universe, but tough titty. Education's still the only thing we're gonna chug, shoot, slam, snort, or inhale in my class and in my corner of the building, so help me God. Amen.

The Film class is watching *The Deer Hunter*. It's after the wedding reception, and De Niro, Walken, John Cazale, et al. are hunting in what's supposed to be the mountains of Pennsylvania but which in reality are the rugged Cascade Range. I explain all this to the class then give them a warning.

- If you don't want to see a deer killed, you'd better avert your eyes.

- Really? They're going to kill a deer? a girl asks.

- They're really not going to kill it. It's a trained deer that's fenced in and's been given a sedative. In real time it takes 30 minutes for the deer to drop but on film it'll look like it's just been shot.

Robert De Niro raises his rifle and the girl puts her head down between her arms. De Niro hesitates, the deer bolts, there's a chase, De Niro gets the shot again and takes it. The deer drops in slo-mo, 4 hoofs straight up. I look at the girl, and her head's still down even though the scene's over and there's no immediate forecast of roasted venison.

A few days later after the funeral scene and the singing of God Bless America a normally quiet girl thanks me for showing this Vietnam classic. I didn't think I was going to like it, she says, but it was really excellent. Happy you enjoyed it, I say and I am. Acceptance and appreciation are not a given and there's nothing better than a student thank-you after you just showed the controversial and put your ass out there. I also like converting the philistines, though no one's called me Moses yet.

Snippets: One of my students nearly runs me down in the hall tooling around on his 4-wheel electric scooter. He's pulling reverse wheelies, going sideways on 2 wheels, cutting people off. He tells me he hurt both his ankle and shoulder so he can't operate a wheelchair. To him it's life now in the EZ Pass Lane. To the elder within me it's extreme asinine sports. To the teen part of me it looks like a helluva lot of fun.

I'm sitting in caf study when there's a loud CLANG! followed by a bunch of girls loudly gabbing. I go over. The metal trim that goes around a sprinkler head in the ceiling's fallen onto their table. Just crashed down. I assure them they're OK, while smiling over the near irony of getting T-boned by the safety equipment.

A student asks me during a vocabulary lesson what my favorite word is and I say, Bentley, what's yours? Incognito, he says. This is a word the student didn't know until a minute ago, and now it's his favorite word? And why's that? I ask smiling. Because I like the sound of it, he says. He also likes the sound of belching, squeaking his rubber soles on the floor, and cracking knuckles so I'm not impressed.

One of my male students is standing outside my room with a Jack Daniel's t-shirt on. I momentarily debate about saying anything because I've had trouble with him before and he's with a girl now and might decide to posture, but I go ahead and tell him it's a really nice shirt but to turn it inside out when he gets a chance. Hours later he walks by me with the bourbon message still L&C so I flag him down and ask, What gives? I did turn it inside out, he tells me, but it had some nasty white deodorant stains and I didn't have anything else. I laugh and wave him on.

Wife Story – She escorts one of her tiny students to the bus line, and out of the clear blue Tiny Tot says, My mother doesn't like any of you teachers. My wife's predictably surprised and says, She doesn't? and T.T. says, No, *her* doesn't. That's why *her* wants to move. . . And out of the mouths of babes.

After over 8 months of deliberation I decide to retire at the end of this year and I submit my paperwork to the state. There've been just too many changes with even more chicken shit planned for next year. For most of a teacher's career it's adapt or be gone. Then you reach a stage when you no longer have to shed the old layer of skin and you can crawl out of the educational swamp and go your own way. It's bittersweet, but exciting, and a well earned advancement up the evolutionary scale to a new world. I toast myself, but tell no one except the state and my wife.

Where's Roff? I ask. I've been asking this same question everyday for a month when I take attendance and everyday his friends tell me the same thing: Rolf's dropped out and he's not coming back. Rolf's one of my zero liners who sleeps in the back of the room and now I'm told he's sleeping late at home, not working, and getting his license. Amazing. Salt of the fucking earth. Where's he getting the money, and why's he getting rewarded with a license for a lame life of zip? I ask into the wind.

A couple of days later I get an email that Rolf's being officially removed from school, and his guidance counselor brings me Rolf's books, new and unopened. This is a student who came to me at midterm with a different counselor wanting to work a deal. What can Rolf do to pass this course? Counselor 1 asks. The Unstated: His average is too low to be legitimately redeemed and he needs a favor from you Godfather. No way, I tell them. You don't get to take a half year vacation in a full year course and pass. Rolf's been warned nearly everyday to start working and that there will be no deals down the road. No-deal *is* the deal. It's not personal, I say like Vito Corleone. So now Rolf's gone and like Luca Brasi sleeps with the fishes, or at least I get to remove him from my seating chart. For now. Most likely he'll resurface back here, but if he doesn't it's OK. The world needs sleepers and dreamers. Sidebar: The national dropout average is 25%, our state dropout average is less than 20%, and the rate's even lower in this school. We don't have many Rolfs. Flunkees yes, dropouts no.

Kidnapped By The Zombie Troupe – *Realize that no school will ever achieve a 0% failure or a 100% graduation rate. But with NCLB you better try.*

Yes We Have Some Bananas – *School's a privilege in some parts of the world reserved for the rich and the very bright/motivated. But here in the U.S.A. we believe in universal education, i.e. school for even the Rolfs. For some of you students there are better things than staying, and worse things than going, and ain't that a fucking trip.*

Since the beginning of the year my zero liners have shown about as much change as the heads on Mt. Rushmore and that's rare. Usually this time of year I'm rejoicing with a bunch of comeback artists, the ones who vie for most improved, and whether or not it's fair, such students get a lot more attention than the ones who work diligently all year and never let up. It's Shakespeare's Prince Hal in *Henry IV*. Hal's hung around with a riotous gang, but those days are done and he talks about how his reformation will glitter over his faults, how he'll seem better now for having been bad.

My own zero liners haven't made the turnabout. One does some threatening, is outplaced for a while, but he's back and works about as well as a dried out pen. Another was pulled out of my class at midterm and put into a tech ed course so he doesn't waste a half year doing nothing. This is totally logical but unprecedented in my years. Students who sprain the brain, usually flunk, repeat the course, and second time around get added support, threats, and breaks. There's a hesitancy to Kevorkian them, to endlessly recyle do nothing lifers till they're old enough to drink and vote, at which time they're legally gone anyway.

Spring in my room is a dead zone with this group and a condition of anal glaucoma for me, i.e. I can't see a bunch of their 16-year-old asses passing, or another bunch getting above D. It's gutter and curb top achievement. Dismal dog shit.

Sort of Good News: Two of the original zero liners are semi-reformed. One's been making an erratic comeback since November. Her license depends on passing the course, and it's going to be a June photo finish. Another original's been getting tutored in lieu of class since early winter and will join the photo finish. Definite Bad News: About a half dozen original non-F-ers have been on a steady downhill slide since late autumn and may or may not pass. I'm not happy about any of it, though the worst dunce caps are not really suffering over grades. In psychological terms they've embraced a status quo bias i.e. they're inclined to keep things as they are and not change established behaviors for anything as abstract as a C, B, or A.

Honestly, and in my heart-of-hearts, I wish all students were motivated or at least responsive to motivation. I wish no one would finish lower than a C, and I wish all/most would excel. Those are my wishes, but psychologically

I'm slipping into a Taoist world where I'm no longer trying to save the world and every last flunky in it. It's wu wei – action through inaction, the idea that by doing nothing everything will be done. I'm not exactly clear on what that means, but it's sure as hell restful.

Do Not Pass Goal, Do Not Collect Squat – *Former Yankees' owner George Steinbrenner withheld positive vibes for anything but the big shit because he believed butt pats, high-fives, fist bumps, etc. meant more when they were really earned. Of course he dealt with adult professionals and some of these teens are barely weaned. Still, D's, marginal efforts, or half-hearted comebacks don't deserve much – maybe a Bronx cheer like, Pfffftt!*

The African American Lit and Film class finishes *Malcolm X*, *The Great White Hope*, and the modern classic *Sounder*. *Sounder's* way under grade level, but it's beautifully written and not every read has to be challenging or even on grade level. I have the author William Armstrong as a guest speaker a couple of times years ago. He's a fascinating man who taught for 52 years at a prep school near here all while raising a family and herd of sheep. He doesn't suffer fools and is reputed to throw an occasional book. But he seems like a gentle man to me and when he reads the concluding paragraphs of *Sounder* to us he gets all choked up. He takes a pause to gather himself then tells us that when he wrote the ending he knew it was good. He adds he does most of his writing at 4 a.m. when his mind's fresh from sleep. The book's preface says the story's based on a tale that an old black man told him so I ask just how much of the book is the old man's story and how much is his own creative flight. Armstrong just smiles. He says that when he's called down to NYC to meet the publisher for the first time there's surprise he's white. They just assumed that anyone who could write so realistically about the joys/heartaches of a black family had to be writing from personal experience. He adds that Cicely Tyson lobbied hard for the part of the mother in the movie.

Here Without Further Ado – *There's no doubt writers can give some fascinating insight. Many of the great ones are introverted neurotics who tend to wreck lives around them but you're not looking to date or marry them. Authors are very safe at the guest speaker distance. Try to get some.*

Professional Sidebar: I'm not sure I'd ever recommend that any student become a writer mainly because if I have to recommend it the teen probably lacks the prerequisite fire-in-the-gut that's fundamental to most scribes. Plus, writing's a lonely profession. It's a perpetual mental solitude that builds on itself and sometimes gets physically lonely too: Thoreau at Walden Pond, Kerouac on Desolation Lookout, Marjorie Rawlings in the Florida backwoods, etc. It's a life of damnable isolation that can result in strange/ skewed thoughts, weird/disingenuous behavior, and substance abuse. A life that sometimes produces little good other than the manuscript itself. Emmy award winning Rod Serling: Writing is a demanding profession and a selfish one. It is compulsive and exacting. I didn't embrace it, I succumbed to it.

I've recommended newspaper work to some students over the years because reporting's more social, more civilized, and it teaches the basics. In the end though all writing comes down to the person and a blank sheet of paper, and if more mature minds than a student's have collapsed under the pressure, shouldn't we teachers be careful just how many blank sheets of paper we assign, and how often?

My sophomores are reading *Maus* by Art Spiegelman in class, and for homework they're nearly done with *Night*, the Holocaust memoir by Elie Wiesel. I ask the open-ended questions in one class: What do you think of Elie Wiesel so far? What kind of young man is he?

A girl's waving her arm like a windshield wiper on max, and I can't tell if she's energetically volunteering or showing off, but I call on her.

- Sierra?

- He's really not a very bright person.

- Why do you say that?

- I think he should of been smart enough to get away before the Nazis got him.

- At the beginning? How would he know enough to get away?

- I don't know. He just should of. Everyone knows what the Nazis did.

- Maybe historically, from our perspective. But how would Elie Wiesel have known at the time? Was there anything in the book? Let's keep our judgments based on the book.

- He just went along with what everyone else was doing. That's not very bright.

- Because of what Moshe the Beadle told them?

- Who?

- Moshe the Beadle, Elie's mentor. Didn't he warn everyone in the village what was going to happen?

- I don't remember that.

- He's on your character list.

- I didn't fill it out.

- So when you say young Elie's not very bright, you're not really basing it on anything in the book.

- It's just the way I feel.

- So it's really an instinct, not an opinion.

- What do you mean?

- Opinions need informed information behind them. Yours doesn't have any. It's just a feeling, an instinct.

- Whatever.

- Do you think yours is an opinion?

- Yes.

- Then your opinion's wrong . . . Even as I say it I realize that Sierra doesn't get the difference, and I'm climbing aboard the Ferris Wheel.

- How can it be wrong, it's my opinion?

- So?

- Opinions can't be wrong. They're opinions.

- But they have to be based on something. Yours isn't based on anything but some vague notions of history. This is a literature class and we base opinions in here on the books we're reading.

- So? It's still my opinion.

- Great. . . Let me ask you this. The Nazis had the opinion it was OK to kill Jews, gypsies, political dissidents, the mentally retarded, physically challenged, etc. Actually, it was a belief, but let's call it an opinion. Was that opinion correct?

Sierra pauses. She feels a trap and takes her time.

- No, it's never OK to just kill people. They didn't do anything to the Nazis.

- But the Nazis said the Jews did plenty to them and tied it all into social Darwinism, purity of the race, cultural inferiority, enemies of the state, enemies of the world.

- I don't know what all those are. Maybe they're not good reasons.

- What if the Nazis were just anti-Semitic and didn't like Jews. Is that a good enough reason?

- No.

- So you're saying that for an opinion to be correct the reason behind it has to be correct? Sidebar: I've had these *opinion* conversations before, i.e. it's an old dance. The progression should be instinct, opinion, belief, each requiring a higher level of thought and proof. Instinct/conjecture/gut reaction is what Sierra's expressing. Opinion has thought; belief has more thought and finality. Key Point: Whether it's an opinion or belief, there has to be the lubricant of thought behind it, i.e. neither can have a foundation of just air. And that's both my opinion *and* my belief.

- I guess so.

- So maybe your opinion that Elie Wiesel isn't very bright isn't correct because your reason isn't correct?

- No, he isn't very bright. That's my opinion.

- It's my turn to pause. Is she serious or just stubborn? Is anything happening upstairs?

Loading-loading-loading. This is painful, the death of a thousand cuts. Perhaps reading more of the book and doing the supplemental materials will change her mind. I don't want her taking away the instinct/opinion that Elie Wiesel isn't very bright. But for now we need to break the loop, get concrete, and move on. In my opinion.

- That opinion, backed up like you just did will get you a zero on quizzes and the test, and an F on any compositions. Historically your opinion may be correct, it may even be correct given the facts of the book but you don't know the facts. Better start reading and be able to cite specific people, quotes, and happenings to prove your points and opinions, or it's going to be a long tough last month.

Sierra looks unfazed and I'm sure my attempt at the Socratic method accomplished nothing more than taking ticks off the clock. Maybe I should just lighten up now and say, Outtasight, groovy opinion. It's like you just know what the man's all about, you feel it. Trust the heart not the brain, right-on. Just cause the dude wrote a book doesn't mean he's bright. I mean, look at his picture. . .

Pull Your Pants Up – *Opinions are like assholes. Everyone has them, and many stink.*

The Good Ship Lollipop – *I understand you like to toss out opinions like you're tossing a salad, but opinions require a little thought. It's reasoning, not seasoning.*

Snippets: Another zero liner in World Lit's pulled out by guidance to concentrate on courses the student stands a chance of passing. This is unprecedented so late in the year but I wish the student luck, offer no protests, and experience no teacher remorse. I offered extra help, but the student was unwilling to meet me halfway, or a quarter of the way, or any way but no-way.

One of the nontenured in the department has an Honors' boy come up to her and say, I've been thinking about this grade you gave me on this composition, and it's bullshit. The teacher looks at the composition and it's 2 months old. She tells him, I don't appreciate your tone or language, and I will not discuss this composition. I tell her, Hell yeah! We're not in the antiques business. And we're not sitting in the dunk booth either.

Two former students stop in after school and it's good to see them. I lose contact with virtually all of my formers, and these two young men gave me a lot of laughs, showed a lot of creativity, and it's uplifting to know they just graduated from good colleges and will make their mark in the world. It's a reminder also that not all of this is for naught or just a paycheck.

I'm going over the rough drafts of the African American research projects. I've been taking the students to the library one day a week for the last 5 weeks so I've kept up with their sources, bibliography, quotes/footnotes, and mandated connections to the different historical periods and literature/film we've covered. The rough drafts are lengthy and complicated, and really time consuming to edit. One of the hardest things is dealing with awkwardly worded, unclear sentences/paragraphs. I can mark them AWK or UNC, but students have a difficult time seeing/hearing it and a worse time straightening the confusing thoughts out. Sometimes I just rewrite key lines myself, but I have to limit myself or I wind up grading my own paper. I sometimes tell them they can't use my exact words but to mimic them.

A major problem is that many don't recognize good and bad writing. They don't have that sense which is essentially the same problem every writer has. Ernest Hemingway once told a would-be writer whose copy he'd been editing that a writer needs to develop a sense of what's good and bad even when the writing's his own. And if you can't develop that sense, maybe you're pursuing the wrong field. A Canadian playwright once told me that it isn't unusual for him to type 10 pages of shit and at the end of the day to toss the whole pile. You need that sense.

Still, it's not easy for professionals to be self critical, and many have doubts over the worth of their writing. It's even tougher and sometimes impossible for the student. To compound the problem students don't like to rewrite. They feel they did the paper once, and unlike sex, once is enough.

In any case it's going to take all weekend to get through these rough drafts. So much for the notion that teachers have a short work week, and golfing and yachting weekends.

The Film class finishes *Chariots Of Fire*. I've never shown this movie before and it's a personal favorite. I ask them at one point how they're enjoying it and they're not. Near the end I hear sniffling. A girl turns around and asks the boy behind her, Are you crying? I don't hear his answer but I know I'm pretty choked up myself.

I pass out *Fences* by August Wilson to the African American Lit class. Since *Malcolm X* I decide to finish the course with a series of short works in an attempt to cover as many writers and important works as possible. There's only so much you can do in a semester, and I'm trying to do more. I should know better. It's the annual sense of urgency and surprise that September crawled, and now time's accelerating? WTF Time might be a variable in science but not NOW, not in English! Dr. Seuss: How did it get so late so soon?

- Today's Tuesday. Act 1 is due Friday, I say.

- Mr. Bentley, they all protest at once, the Senior Picnic's Friday!

- Really? Shit. . . I stop, they gasp, crocodile tear time. . . Sorry about that. It slipped out. Well, this throws off the whole reading schedule. Guess we'll just have to have the whole play due next Tuesday. No problem.

- The whole play? they say in unison. By Tuesday?

- That's a week. It's a short play, easy too. Besides, you people haven't been reading anything I've given you so what's the difference when it's due?

- They know I have an excellent point and that most are not going to read this so the buzz lowers to a drone. Then I get crazy.

- You know, I say, maybe I should pray for rain for your picnic. I'm in pretty good with God. Maybe it should rain to punish you for not doing the reading in this course. . . I'm kidding them, of course, but I'm also on thin ice and I know it.

- That's not fair, a girl says.

- No, it's justice.

-That's not justice. It's really selfish. Everyone gets punished because we're not reading?

- You're right. Forget it. May the sun shine brightly on your picnic.

I go to start the film, but something's wrong and the data projector's only projecting a bright rectangle.

- God's punishing you Mr. B, a boy says and the class laughs.

- You're right, I say and I give a perfunctory chuckle. I shouldn't have made light of the whole thing.

I check the connections. The audio plug is in the video input and the data projector is on the wrong source. Incredible. How did this thing get so fouled up? I make the changes. As the ending of *The Great White Hope* starts I pause it and tell the class, I apologize for the delay and stupid glib remarks. Hope you really do have good weather.

Blessed Are The Contrite And Truly Sorry Asses *– We used to say the Lord's Prayer in school, then came a minute of meditation, now there's nothing. If you decide you want to invoke God anyway, be advised that school officials and God have excellent ears. And when they answer you may not like it.*

A few years ago we have a diversity assembly where people talk about diversity and the importance of being accepting. Following the keynotes, students one-by-one share their thoughts and experiences with us. Because we're not a very racially/ethnically/culturally diverse school the revelations tend to be superficial and more personal gripes than anything, e.g. I'm naturally big-boned and it'd be nice if people didn't judge me by the number of lunches I eat. One young man talks about being accepted as a gay and no one thinks anything of it till an adult steps to the mike and says something like, I don't wish anyone here ill but my religion will just not let me accept a gay lifestyle in others. The gym grows quiet, and everyone's looking at each other but nothing's said. Months pass and a new school year starts but the nonaccepting adult is no longer with us. I don't know if the person voluntarily resigned or if the decision came from higher up, even way-way-way up. But there's a vacant seat. Final Thought: I don't know if the silent/meek really will inherit the earth, but they stand a better chance at keeping their jobs.

Film class turns in their final video projects: I Wanna Be Fat, America's Next Top Model (tv show parody), Remember the Quad Stackers (football movie parody), Unreal America (zombie humor), Infamous Riders (stunt bike documentary), et al. As always students love to watch themselves and their classmates. The humor and satire is basic, even corny, but it doesn't matter. It's show biz high school and it's a big hit.

Back in my junior high teaching days I'd be on a 5-day field trip now to Washington DC where we'd see students from all over the country already done with school. Those years of visiting DC grew hot, hotter, and finally broke a record. It's getting hot here too but the stretch run's in sight so let it pour down. I feel like Donovan's Sunshine Superman.

June – Hold The Applause

June, there isn't a better sounding word to me right now, not even Bentley. Traditional Teacher Joke: What're the 3 reasons for becoming a teacher? Answer: June, July, August. The official final day's June 20 which also happens to be the summer solstice – the official start of summer. But Memorial Day weekend's the unofficial start as everyone knows. It's tacking against a real summer breeze now to get students to work. The mental set is sandals and cutoff jeans. Thoreau: It is dry, hazy June weather. We are more of the earth, farther from heaven these days. . . There're two weeks of classes left and a week of final exams. The end's in sight, but it's hardly an unhassled stroll in the sun. Emerson: Do what we will, summer will have its flies.

I'm sitting by the door in caf study with my 70 flies and the other teacher's 60, and it's noisy and hard to concentrate. I'm trying to take attendance and sign out students, and just when I think it can't get any worse a large group walks in and looks around like maybe they just stumbled into the promised land.

- Where do you think you're going? I ask the lead ones.

One hard branded wise-ass looks back over his shoulder and I follow his eyes to a teacher trailing the group. The semi-veteran educator stops dead in front of my table while his students seek out friends and distant corners, then he sits down.

- What's going on? I ask.

- It's too hot in my room to work, he says like we're co-conspirators.

- What?

- It's 88 degrees.

- You're kidding me. So you're not going to teach? You're just keeping your students in here for the period?

He looks at me hard, realizes he doesn't have an ally, gets up, and moves to another table. I'm looking at him like maybe he needs to be tested for whimpism, like maybe if he thinks 88 is a sweat box he needs a Middle East tour in a bio-chem suit. This caf's air-conditioned and it *is* nice in here, but I'm figuring we already have enough students doing nothing. His aren't needed or wanted, and if he wants to use the facility he ought to at least keep them together and try to run a lesson. Sidebar: I'm thinking like an administrator on the verge of writing up a teacher and what's *that* all about?

It doesn't take long and the hard-branded wise-ass starts to act up. I look over at his teacher but the guy's oblivious, or pretends to be. I don't like to usurp a teacher's authority but this one's in here because he doesn't want to do anything so what're the chances he suddenly wants to get involved? I wait, and wise-ass and his buddies get to their feet and start pushing and laughing and acting like this is a fucking elementary school playground. Oblivious teacher's still got his head down reading a magazine. I finally get up and walk over, the devil nipping at my heels.

- Excuse me, enough, stop. Knock off the fooling around and sit down, all of you. You're getting on my nerves.

- What? Whatta we doing wrong? wise-ass wants to know all innocent like.

And just like that I'm in an abbreviated conversation with a bunch of constipated circle jerkers, boondogglers who specialize in random acts of stupidity, students who shouldn't even be in here. . . Of course I don’t say any of it, or even think most of it, but I certainly *feel* it. I try to inwardly smile, breath slowly, control breathing/heart rate, keep that blood pressure around 120/80. TM, drift into The Zone.

The Outhouse Shit Needs To Be Burned – *We're all be in this together so don't be a clueless corn-hole. If you don't want to teach, can't maintain behavior, would just like to be left alone, for heaven's sake go into administration, the State Department Of Ed, or college teaching. With the latter you can get sabbaticals. All provide pensions and benefits.*

Only You Can Prevent Forest Fires – *For some of you students standing's an open invitation to get physical. It's like when you stand all the blood goes south, but there's not much south of the neck that you need in school.*

This class is a lot tougher than my last one, the teen says to no one in particular, and immediately he has everyone's attention.

- Your last one was one-on-one tutoring, wasn't it? I ask.

- No, there were 30 students, 6 teachers.

- Pretty nice.

- It was.

The conversation should end here but another students chimes in with, That's the way it is in the dummy school.

- It wasn't a dummy school, the first lad corrects him.

- What was it? second lad wants to know.

- A school for people with behavior problems.

- No, it was a dummy school.

I break it up before it can get really insulting. Lad 1 isn't offended up to this point and seems to be good naturedly enjoying the talk about his alma mater, but the explosive potential is there. I mean, didn't he just confess to a previous behavior problem? And is it really dormant?

A little while later Lad 2 offers an unsolicited correction on his loss of credit yesterday for not having his book.

- Mr. Bentley, I did have my book yesterday. I was just too dumb to find it in my backpack.

- Guess you belong in the dummy school.

- The class laughs including Lad 1.

- Guess so.

- You walked right into that one, didn't you?

- Yes I did.

To an impartial observer this exchange might not seem very p.c., but every class has its own dynamics and it's up to the teacher to know and understand them. In this particular class I have two students who work hard all the time and like being held up as good examples. There're another 4 or 5 who'll work most of the time if there're no outside distractions and are fine playing the parts of proverbial good kids. There's one who's spacey and likes the attention it brings, and 4 who would prefer to remain x-ray portraits of invisible people. All are fine with kidding around that doesn't involve them, and there're are no natural enemies. Two have permanent deflector shields up to ward off the negative/personal, and demand sensitivity and seriousness even in private. Three practice self-deprecating humor, all consider me fair game for almost any question/comment, e.g. Mr. Bentley you seem rich, are you? Mr. Bentley you should get a tattoo.

The Lifeguard Is On Duty – *It's fine, even ideal that students exchange ideas, differences of opinion, even humor amongst themselves. But you have to monitor it all and be ready to intervene. Be gentle with them and insist* *they be gentle with each other. Disagreement doesn't have to be confrontational. We're not clubbing baby seals here.*

The Womb Is Not A Condo – *Interpersonal and interclassroom debates/ discussions are an important part of school. Be passionate about your opinions, disagree amicably, be generous and willing to concede points, and know enough when to stop. Just like in sex, you don't need to go all the way.*

Early morning before first period a father shows up in my room unannounced and unscheduled. I don't recall this ever happening before but I'm fine with it. He's a good guy and he's concerned about Nigel.

- My son won't be in today, he says. Nigel claims he's sick.

- Sorry to hear that, I say. Tell him I hope he feels better soon.

- I don't think he's really sick. I think he's home gaming on the internet.

- Gaming on the internet? What's that?

- Students compete on-line. They play a variety of popular games. They can network with friends. It's what school and your homework have to compete with.

Interesting, I think. *Guess I heard the term gaming before associated with the computer but I never really thought about it.*

- Is there a major assignment due today? dad wants to know. I'm checking with all of Nigel's teachers.

- No, nothing today. There was a test yesterday on *Night* that Nigel did so-so on. And then we started *Dawn*.

Dad's gone and later I ask one of my classes about gaming.

- Oh yeah, says one of my late nighters. I was playing against a kid from France last night.

- You were? I ask. How? I'm sure you don't speak French.

His answer's a bit confusing but I do catch his point that outbursts and swearing are uni-language. I forget to ask him about the time difference – is he up really late, or really early, and what about Jacques? Hope my man's savvy enough to use any time advantage, though I doubt he sees being wide awake as an advantage. He never does in class. In any case it's U.S.A. vs France and here I was concerned about my man reading *Dawn*.

Lightbulb Moment: It occurs to me that this on-line gaming vis-à-vis with international competition could be tied into World Literature, i.e. it is a cyber field trip across cultures, national boundaries, oceans, and datelines. Must be some related unit I can come up with, possibly as extra credit, that would hook my non-bookish potentially failing students. . . It's a great seminal idea but it's too late for this year, and too late for me, period. Still, it's funny how far a basic idea's come that started with a simple pop-in visit from a father.

Stop Look Listen – *Life's organic. There are new and fresh ideas all around. Be receptive. An old meditation says, Slow me down Lord. . . Good ideas come when you slow down and least expect them.*

Spring sports are over for most. Our boys' volleyball team tries to capture their third straight state title but gets beaten in the finals. A senior spiker complains to me the underclassmen choked, but I remind him it's a team sport. Other athletes are still in the throes of state competition, most notably our best runners. Most are happy that practices and games/meets are finished, which is ironic since sports aren't mandatory so why is it such a joy when something you volunteered for ends? It's ironic, but I guess it's sort of like work, or marriage, or a prostate exam.

There's no better feeling for me than when baseball season ends my first year of teaching. I'm a terrible baseball coach, know little about the sport, and only agree to take the junior high team because it goes along with getting the teaching position. When I'm asked in the job interview if I can coach baseball I tell the principal that baseball's practically my middle name. I do what I have to do to get the job and now every night after practice I phone my brother who's a fine player and coach, tell him how the session went, and he tells me what to do the next day. He coaches the coach.

Unfortunately he cannot give me his hard won insight or eye-hand coordination, and it's a long, long season.

Flashback On the Flashback: I cut an 8th grader who missed the second tryout and I get called into a conference with the father and an administrator. Father gives me hell and calls me sonny. I get to my feet and tell him, I'm a veteran, no one calls me sonny, this meeting's over. Administrator hops to his own feet and manages to calm things down. I reluctantly agree to give the real sonny another tryout. The lesson I take away is that parents who don't get upset at all about poor grades go stratospheric when it comes to sports as if the real sonny is about to be drafted to the big show.

It's just one-thing-after-another during that long ago season. We're way behind in a game so I take out my starting catcher to give his backup some experience. The starter goes into the stands and sits with his girlfriend. I motion him back to the bench but he won't come and tells me, If I'm not going to play I'll sit where I want. I tell him to either rejoin the team or turn in his uniform. I get the uniform.

We're warming up before a game and I go to hit a fly ball to the right fielder but instead I top it and hit a line drive at the first baseman. He gets his glove up but not enough and the liner bends the top fingers back and the ball smashes into his mouth. He jerks backwards into the air like he's been shot and is flat on his back when I get to him. His hand's covering his mouth, there's blood all over. I gently remove this fingers and there're no teeth showing. The front ones have either been knocked out or bent back like they're on hinges. It's the worst moment I have in education. Fortunately he has insurance and is very courageous about it all.

Hara-Kiri Takes Balls – *If you don't want to coach or take extracurricular activities I understand. While they can be a source of great reward and joy, they can also be damn tiring and frustrating, and can whop your ass royally.*

We don't finish with a winning percentage, the mercy rule's invoked against us once, and late in the season I have to recall players I initially cut because players are quitting or getting tossed. An administrator gives me the worst chewing out I ever get to this day. He's yelling so loudly at me in front of my class that a teacher at the far end of the hall closes his door, and all because I tell a parent who's trying to schedule rides I don't know exactly what time our game will end. To his credit the honcho meets me at the door the next morning when I arrive and apologizes. No problem. If baseball serves to make adults out of teens, it also serves to make teens out of adults, and we've all been there, a bit over-torqued.

The season ends, the 8th graders graduate, and I never see most of them again. One eventually becomes a musician, the squat powerful leader becomes a mason, another works as an electrician. A teammate joins the Corps and survives only to have his life fall apart and die young. One is eventually convicted of murder.

Did playing that one season of baseball improve anyone's life? Did it do anything more than fill afternoons and keep everyone off the streets? Is baseball the answer for anything, or is it just a game like any other game, at best a temporary hideout from life's real problems?. . . I don't know the answers. I do know it was a learning experience for all of us and we had some fun too. And I do know it would've been nice to win a few more games and not be responsible for a young man losing his teeth.

It's a scorching 96 degree Monday with high humidity that makes it feel like 102. At 9:30 the announcement comes on: lunch's cancelled, afternoon classes won't meet, school will be dismissed at 11:30. Students go from dripping to tripping. I hear cheering ringing up-and-down the hall, and I'm pretty happy about it myself. Nothing like the unexpected and this is unprecedented. It's been this hot before, but for all the decades we just hung tough like desert Bedouins. I get out of my last ever caf duty and my two senior p.m. classes. I don't expect many seniors to show up anyway. It's senior skip day following prom weekend and the only ones who will be here are the few who either didn't go to the prom or are still concerned with grades. The ones with simple paperclip lives. Sidebar: There are post-prom Mondays I continue on as usual even if there's a mass diaspora to the beach. This may not be nice or educationally sound, but I feel no obligation to accommodate what Walt Whitman called mad, naked summer. Not just yet anyway.

One of my former bubbly students is subbing in the room next to me. I recognize her face but it takes a minute to come up with the name. She was a fine student for me and is set to begin her career now as I'm about to bow out of mine. One generation passeth away, another generation cometh. . . It's said that power doesn't concede easily, not that I have any real power, but whatever authority I do have I don't have a death grip on. In the past I've actually told older teachers who've hung on too long it's time to step down, make way, a new world's awaiting. And I'm prepared now to follow my own advice. Ecclesiastes: To everything there is a season and a time for every purpose under heaven. I've always loved those lines but up till now they've pretty much just been words. The bubbly miss tells me she just graduated and I give her a pennant from her college that was hanging in my room. In that gesture I pass on the scepter, or at least sow some good final seeds. There's not much time left for goodwill gestures.

Mourning Becomes Electra – *Dylan Thomas said, Do not go gentle into that good night. It's great poetry but bad advice. Gracefully relinquish the past. You had your day.*

The Bell Tolls For Thee Schmuck – *Get ready. You think your day's far off, and maybe it is, and maybe it isn't, but guaranteed it's a-coming. It's one truth we all wish wasn't.*

I'm sitting in the faculty room during my planning period reading the newspaper and talking to two other longtime teachers. I almost always work through my planning period alone in my room, but I feel the need today to break out. Three female students come in without knocking, go right to the refrigerator, and take out a container of food. Noisily. It's not unusual for students to use the faculty fridge for club or class functions, but now the girls load up the microwave, punch in some numbers, and while the food spins they gab away like this is the powder room or an iChat. I look at the two other teachers, they raise their eyebrows, and I give a loud harumph.

- Excuse me ladies. How long does your food have to cook?

- Seven minutes, one of them says looking annoyed that I interrupted. A real alabaster princess type.

- How about you find somewhere else to heat it?

- Where else is there? Her Little Miss Coppertone friend joins in aggressively like maybe the faculty has the only microwave in existence.

- There's a microwave in the back room of the main office. Try there. Or Culinary.

They're not happy, but they take their food out without too much grumbling and leave.

There's a simultaneous look of exasperation from us as the door closes behind them. We agree it's a battle we've fought too often before, i.e. students are not allowed in the faculty room and as I frequently point out to trespassing ones, that's why it's called the *faculty* room. Flashback: I'm a student teacher and one of my students knocks on the faculty room door. Mr. B, could you answer a few quick questions? she asks. Sure, I say, I'm in the middle of lunch but come on in. She sits down opposite me, I continue eating, and the Q&A is over in a minute or two. After she leaves my cooperating teacher sits in the still warm chair and tells me not to ever do that again. Teachers talk informally here, she says. We pass off-color remarks and talk frankly about administration and students. This is our well earned oasis, she concludes. She doesn't mention it but I also notice that teachers smoke and they smoke a great deal. The faculty room's a haze of palpable white air. I never make the mistake again and become a champion of literally showing students the door. . . And now we three agree that it's up to the new generation of young teachers to fight the fight. Or not. But we've had enough. I'd rather try to teach teens to eat soup with a fork.

It Never Was Ever – *The faculty room is just that even if many of you are too busy to use it anymore. Still, try to shake loose some time and see what your colleagues are up to. This room is more than just 4 walls and a door. It's the spirit, life, animus, ka, the soul of the school when you're here.*

Student Shoutout – *Maybe you're in a school that has a commons area, a student lounge, or really big lockers that can accommodate you and a friend. We all need some inner and outer room. Find yours even if it means getting nano.*

Three of the 8 teachers in English department are ecstatic. Two of the nontenured ones that I wrote recommendations for have just gotten hired by gold coast communities down on Long Island Sound. For one it's a $10-K raise, the other gets a $5-grand increase. And with no extra-curricular pressure, fewer observations, fewer meetings, and what they see as more congenial attitudes regarding staff. The third teacher gets a transfer and of course I'm retiring. The department's getting wiped out as I predicted but what's bad news for the school is good news for the individuals. I remind the emigrants to insist on exit interviews if they're not offered. Eyeball-to-eyeball, town crier stuff. You have an obligation to your colleagues, I tell them, to air your gripes and not leave administration thinking it's all about money. Proprio motu – You're leaving of your own volition, sure, but a lot of our policies led you to the door. Let 'em know. Add political action to your final movement.

N-S-E-W – *T.S Eliot says in his poem The Hollow Men that the world will not end in a bang but a whimper. How will your world end? If you don't speak up when you're leaving, it's a whimp ass whimper.*

***Bilbo Baggins** – Things not working out? Think life would be better somewhere else? Maybe it will be. You won't know till you go. But remember to talk it out first, try to make life work where you are. No talk, no corrective action, then you're not leaving you're retreating. Fucking surrendering.*

The Film course ends with *Bowling For Columbine*, *Crash*, *Summer Of '42*, and *Do the Right Thing*. As always I fast forward through the love making scene in the Spike Lee Joint, i.e. it's one thing to hear the mega use of the word fuck, it's something else to actually see it performed.

Summer Of '42 is a first in this course and I'm surprised at the student reaction or lack of, i.e. they're very so-so on it and that's across the aisles. They don't even think the coming-of-age sex scenes are funny or poignant. Hermie goes to buy a prophylactic, is very embarrassed, and pretends he wants it as a balloon. I'm laughing, the class is like, What a dope this kid is. Ditto on the scene in the movies when Hermie thinks he set a personal record of 11 minutes for copping a feel only to find out he's been too far east and has been squeezing her arm.

The impression seems to be that the humor's dated and that these aren't real life experiences anymore. Amazing. I know this group is more sophisticated than 1940's teens, but to not even appreciate the movie in the historic/social/pre-Kinseyian context is puzzling and disappointing to me. I think the summer setting, the earthy tone, and Hawaiian backdrop perfectly match June, their age, and a place they'd like to be. And the theme of a young man and older woman is nothing more than a variation on the Benjamin/Mrs. Robinson theme from *The Graduate*, which this class liked a lot.

What's the difference in the movies? Why did one succeed and the other flop? Did I fail to set this one up properly or fall short in filling in the relevant background information? Maybe I laughed too much at scenes that were a joke to me but serious stuff to them, e.g. I cracked up when the boys were reading Benjie's parents' sex book and Oscy says, Foreplay, it's called FOREPLAY!. . . My gut is to say, How can you not like this? Everybody LOVES this movie! Then I realize, everybody *my* age.

Sophomores start the graphic novel *Persepolis* by Marjane Satrapi, her autobiographical account of an Iranian girl growing up in Tehran. It's an appropriate ending to the year and to our Middle East unit. Anything with pictures or illustrations the students like and it's a refreshing assignment for the nonreaders just as *Maus* was. They'll view and read, and view some more, and wrap up the year on a positive note.

Meanwhile I'm collecting the *World Literature* anthologies they've had all year. I'm having trouble getting them all turned in despite counting it as a homework assignment. Oswald tells me he's not turning it day-after-day because he can't find it.

- Honestly Mr. Bentley, he says, I looked everywhere. I guess I lost it. My mom's upset. We tore the house apart.

Because it's a $45 text I foresee getting a phone call on this, i.e. parents tend to get upset when they have to write substantial checks to cover avoidable end-of-the-year gaffes. I'm more than willing to try one more option.

- Maybe it was found and put back into the book room, I say. It's not likely but it is possible. . . I don't tell him he'd have better luck finding a Gutenberg Bible.

- Can I go look for it now?

- You *may* come back later either before or after school. I'll write down your book number and let you in. The door's locked.

Oswald's back right after the final bell and I leave him alone in the book room with his number and salvage aspirations. There are many stacks of heavy anthologies to go through, and the room's a sauna because of zero ventilation and a large floor-to-ceiling electrical panel that radiates heat.

Oswald's back in 5 minutes with what I later judge to be a nervous look.

- I found it Mr. Bentley.

He hands me a ragged-ass book, I glance at the inside number and tell him, Congratulations. He looks relieved, perhaps a bit more than he should, and leaves. It isn't until he's gone that something clicks and I double check the number. It's been neatly and darkly written over, but the original one's still faintly visible. The original number's also written boldly in magic marker across the outside edge of the pages. It's a fail-safe backup, i.e. the outer number's unalterable without a matching magic marker and the eye of an engraver. But the numbers don't match i.e. the inside and outer edge ones. Oswald's also written his name in pencil on the inside cover and to me it looks like he smudged it a bit to give it an aged appearance. It's a red herring but isn't enough to fake me out.

Gotcha! I think, *for $45, a whopping lie, and an amateurish counterfeiting job.* I feel like Agatha Christie, an author Oswald was supposed to read last year when freshmen were assigned *And Then There Were None*. I doubt he read it, he certainly did not internalize the lessons that crime doesn't pay and that Agatha solves all in the final chapter.

I make a note to talk to Oswald privately, and debate the penalties. Of course he'll have to pay for the book, but anything beyond that? Strangely, I'm flirting with the idea of mercy. He's going to fail the course anyway, and coupled with $45 for an old beat-up text it's probably enough. Actually, $45 is probably too much and maybe I should figure in depreciation. I don't normally, but as a farewell gesture to Oswald and myself. . .

And how much of this damage is Oswald's? I look at the book receipt he filled out back in September and read his description of the book's condition: binding loose, tear on spine, pages dog-eared, ink on cover, et al. I look at the book. Son-of-a-bitch, some of it matches. Not all but it's a close enough match between the book's condition and Oswald's description that this actually *could* be his book. Could be. There are real differences, but intersecting points too. Reasonable doubt? If I accuse Oswald of doctoring the number he's only going to say the number was that way when he got it and that he never noticed that it didn't match the outside magic marker number. . . My daydream of bestowing an 11th hour pardon slowly vanishes along with imparting a little Shakespeare to Oswald: The quality of mercy is not strained. I had to memorize that speech from *The Merchant Of Venice* back in my own high school days and I now miss the chance to complete the circle and leave it from whence it came: classroom-to-classroom.

I rip up the receipt and toss the book on the return-to-book room pile.

Pardon Me Pardon You – *If the numbers fit, you must acquit.*

Laying On The Dog – *Cheating can pay in the short-term. I know a student who saved $45 short-term but lost a teacher's trust long-term.*

I'll never know with 100% certainty if Oswald doctored the book number or not, but I do know he's no Hardy Boy and *is* a Triple A League pain-in-the-ass who could use a session or two with Deepak Chopra. He reminds me of what Damon Runyon said about NYC Mayor Fiorello La Guardia: The fella will deny he's having a sandwich while he's chewing on it. . . But he's going to draw a bye anyway. It's time for me to detox myself of all these schmos. And I feel sorry for the parent who'll have to write the check. R.I.P.

Snippet Timeout: I'm told English students from other systems have recently written: Holden Caulfield (*Catcher In the Rye*) thinks most people are phones. . . Hamlet, he jes set aroun and do nothin. . . In *Color Purple* Shug asks Cellie if she ever look at her female gonads. . . Don Quixote's sidekick Squanto. . .

I go to the State Open Track and Field Meet. One of my former students wins the girls' 1600 easily in 4:55 and looks great doing it. Another former takes 3rd in the boys 100 meters in 10.79. There's something elevating and just plain feel-good about watching the young, and actually anyone, excel at something they're really good at. Celebrity Anecdote: At the Stand Up For Heroes benefit at the Beacon Theatre in NYC John Stewart and Jerry Seinfeld are watching Bruce Springsteen play a few licks on the Steinway, and Stewart says, If you could do that, you would. That's what you'd do. Seinfeld agrees. And watching my former students, I agree too.

I'm backing up with a cart that holds the data projector, external speakers, DVD/VCR, and I'm going, Beep, beep, beep in a fast high-pitched voice. Some of the class get it and laugh. It's stupid and silly and I'm laughing myself.

Wife Story – Out of the clear blue one of her tiny tots says, Mrs. Bentley, my little sister couldn't go to pre-school today. Yeah, her bottom's leaking.

A girl comes in during her study to make up a missed reading quiz. She breezes through it and turns it in before I can say, academic dystopia.

- Are you sure you're done? I say looking at the one line answers.

- Yes.

- No questions?

- Nope.

- Want to wait while I grade it? Shouldn't take long.

- OK.

I grade it in less than 15 seconds. She's watching me without expression as I cross out every single answer.

- You got a zero.

- Really?

- You didn't know anything about the reading. So why did you even bother making up this quiz?

- What do you mean?

- Why not just take a zero and save us both the time and energy?

- We're supposed to make up work.

- When you know something, yes. What was the point of this? . . . I'm thinking if I close my eyes and open them maybe she'll be gone or transformed into something beyond a binary 0-1 code. I try it, but no, she's still fucking here.

- I knew some of it. I just didn't know what you asked.

- But you had all the questions ahead of time. There weren't many and I asked you the easiest ones.

She shrugs and I agree. Why go on with this? This is bushwhacking to flush out quail that just aren't there. Getting my freak on. For some reason I think of the story about a person who hops into a freshly dug grave, lies down, and looks up to experience what death will be like.

Flashback: In a long ago era a 14-year-old comes in to make up a grammar quiz on agreement of subject and verb. You missed the last class, I say. Let's go over what you missed, OK? OK, she says with a cheery agreeableness. I cover the lesson, clear up her questions and give her the short answer quiz. She fails with a 30%. I go over all the answers, explain the reasoning and rules behind each, and ask her if she would like to retake the quiz. She's all smiles and I give her the exact same quiz again, and again she fails, this time with a 55%. I go over it all a third time, answer more questions, and she takes the exact same quiz within 15 minutes of taking the first. This time she gets a 70%. I rip up the first two quizzes and congratulate her on the improvement. She's all smiles and flushed with victory. There's no doubt that tomorrow she'd fail the same quiz, but that tomorrow ain't coming.

Déjà Vu All Over Again *– Allowing a student to retake the exact same test, quiz, or exam is not generally a good idea. This isn't t-ball where tiny tykes get to swing away till they connect. On the other hand realize that for some students it's not the exact same test/quiz/exam even if it really is. They see colors, but not much beyond that.*

Rubber Ball *– Isn't it nice when a teacher lets you retest, and retest, and retest and doesn't change a thing, or changes so little that with some practice a horse could paw out the answers?*

A few days later one of my downwardly mobile types, whose behavior's an argument for reverse evolution, is the first one into the room. He comes right up to my desk and looks around to be sure we're alone. I figure maybe it's to apologize for a year of oscillating grief, but I must be confusing me with him.

- Mr. Bentley, can I have that sign now? You said you might give it to me at the end of the year. . . He's referring to a No Turkeys Allowed In Here plastic wall hanging that I once said I *might* give to him. And he's smiling, I guess, to try to charm me into mindless generosity.

Ha, I think, w*hen you can put your head between your legs and kiss your ass.* It's like this, I say to him. Your behavior this year was marginal, so were your academics. If that were all I still might give you the sign, but do you know why you're not going to get it?

- Why?

- Because of what you said to Mrs. Darling.

- Who's that?

- Your study hall teacher. She's my good friend. She told me. You know, you've got a really dirty mouth. . . The class is coming in now so I finish with, Do you know that teachers talk and that sometimes our main topic of conversation is you students? Absolutely.

I don't have to finish, he gets it. Solidarity, esprit de corps. Fuck over one teacher and you just screwed us all. Not all teachers feel like this and certainly not all the time. There are particulars, but overall all it's strength in numbers; one for all, all for one; yeah baby yeah. This student's rude behavior is practiced across the school, and my parting gift to him is to let him know that I know it and that there are consequences. It's a fuck over, sure, but it's also an intervention. And it's a better gift than a movie poster. Envelope please. And the winner is. . .

End Of the Year Snippets: One of my zero liners tells me he's not coming in to take the final exam. What's the point? he says. I can't pass anyway. Of course he's right. I call it a sagacious use of time. It's the wisest he's been all year.

I ask a girl for her very late composition. I don't have it, she says. Then it's a zero, I say. I know, she says, I suck at life. I don't know about that, I say, but you suck academically at World Lit. Think it could be effort?

A boy's throwing a tennis ball around in study hall and the teacher goes over and asks him for it. The boy puts the ball down the front of his pants, and still holding onto it asks the teacher if she still wants it. Without answering the teacher starts a countdown: 5, 4, 3. At 2 the groper yanks the tennis ball out and hands it to her.

Wife Story: One of her chirpy little girls is getting taken out of the classroom for the upteenth time for more testing and she says to the escorting lady, I hope this isn't going to take too long. I have important things to do in this class.

I'm collecting *A Soldier's Story* the final book of the year in African American Lit. One student I've criticized privately for not reading puts the book on my desk and says proudly, I read this book Mr. Bentley.

I think to myself, *Your grades on the quizzes don't show it*, but I say nothing and only look at his copy now sitting in front of me. It was brand new when I gave it out and very tight. I notice that the pages are still tight, untouched, unread, except for a few at the beginning that appear riffled.

- Wait a minute, I say. Look at this, and I wave him back. I point to the edge of the book which clearly shows a dividing line between the used and unused portions. I delicately and slowly like a surgeon insert my pen into the break and open the book. . . Page 20, I say. Looks like you read up to page 20. There are 100 pages in this playbook so it appears you read 20%. Congratulations, I continue, it's more than you usually read.

- At least I read some of it, he says not denying it.

He has a point. A good, logical, end-of-the-year point.

Decelerate Deprogram Depart *– Unless you teach surfing, sunbathing, beach volleyball, grilling, etc. you'll be skipping stones across still waters if you push too hard now. But do what you have to do. Like them, you will anyway.*

Max Factor Closeup *– Poet William Carlos Williams said, In summer the song sings itself. It's true. Unfortunately the work doesn't work itself, compositions don't compose themselves, reading doesn't read itself. Still, you're only young once so why worry about it? Like Walt Whitman, sing the body electric! Just don't short-circuit.*

Because I know what June's like, what I'm like, I plan ahead. We don't sprint into the summer. My classes hit the ground running in September, maintain a steady pace, and start to decelerate after Memorial Day, gradually going slow, slower and slowest till by the last few days there's nothing to do but cheer the victors and bury the dead.

For the first time ever the Film class will not have a final exam. Their film project counts both as a project and the exam. They know this from the first. No exam, no presentation on exam day, no final course evaluation, no exit polling/septic tank cleanout, nothing other than the tradition Tibetan parting, May there be a road.

It's the same deal in the African American Lit and Film course, i.e. their research papers are both project grades and the exam. I've already corrected the papers and given them back. Anyone who wishes can make the corrections, follow the suggestions, and resubmit for recuperation of lost of points. Exception: If I made corrections/recommendations on the rough drafts that were not followed on this finished copy, then there's no second try now to remedy it. It's not the first time I've done something like this, but it's been a long time. I do it now because I feel a twinge of guilt that 12 accommodated me by signing up for the course so it could run, and then I assigned more reading than they expected, though no one will fail.

With finished papers now in hand the class has to present them. It should be worthwhile and entertaining. Their final papers are impressive.

I start reading off their names: Blake, Andre, Prunella, Jose, Ruth, Augustus, Faye. I get yes, no, no way, yeah, nahh, OK. I go through the class roster and by the end 50% agree to present, the other half opt to loss the ten points I'm counting for the presentation.

- Come on , I appeal, share! It's not like your papers are fair or poor, they're terrific. You should be proud. . . I get head shaking and 7 students who are content with their final grade with the 10 point loss. Hindsight: Should I have counted the presentation more? I put it to a group of teachers who tell me that for 10 points they wouldn't present either. What! Suddenly a full letter grade deduction isn't enough of a tectonic shift? Obviously like Yeats these seniors have already left port, sailed off to Byzantium, the land beyond age and high school.

- Well, I say, if you change your minds once we start, no problem. Volunteers?

I tell the sophomore classes, This is the time of year I spoke about back in September. If you established a high average back then and maintained it for awhile, the final exam won't pull it down. Congratulations, you'll soon be juniors. If you established a low average right off, didn't do much since, the final exam won't rescue you now. I appreciate that some of you earlier failures have worked hard this last month, but it's too little too late. Better make summer school plans. Unstated Bubble: No child left behind? I'm gonna leave a few of you dim dolts behind. There's no affirmative action for the lazy and unmotivated. It's time to pay the piper. Mea culpa. Fait accompli.

I could close with a little George Carlin: If you try to fail and succeed, which have you done? But I keep it to myself.

It's my final homiletic preaching. Not exactly the stuff of Randy Pausch's *Last Lecture*, but I've given enough motivational talks this year, thrown out enough messages in bottles that those who could be moved already have been. I wish I were a student whisperer and could look into each and every student's soul and meet his/her needs. But I'm not, and I can't, and I've grown tired trying with some. Groucho Style Reflection: If you lecture to a student, he hears you while you're talking. If you teach a student to lecture himself, there's going to be a lot of mumbling in the class.

Any leanings I have towards re-evaluating the detritus of low averages, demonstrating last minute empathy towards the vanquished disappears when I look at the faces of the many teens here who worked hard all year and for little more than a smiley face on a paper, a verbal compliment, and a number punched into a computer.

I metaphorically switch on the applause sign for all those who did the job, fought the fight, kept the faith, and won. This is their finest hour.

The day before exams start we have a homeroom period and locker cleanout. I have to check each locker and collect school padlocks. Many share lockers or live out of backpacks, and they don't know their assigned locker numbers or combinations. I have all that information and I'm very busy trying to get every locker opened and emptied amidst a crush of noise and bodies.

The lockers are skinny broom closet affairs crammed to the top. Some have homemade shelving; many have inside doors covered with pictures, stickers, buttons, streamers, glitter, mirrors, etc. There are large trash barrels every 25 feet and they're brimming over with defunct notebooks, flyers, notes, course papers, articles of clothing, moldering antediluvian lunches, and books. Teachers are trash trolling to get the books.

Flashback: Years ago I find 7 of my grammar books in one student's locker on the last day. I'm seriously pissed off because the books have been disappearing all year, I've been begging students to return them if they mistakenly took them, and I'm scrounging and hard pressed to keep a class set. I give the boy a detention for that day, he skips, and when he returns in September I give him a double detention for skipping. He appeals to the principal who tells me, You can't carry over a detention from one year to the next! I argue, It hasn't been a year, only 8 weeks, and a detention's a detention, a thief's a thief, and a duck's a duck. I want the thief and detention. Principal rules for the defendant, but it's only a temporary reprieve. The thief eventually hangs himself with me over something else.

No problems this year except for one student who doesn't know where his school-issued lock is and I have to turn in his name.

There are five exam days but I only have to administer 3 sophomore exams which means the last week of my teaching career is filled with almost as much free time as an athletic director and coordinator. Students are finishing the exam 30 minutes early which means this final assessment isn't a marvel of planning. I could give them a final course evaluation like I used to do but

I'd only toss it anyway. Once everyone's done I fill in the remaining time by playing guessing games and asking them riddles.

I'm giving out the little that's left in my desk for prizes: skittles, Hershey kisses, a tennis ball, a nerf ball, pens, pencils, magic markers, and foreign coins pre-Euro. It's all junk to me, treasures to them.

Only one student's absent. If this student doesn't make up the exam and takes a zero, he fails the course. I talk to guidance and call mom, and the boy comes into my room the next day to tell me he'll be in on the very last day to make it up. I'm like, whatever. This student has failed to make up a lot of work in the past, has mouthed off, and show or no show, makeup or no makeup, summer will be summer. And very soon.

When Exams Were Exams. **Snippet 1**: The class is getting ready to start the exam, and a girl tells me she forgot her notes at home. This is not a good student, and she needs to pass this exam to pass the course. I'm tempted to allow her to retake the exam another day, and briefly consider it, but this would lead to all sorts of protests from other students who would also like to put off the exam. I don't even know that she has notes at home. She takes the exam, fails it, and fails the course. Mother acts like it's my fault, and I don't feel good about the girl failing, but I know it's not my fault, NFW.

Snippet 2: A student has really bad handwriting made worse when he rushes. There are portions of all his tests I can't read. I know he has a laptop – back when laptops were first generation – and I suggest he use it on the essays. He does, and we're both happy. Years later another student has an IEP that says he thinks better at a keyboard and can go to the computer room for essay writing. I don't think twice about this one. SPED students usually leave the class for exams; many are allowed alternative test sites. No problem-o.

There've been a few cheating incidents, but out-of-class, out-of-my-control. I've tried complaining, even had three retested one time, but it's not like they're vying for National Honor Society/class valedictorian.

Snippet 3: A student wants me to reissue the semester's books to him so he can work at home. I tell him, The exam's next week. You didn't read the books first time through, and now you're going to read all those books in one week? And take notes? I want to try, he says. You're wasting my time, I say, and your own, but OK. I go to the book room, grab single copies, and reissue them. Student takes the exam and fails it badly. I thought you were going to read the books, I question him later. He shrugs, and I let it go. Shrugging is an accepted coping strategy, and it sort of says it all.

The last exam I ever give is uneventful with the exception of one swivel-headed boy whose ramblings and laughing are using up too much oxygen. I give him several warnings about his spasms, then with a symbolic back of the hand I toss him with 20 minutes to go. He becomes the only student I ever toss out of an exam and I think, What a fitting way to end this year and my career. But then some students hang back after the bell to wish me a happy summer and tell me they enjoyed having me. These are great kids, the wonderful students, and if only they could be cloned to fill the school. I'm feeling good now, happy. Hi-dee-ho. All's well that ends well.

We get an email telling us to delete our emails, the server is nearly full. The irony is that for years we've been told not to delete any emails, and especially emails regarding students. I've never listened and always delete everything on a daily basis, i.e. I delete my Inbox, my Sent Items, then I delete the Deleted Items box, refresh/recover it, then permanently delete each individual email. Anyone checking my email bins at virtually any time of the day finds nothing. And that's my attitude regarding email, i.e. send it all to the Trash Bin.

I keep the computer humming, go into my documents, and delete them all till there's notta left of Bentley's mojo. There'll be no dead hand control. I'm leaving and so are my creations and influence. Bring it on home.

It's June 20th, the last day. Surprise of surprises the boy shows up to make up his exam, does well, and passes for the year. I find a stink bomb in its small red box in the way-back of a desk drawer. It's a souvenir from past decades that I forgot I had. What to do with it now? I'm tempted to lay a booby trap in some distant hall, but decide I'll be grownup and I pass it onto a younger teacher. Maybe 30+ years from now he'll have the same dilemma.

I turn in my corrected exams, verified grade sheets, obligation list (you lose or damage a book you pay), failure list, AV equipment, and book inventory list. Years ago the last day at the junior high meant a faculty/ student softball game, which we always won. By 10 a.m. the busses arrived, the students left screaming and cheering, and by 11 a.m. we had a cooler of beer in the faculty room. At noon we adjourned to an all-afternoon, all-evening party at someone's house with volleyball, horseshoes, swimming, a campfire, and general revelry.

So many last days, so many long ago goodbyes, so many departed faces – where did they all go? Where is that "incommunicable past" of Fitzgerald and Willa Cather? That past we'll never see again, can never communicate to others, that past that grows increasing dim even as the years steal our memories and most heartfelt friends.

I'm feeling emotional, sad and elated, and I'm a bit puzzled about the mix. I mean, damn! This is the moment I've waited for, for a long long time, and now that it's here I'm dimming the lights and pulling out a body bag?

I'm surprised.

It's time for a last walk.

The high school is quiet now. Today's a makeup exam day with a later senior rehearsal for tonight's graduation. Teachers are scrambling to tie-up loose ends and few students are in the building. There's something about a nearly empty school that brings out the ghosts and memories. Footsteps echo in deserted halls and the walls hold their silent witness. How many thousands of students and staff have lived some of the best years of their lives here? How many voices and how much laughter bounced off these walls to resonate and reverberate, kalpa after kalpa, aeon after aeon, forever in the minds of those who experienced it all? Edgar Cayce said, There is a river. Life is a flow, an ending stream of spirit and meaning.

But my life here is over. Goddamnit! it was a ride.

I take a few photos of staff members and have my picture taken with an administrator. We're civil now, almost friendly, what the hell. I turn in all my keys and go back to take one last look at my room. I stand in the doorway looking at the posters I left up, the rows of traditionally arranged seats, the empty file cabinets. I remember Dean Jagger in *Twelve O'Cock High* looking over the deserted WWII British airfield and remembering back when it was a scene of frantic activity while a voiceover chorus sings, Bless us all, bless us all, the long and the short and the tall.

Without me, without the students, it's just a room: four walls with a view of the guidance wing 25 feet away.

I turn off the lights and leave the unlocked door open.

I walk out the front door into bright hot sunshine. The back of my t-shirt says Les Miserables, Victor Hugo's message of a hope and ultimate redemption.

Bentley has left the building.

My work here is done.

I'm going home.

Epilogue

Elie Wiesel in a PBS Special said that life is not made up of years, but of moments. Like all teachers I've had enough educational moments in 32 years to fill volumes and I wish I wrote them all down. The students, conversations, and events I do portray here represent only a tiny fraction of all that happened, a microcosm of a microcosm.

I suppose in the grand scheme it doesn't add up to much, but it does represent my version of a teacher's life, a life that gave me great satisfaction most of the time.

More than anything else being a teacher's defined who I am with the exception of saying I'm a part of the planet first, a piece of John Donne's main. A business executive once berated me for not wanting to be more. You're just going to *stay* a teacher? he asked incredulously as if I were opting to try to set a Guinness record for most continuous roller-coaster rides. Why not? I said. I'm helping people, not taking advantage of anyone, not profiteering, not selling the public an unneeded/unwanted bill of goods. Can you say the same thing? I asked him.

And now like Oscar Wilde's Dorian Gray I shall grow old, and horrid, and dreadful while the student portraits I helped to create will remain always young in my memory: Acker, Adams, Alger, Banatoski, Barham, Barney, Bartlog, Battistoni, Bean, Bednarski, Beliveau, Black, Blais, Bonito, Braddock, Brasche, Bredefeld, Brunelle, Brunetti, Burzynski, Cahill, Calusine, Chalker, Ciarcia, Cimelli, Clark, Criss, Crotty, Crovo, Cruz, D'Amato, Deveau, Dias, Donaghy, Doninger, Dumond, Durstin, Elder, Ereminas, Estes, Febbroriello, Figlewski, Fortin, Frauenhofer, Frost, Galusha, Gioscia, Godenzi, Goode, Grieco, Grindal, Hansen, Harden,

Harding, Hart, Hennequin, Heredia, Holt, Horner, Iacino, Jankowski, Jeans, Kaherl, Kaseta, Kay, Keepin, Kirchofer, Kolessar, Krasner, Kula, Kulhowvick, Labrecque, Lavinio, Leeds, Leone, Lindquist, Liftman, Lonkoski, Lorenc, Macri, Mensel, Mooney, Orefice, Orie, Painter, Patridge, Peabody, Pedra, Pelletier, Pickard, Poole, Powers, Ramsdell, Reed, Rinko, Rivera, Rosinski, Rotondo, Rousseau, Rusin, Russell, Satherlie, Schleich, Shea, Silano, Simonin, Slabinski, Soden, Steele, Stinton, Sutak, Szafranski, Szydlo, Teller, Thierry, Tracy, vanNoordennen, Vilardi, Visentin, Vollono, Willey, Yakubowski, Zeller, and so many, many more.

To all I wish a long, prosperous, and happy journey. May the road always rise to meet you.

To my teaching colleagues I say there may not be a comeback chapter like Roy Hobbs in Malamud's novel *The Natural*, or a last hurrah like Frank Skeffington got in Edwin O'Connor's novel, or any final quest as in Tennyson's *Ulysses*. But neither is there a womb of anonymity. The thousands of lives we touched really *do* go on through the endlessly repeating, interlocking generations.

It's a rich legacy that makes us all a part of the same genealogical tree, the same flowing river, and it's enough. It has to be.

Dante: Night then saw all the stars. We were filled with gladness which soon turned to tears until the sea closed in on us.

Made in the USA
Charleston, SC
02 January 2011